Young People and Politics in the UK

Also by David Marsh

THE CONFEDERATION OF BRITISH INDUSTRY (*co-author with W. Grant*)

ABORTION POLITICS (*co-author with J. Chambers*)

THE NEW BRITISH POLITICAL SYSTEM (*co-author with I. Budge* et al.) (New edition as THE CHANGING BRITISH POLITICAL SYSTEMS: Into the 1990s)

PRIVATE MEMBERS BILLS (*co-author with M. Read*)

THE NEW POLITICS OF BRITISH TRADE UNIONISM

POST-WAR BRITISH POLITICS IN PERSPECTIVE (*co-author with members of the Birmingham Political Sociology Group*)

CHANGING PATTERNS OF GOVERNANCE IN THE UK: Reinventing Whitehall (*co-author with D. Richards and M. Smith*)

PRESSURE POLITICS: Interest Groups in Britain (*editor*)

CAPITAL IN EUROPE (*editor*)

POLICY NETWORKS IN BRITISH POLITICS (*co-editor with R.A.W. Rhodes*)

IMPLEMENTING THATCHERISM (*co-editor with R.A.W. Rhodes*)

THEORY AND METHODS IN POLITICAL SCIENCE (*co-editor with G. Stoker*)

COMPARING POLICY NETWORKS (*editor*)

MARXISM AND SOCIAL SCIENCE (*co-editor with A. Gamble and T. Tant*)

DEMYSTIFYING GLOBALISATION (*co-editor with Colin Hay*)

THEORY AND METHODS IN POLITICAL SCIENCE (*co-editor with G. Stoker*) (All new second edition)

THE STATE: Theories and Issues (*co-editor with Colin Hay and Michael Lister*)

Young People and Politics in the UK

Apathy or Alienation?

David Marsh
Professor of Political Sociology
University of Birmingham, UK

Therese O'Toole
Lecturer in Ethnicity
University of Birmingham, UK

and

Su Jones
Research Associate
University of Birmingham, UK

First published 2007 by
PALGRAVE MACMILLAN
Houndmills, Basingstoke, Hampshire RG21 6XS and
175 Fifth Avenue, New York, N.Y. 10010
Companies and representatives throughout the world

PALGRAVE MACMILLAN is the global academic imprint of the Palgrave
Macmillan division of St. Martin's Press, LLC and of Palgrave Macmillan Ltd.
Macmillan® is a registered trademark in the United States, United Kingdom
and other countries. Palgrave is a registered trademark in the European
Union and other countries.

ISBN-13: 978-0-230-00131-2 hardback
ISBN-10: 0-230-00131-9 hardback

This book is printed on paper suitable for recycling and made from fully
managed and sustained forest sources.

A catalogue record for this book is available from the British Library.

Library of Congress Cataloging-in-Publication Data
Marsh, David, 1946–
  Young people and politics in the UK : apathy or alienation? / David Marsh,
  Therese O'Toole and Su Jones.
      p.   cm.
  Includes bibliographical references and index.
  Contents: The study of political participation—The context and
  consequence of political participation: citizenship and governance
  in the UK— Methodology—The politics of youth—Class as a lived
  experience— Gender and participation—Young people and the
  politics of "race", ethnicity and identity.
  ISBN-13: 978-0-230-00131-2
  ISBN-10: 0-230-00131-9
  1. Youth—Great Britain—Political activity. 2. Political
  participation—Great Britain. I. O'Toole, Therese, 1970–
  II. Jones, Su. III. Title.
  HQ799.G7M355 2007
  324.0835'0941—dc22   2006049320

10   9   8   7   6   5   4   3   2   1
16   15   14   13   12   11   10   09   08   07

Printed and bound in Great Britain by
Antony Rowe Ltd, Chippenham and Eastbourne

For Suzy, Holly, Michael and Rosie

Contents

Acknowledgements

We wish to thank the ESRC for its support for this research (ESRC reference: L215252015, *Explaining Non-participation: Towards a Fuller Understanding of the Political*). Thanks also to all our contacts at the schools, college, hostel and training centre in Birmingham where we carried out our fieldwork for giving us their time, expertise and support. Most of all, we wish to thank all the young people who participated in this research, from whom we have learnt so much.

Introduction

The issue of political participation has received a great deal of attention in recent years, both in the UK and beyond. Much of the academic literature, and indeed public debate, identifies three crucial concerns with which this book engages: first, there is considerable evidence of a decline in key forms of political participation in the UK and more generally. Secondly, there is particular concern about the decline in political participation among the young. Finally, both these concerns are potentially crucial issues for the future of liberal democracies and governments have begun to engage with what many see as an emerging democratic deficit.

A decline in political participation

In the UK, the reason for concern about political participation is strongly linked with declining turnouts for local, national and European elections and falling party membership. For example, the turnout in the 2005 General Election was 61 per cent, only 2 per cent higher than the 2001 General Election turnout of 59 per cent, which was the lowest in the post-war period (when turnout was 12 percentage points down from the 1997 Election and 25 percentage points lower than the post-war high of 84 per cent in 1950). In relation to young people, the picture was even more disturbing; MORI's (2005a) figures suggest that the turnout rate for 18–24-year-olds dropped from only 39 per cent in 2001 to 37 per cent in 2005. Similarly, membership of political parties has declined significantly (see Mair and van Biezen, 2001). Party membership is ageing (see Seyd and Whiteley, 1992; Richardson, Seyd and Whiteley, 1995) and youth political parties barely exist in numerical, if not in organisational, terms (for the best recent work on youth parties, see Lamb,

1

2002). To put it another way, the combined membership of British political parties is less than two-thirds that of the largest UK interest group, the Royal Society for the Protection of Birds (Walker, 2001). These figures worry politicians, journalists and the 'chattering classes'.

These trends are not confined to the UK and there have been numerous studies charting the decline in citizens' engagement in representative politics in advanced democracies since the 1990s (for a summary of this literature, see Norris, 1999).

The issue of youth participation has, however, evoked particular concerns. As Norris (2003, p. 2) argues, 'Political disengagement is thought to affect all citizens but young people are believed to be particularly disillusioned about the major institutions of representative democracy, leaving them either apathetic (at best) or alienated (at worst).'

Certainly, the view that British young people's interest and participation in formal politics are declining is supported by several survey research studies. In this vein, Pirie and Worcester's (1998) data suggest that the 'Millennial Generation', their term for young people who reached the age of 21 just before or just after the turn of the millennium, are: less involved in politics than the equivalent age group were 30 years ago; less likely to vote in national or local elections than older people now or young people 30 years ago; and have little knowledge of politics at local, national or European levels. They conclude that this generation is an 'apolitical generation'. Similarly, Park's (1998) study of social attitudes among British youth indicates that teenagers and young adults are less likely to be: involved in conventional politics; knowledgeable about politics; have an attachment to any political party; or view voting as a civic responsibility.

Such trends are also evident in many other countries, with a number of studies reporting declining levels of political engagement and participation among young people worldwide (Norris, 2003).[1] For example, data from the Institute for Democracy and Electoral Assistance suggest that in Western Europe, the USA, Russia and Latin America, there is a consistent pattern of young people being less involved in the electoral process than older cohorts[2] (IDEA, 1999). Similarly, a report commissioned by the European Union notes that 'declining political engagement and traditional societal participation among youth is perceived as a threat to the future of the representative democracy' and is a particular source of concern in several European states, such as the UK, Sweden, Finland, Norway, Austria and Luxembourg (Istituto di Ricerca, 2001).

A growing democratic deficit?

It is clear then that many people identify a growing democratic deficit in advanced democracies, such as the UK, that is associated particularly, although by no means exclusively, with the young, which they see as a matter of concern for the future health of democracy. Thus, within the UK, observers like Pirie and Worcester suggest that a 'generational effect' is taking place, whereby today's young non-voters will become tomorrow's adult non-voters. This interpretation is supported by Phelps (2004 and 2005), whose analysis of turnout data for UK General Elections in the post-war period suggests that a generational effect is taking place. Norris (2003, p. 8) draws attention to the broader putative consequences of such disengagement:

> many are concerned that widespread mistrust of government author-
> ities in the mainstream culture may foster a public climate which
> facilitates the growth of anti-state movements and, at the most
> extreme, the breakdown of the rule of law and sporadic outbreaks of
> domestic terrorism by radical dissidents – whether the bombing of
> abortion clinics in America, threats of biological terrorism in Japan,
> the assassination of elected officials in the Basque region, violent
> racist incidents in France and Germany, heated ethnic/religious
> conflict in Sri Lanka, or splinter terrorist groups sabotaging the peace
> process in Northern Ireland and Israel/Palestine.

In a less dramatic vein, some UK observers have suggested that young people's disengagement from political institutions and processes is also linked with a variety of broader democratic and social problems, such as disengagement from local communities and lack of social integration – a viewpoint that was raised in the post-hoc analysis of the disturbances in Bradford, Burnley and Oldham in 2001 (see, for example, Cantle, 2001).[3]

The UK Government is concerned about declining turnout because it raises questions about its legitimacy. Consequently, although it is worried about current turnout, there is greater concern both that the current younger generation will continue to stay at home and that the next generation will follow suit. If this happens, it would be difficult for any government to claim legitimacy when less than 50 per cent of the electorate voted.[4]

Given this concern over declining political participation among young people, the UK Labour Government commissioned the Crick Report, *Education for Citizenship and the Teaching of Democracy in Schools*, which was published in 1998. The Crick Report recommended that, in order to tackle problems of declining political and civic participation among young people, citizenship education should be compulsory for secondary school pupils. The Government subsequently introduced citizenship classes, making up 5 per cent of the national curriculum, from September 2002. In addition, the emphasis on active citizenship reflected in the Citizenship Education curriculum is also evident in the Government's volunteering initiatives, many of which are targeted at young people (for example, Millennium Volunteers and the inclusion of voluntary sector work experience within the New Deal for Young People Programme). At the same time, there have also been a variety of other participatory initiatives, sponsored by central and local Governments, including: the United Kingdom Youth Parliament (UKYP); locally focused Young People's Parliaments in many British towns and cities; local (ward-level) youth forums; and youth-focused neighbourhood renewal projects. More broadly, there has also been increased emphasis on youth consultation within local democratic institutions.

The issue of declining participation has also proved interesting to social scientists and to funding bodies. In particular, the Economic and Social Research Council (ESRC) established a *Democracy and Participation Programme* with £3.5 million, funding 21 projects, which ran from 1999 to 2003,[5] to investigate declining political participation in the UK. The project which this book reports was funded by that Programme, while the major quantitative study was by Pattie, Seyd and Whiteley (2004) and we consider their work in detail in the next chapter.

Our argument

This book then is located against the background of concern about the decline in the political participation of young people. However, it is a book which offers a critical assessment of the idea of youth political apathy. Essentially, we develop four main arguments. First, we argue that the mainstream literature has tended to operate with a narrow, imposed conception of the political and hence of political participation. It therefore fails to engage with how young people themselves conceive of the political and does not attempt to investigate their political imaginaries. This tendency is, to some extent, driven by a reliance on quantitative survey methods that aim to measure political engagement and in our view there is a need to investigate young people's own conceptions of the political through the use of qualitative methodologies.

Secondly, this narrow conception of political participation, reductively and erroneously, equates non-participation by young people in a range of activities specified by researchers with political apathy. In our view, it is crucial to take a more nuanced view of non-participation and acknowledge that apathy is not necessarily participation's 'other' (DeLuca, 1995).

Thirdly, the conception of the political within much of the literature on participation is generally premised on a separation between the public and the private and fails to take account of the politics of the personal and, thus, the politics of identity. Following feminist critiques of the separation of the political from the personal, we argue for a conception of politics that understands it as a 'lived experience'.

Finally, the dominance of behaviouralist, indeed intentionalist, approaches to political participation has meant that insufficient attention is paid to the features of the political system itself and how these shape political participation (beyond the specific jurisdictional issues pertaining to the British constitution). Turning to recent political sociological literature, we engage with the argument that changing governance practices and the emergence of 'reflexive individuals' may have a profound impact on the extent, objects and repertoires of political participation. Here, we suggest that Henrik Bang's (2003, 2004) work on the development of 'culture governance' and the emergence of new types of participants, 'Expert Citizens' and 'Everyday Makers', strongly resonates with our findings. Following Bang, we suggest that the changing nature of the relationship(s) between the state and the citizens invokes new democratic challenges. More specifically, as Bang argues, the key problem of contemporary political participation is not a 'free-rider' problem, with non-participation a reflection of the political apathy of unengaged citizens who, nevertheless, enjoy the benefits of citizenship, but rather a problem of political exclusion, with many alienated from a political system which they experience as unequal and unfair.

These arguments are explored through: a critique of the existing literature; our advocacy of an alternative methodological approach to studying political participation; and an analysis of findings from our qualitative empirical research on young people's engagement with politics, based on work from our ESRC-funded project *Explaining Non-Participation: Towards a Fuller Understanding of the 'Political'*.[6]

The book's structure

In Chapter 1, we begin with a critical analysis of the most recent, comprehensive data on political participation generally and youth participation particularly: Pattie, Seyd and Whiteley's (2004) work on citizenship and participation in the UK; and Norris' (2002 and 2003) comparative study of political engagement.[7] Whilst these studies tell us a great deal about particular aspects of political participation, in our view they operate with a narrow conceptualisation of the 'political', which is imposed upon respondents. In contrast, we suggest that it is crucial to focus on how young people themselves understand politics and, in effect, to view politics as a structured 'lived experience'. These arguments are developed in the second section of Chapter 1.

As we have already indicated, debates about the extent and form of political participation have broader resonance for questions about the nature of both contemporary citizenship and contemporary governance and the relationship between citizens and states. In Chapter 2, we identify our position on, first, citizenship and, subsequently, governance. It is clear that different conceptions of citizenship are related to different notions of politics and 'the political' and, thus, of political participation. As such, we consider three broad conceptualisations of citizenship: rights-based conceptions; responsibilities-based conceptions; and participatory-based conceptions. We then consider Henrik Bang's argument that new forms of political participation and types of citizen have developed as a result of changing patterns of cultural governance. In our view, Bang's work poses an important challenge to much of the contemporary political participation literature. Finally, we argue that the British political system has historically taken a top–down approach to citizenship, which is inimical to more participatory conceptions of citizenship, and that such tendencies persist under New Labour – despite its professed commitment to neighbourhood and civil renewal and active citizenship.

As we emphasised, our empirical work aims to examine how young people themselves understand and experience politics, rather than measuring their engagement in a set of predetermined activities. This aim has methodological implications. In particular, given our critique of the quantitative bias of much of the existing literature, we needed to employ a method that set out to understand our respondents' own conceptions of politics. To this end, we elected to use open-ended methods that allowed our respondents to discuss their understandings of politics in their own terms, with minimal direction from the researchers. To achieve this, we presented focus groups of young people with a series of images including: overtly political images (for example, party candidates, demonstrators and protestors); images of social inequalities (for example, a young woman and baby, a man and child, a homeless hostel);

images relating to identity and belonging (for example, sporting events with fans in national colours, flag-waving groups); and images of public services and public spaces (for example, school, hospital, public park, police). Each focus group circulated two copies of each image and the group were asked to free-associate with the image. After the group had discussed all the images, they were then asked to conduct a sort of the images, into those they considered to be 'political' and those they did not, giving their reasons for doing so. Subsequently, follow-up individual interviews were conducted with all of the focus group participants who were willing. These interviews dealt with their more personal experiences of and engagement with politics, in the light of the focus group discussions. The method is discussed and justified at more length in Chapter 3. The key point here is that the method stems directly from our criticism of the mainstream literature and the concerns which develop from that critique.

In Chapters 4–7, we analyse the findings of our study, which investigate the ways in which age, class, gender and ethnicity are both aspects of, and shape, our respondents' lived experiences and, consequently, their conceptions of politics. In doing this, we are arguing that these aspects of identity should be seen not merely as independent variables as they are in most studies of participation, but as formative influences on young people's political imaginaries. So, age is not best viewed as a variable that affects political participation, it is rather an experience that has strongly political dimensions, in which we can see structures and agency interacting. So, in this book we shall examine how our respondents live politics, through the lens of their experience of age (in Chapter 4), class (in Chapter 5), gender (in Chapter 6) and ethnicity (in Chapter 7).

Conclusion

Although, low levels of engagement with electoral and parliamentary processes, particularly among young people, have often been read as evidence of political apathy (Toynbee, 1997; Wilkinson and Mulgan, 1997; Pirie and Worcester, 2000; Hiscock, 2001), there is an emerging recognition that apathy does not adequately account for (young) citizens' disengagement (Power Inquiry, 2006, especially Chapter 1). So, there are a number of studies indicating that widespread dissatisfaction and distrust towards mainstream political institutions and processes sit alongside high levels of civic engagement (Pattie, Seyd and Whiteley, 2004) and unconventional (Norris, 2002) and postconventional (Micheletti, Follesdal and Stolle, 2004) forms of political participation. In essence, our study seeks to understand why young people appear to be disengaged from mainstream politics, without assuming that this results necessarily from apathy, in order to open out investigation of how young people respond politically to the world around them.

At the same time, we are concerned to relate this consideration of political participation/non-participation to developments in governance and citizenship. As such, we return to those broader issues in the conclusion, paying particular attention to Bang's work. Broadly speaking, the UK Government's strategy for achieving 'democratic renewal' has concentrated on increasing citizens' political literacy and encouraging participation in local and neighbourhood initiatives (or 'low politics'); we argue, however, that political literacy cuts both ways and that democratic renewal must take place at the level of 'high politics' in relation to the structures and practices of mainstream political institutions.

1
The Study of Political Participation

The study of political participation has undergone some key changes since Barnes and Kaase's (1979) and Parry et al.'s (1992) seminal studies. In particular, both the traditional distinction between 'conventional' and 'unconventional' modes of participation (Barnes and Kaase, 1979) and the view of participation as essentially focused on influencing public officials (Parry et al., 1992) have undergone refinement in recent years. According to Norris (2002, pp. 215–216), there has been a diversification in terms of:

> (the) *agencies* (the collective organizations structuring political activity), the *repertoires* (the actions commonly used for political expression), and the *targets* (the political actors that participants seek to influence).

The notion that the agencies in which people politically participate are evolving and diversifying arises from the contention that, since the 1960s, new forms of collective organisation, such as social movements, have emerged that differ from traditional forms of political organisation, such as trade unions, political parties and pressure groups. Following the emergence of feminist, civil rights, gay rights and environmental movements, we see a more fluid conception of membership of political organisations that grow out of social networks and 'contentious politics' (Tarrow, 1998), and which engage in a variety of forms of collective action (from disruption, use of slogans, music or dress or renaming of familiar objects). Indeed, Tarrow debates whether the late 20th century may have produced a 'movement society' (1998).

In relation to the changing repertoires of political participation, many point to the development of new forms of action as a consequence of technological innovation, such as Internet activism (Bennett, 2004) or

9

text-mobilisation, as witnessed in the demonstrations against Suharto in Indonesia in 1998, alongside the evolution of older forms of action. For instance, whilst there is a long history of economic boycotts with a political purpose (Shapiro, 2000), such actions have in recent years developed into more focused forms of mass political consumerism, such as the No Sweat or Fair Trade campaigns (Micheletti *et al.*, 2004).

Finally, the argument that the targets of political action are changing acknowledges that political power and authority in the contemporary (globalising) world are changing and, hence, also the nature of political campaigning and action. In this scenario, the nation-state is no longer seen as *the* primary target of action for a host of different groups, for whom supranational agents may have greater significance, such as transnational corporations (exemplified in the boycott Nike campaigns) or international bodies (as witnessed by the anti-G8 protests).

Alongside these transformations in political organisation, action and aims, it is suggested that new citizens are emerging who are much less collectivist than previous generations, more individualistic and issue-oriented and concerned with 'postmaterialist' values (Inglehart, 1990). For many, such trends are particularly exemplified in the young.

Much contemporary British political science has been rather slow to address these issues of change, however, and there has been a continued dependency on traditional categories of participation. In part, this reflects a reluctance to lose the longitudinal power of established survey instruments, but, in our view, it also reflects a focus on intentional, rather than structural, explanations of participation. Indeed, it seems to us that a great deal of recent British political science work on political participation has been primarily concerned with the decline of traditional forms of participation, rather than with theorising the significance of changing patterns of governance and participation more broadly conceived. In this chapter we set out our dissatisfaction with much thinking around the crisis of political participation, whilst in the next chapter we pay more attention to broader conceptions of citizenship and how these relate to changing aspects of governance.

1.1   Quantitative survey studies of youth political participation

1.1.1   Pattie *et al.*'s study of citizenship and participation

We begin by examining the approach and findings of the major study of citizenship and participation in the UK, by Pattie *et al.* (2004). This was a large quantitative survey project undertaken within the ESRC's Democracy and Participation programme of which our study was also a part. We pay particular attention to Pattie *et al.* (2004) for three reasons: first, they provide the most up-to-date and the most recent, comprehensive work on political participation in the UK, and our empirical work focuses on the UK. Secondly, their work represents a major advance on the previous equivalent work on the UK published in 1992 by Parry *et al.*, which operated with a much narrower understanding of politics. As such, this study in many ways represents an advance on previous survey research, particularly because it broadens the range of political activities it considers. Third, in an important sense, our work represents a response to the approach they adopt.

Pattie *et al.* report the results of three separate surveys based on representative samples of the population of England, Scotland and Wales. The main merged sample, which is the basis of the results we consider here, included 12,163 respondents from face to face and mail surveys conducted in 2000.[1]

Pattie *et al.* considered naming their book the 'Atomised Citizen' and suggest (2004, p. 275) that 'this reflects many of the trends we are observing in contemporary Britain'. More specifically, they identify a number of characteristics of participation in modern Britain. In the first place, they suggest that citizens have not in fact contracted out of politics; rather they are engaged in a large number of non-traditional forms of political participation. Whilst collectivist forms of participation have declined, overall, individualistic forms of political participation have increased. In particular, there has been a notable rise (since the Parry *et al.* study conducted in 1984) in consumer boycotts (2004, p. 81, Table 3.12). Pattie *et al.* argue that this pattern of individualistic engagement makes it meaningful to talk about 'consumer citizenship' (2004, p. 267). In contrast, there is a decline in party membership; now if people join organisations they are usually motoring, fitness, sport and work organisations (2004, p. 98, Table 3.13). In addition, membership of political parties is largely passive (2004, p. 268, Table 3.14). Alongside this decline in more traditional forms of participation, there is a great deal of micro-political action. So, 43 per cent of their respondents had taken action to try to improve their working conditions, while 24 per cent with children in school had taken action to attempt to improve their child's educational provision and 11 per cent had taken action to try to change their medical treatment (2004, p. 114, Figure 4.1). However, this action is individual and politicians are rarely involved (2004, pp. 117–119, Figs 4.2–4.4).

In relation to trust, they found that trust in others is quite high, but trust in politicians, especially national politicians, is low (2004, p. 36, Table 2.2, and p. 38, Table 2.3). Their findings suggest a feeling that government is indifferent to citizen's opinions with fairly low levels of political efficacy (2004, p. 43, Table 2.6, and p. 45, Table 2.7).

In relation to attitudes towards rights, citizens have a significant sense of individual rights, such as the right to die, have an abortion, or take fathers' paternity leave, although they are much less tolerant of gay rights or gay marriage. The majority also believe in state-provided rights, such as housing for those who cannot afford it and government action to reduce inequalities. As far as individualistic rights are concerned, there is a division between those who think the state should provide and those who think individuals should decide (2004, p. 55, Table 2.12).[2]

In relation to attitudes towards the duties of citizenship, they suggest that the sense of civic duty to vote runs deep, but there is little sense among their respondents of a duty to be more broadly politically engaged (2004, p. 50, Figure 2.7).

Finally, they find that all forms of political participation are related to age (discussed next), education and socio-economic status, but not to gender or ethnicity (2004, p. 86, Table 3.4). Perhaps most crucially, it is the disadvantaged who feel they need the state, while the privileged are able to achieve their own ambitions.

With regard to youth participation, the main conclusions of Pattie *et al.* covered areas relating to political and civic activity, interest and attitudes. In relation to activities, they found that the sense that voting is a duty is lowest among the young, that is those aged under 24 (2004, p. 70), and that people are most likely to be politically active in their middle age, with the young and the old more likely to be disengaged (2004, p. 86). Whilst collective political action is relatively more common among the young and more educated (2004, p. 87), they suggest that the young, together with the old, women, the working class, the poor and the less well educated, are less likely to belong to formal organisations (2004, p. 104), and the young especially are more likely to be found in informal networks or friendship groups (2004, p. 105). Overall, in all the participation models that the authors examined, they found that youth inhibits participation (2004, p. 173). With regard to political interest, they found that the young, together with the poor and the working class, are the least politically knowledgeable and interested (2004, pp. 90, 92). Finally, in relation to attitudes, they found that young people tend to be liberal, rights-oriented and less trustful than most other groups. So, they found that liberal values are stronger among the young than in almost all other groups: 'the younger the person, the greater the likelihood that he or she supports gay relationships having equal status to marriage, and the older the person the more likely the contrary point of view will be held' (2004, p. 71). Furthermore, the young, together with the poor and the working class, are more committed to state-provided rights – education, health, social security and so on (2004, p. 72) – whilst both trust generally, and particularly towards the police, only matched by the levels among minority ethnic groups (2004, pp. 61–63), and respect for the law are lowest among the young (2004, p. 68).

As such, the general picture about young people and political participation to emerge from Pattie *et al.*'s study is that the young are less knowledgeable, interested and efficacious about politics and less likely to vote, engage in civic participation or join any formal political organisation, particularly political parties. However, at the same time, they are more likely to be members of informal groups and more likely to be involved in protest politics. The picture appears one less of apathy, or even inactivity, and more of different forms of engagement.

1.1.2 Norris' studies of the agencies, repertoires and targets of political participation

This is a picture confirmed by both Norris' comparative work and other, more qualitative, work on young people's political participation in the UK (Eden and Roker, 2000; White *et al.*, 2000; Henn *et al.*, 2002). Norris has published three contributions which are relevant here: the *Democratic Phoenix* (2002); 'Young People and Political Activism' (2003), which focuses on a comparative analysis of activism in Europe; and 'Who Demonstrates? Anti-State Rebels, Conventional Participants, or Everyone' (2005), which looks both at comparative material on protest politics taken from the World Values Study and at a detailed case study of protest in Belgium.

Norris consistently makes the point that there has been a diversification of the repertoires of political action. She also contends that young people's political repertoires are different to other cohorts, in that they are more likely to engage in demonstrations and consumer boycotts. In this vein, she distinguishes between citizen-orientated actions, relating mainly to elections and parties, and cause-orientated repertoires focusing on specific issues or policy concerns, that is consumer politics, demonstrations and petitioning (2003, p. 4). This distinction leads Norris to broaden her approach to politics in comparison with most classic studies of political participation. So, she contends first that: 'An important characteristic of cause-orientated repertoires is that these have broadened towards engaging in "consumer" and "life-style politics", where the precise dividing line between the "social" and the "political" breaks down even further' (2003, p. 5). She continues, 'identity politics around issues of ethnicity and sexuality also commonly blur the "social" and the political' (2003, p. 5). Finally, she contends: 'Another defining characteristic of cause-orientated political activity is that these are directed towards parliament and government, but also towards diverse actors in the public, non-profit and private sectors' (2003, p. 5).

Interestingly, this brings Norris closer in many ways to our under-standing of politics 'as lived experience' which we shall discuss below. Unfortunately, however, despite these acknowledgements, and, at least in part, because of the quantitative surveys she relies on, her results do not really reflect that theoretical sophistication. Rather, in all her empirical work reported here she treats ethnicity, and indeed age, class and gender as independent variables, not identities, while, like other studies, including ours, she has no information about sexuality as a variable, let alone as an identity.

Norris (2003) identifies three competing interpretations of the rela-tionship between age and participation, interpretations that focus on: generational effects, life-cycle effects or period effects. She tests these three interpretations of what may be happening to youth participa-tion. Because she has no longitudinal data, she uses panel data from the European Social Survey (ESS). This involves data from a represent-ative sample of the population of 14 European nations and Israel:7 in Northern Europe (Norway, Sweden, Finland, UK, Ireland, Netherlands and Switzerland); 4 from the Mediterranean (Greece, Spain, Portugal and Israel); and 4 from East Central Europe (Czech Republic, Hungary, Poland and Slovenia). The data were analysed to establish whether there were linear trends in activism over successive age cohorts (for example, if, as cohorts grew older, there was more voting and less protest participation). If there are linear trends, that would tend to support the generational interpretation. In contrast, life-cycle effects would be reflected in a curvilinear pattern across successive cohorts; for example, in which youngest and oldest vote least. Finally, period effects would be reflected in a significant change in participation at one time, following a key event.

In relation to the relationship between age and citizen or cause-oriented political action, Norris found that, across the 15 countries, citizen-orientated acts attract an older profile and a 'significant age gap

[is] apparent in all citizen-orientated repertoires of action, including voting, contacting, donating money, party membership and party work' (2003, p. 11), whilst cause-orientated acts attract a slightly younger profile (2003, p. 11). Thus, 'contrary to the thesis of young people's apathy, the age gap [is] both substantially larger and also reversed for all the cause-orientated forms of activism' (2003, pp. 11–12). She concludes then that there are differences of age 'even after including all relevant controls, however, age (in years) remained not only statistically significant but one of the strongest predictors of citizen action' (2003, p. 12), whilst 'the age profile remained significant even after including the full battery of controls and it was consistently reversed, with young people more likely to engage in cause-orientated forms of action, not less' (2003, p. 13).

She comes to somewhat different conclusions as to whether these age differences reflect life-cycle or generational effects, however. In the case of citizen-orientated activism, this tends to be expressed in curvilinear form (2003, Figure 3) in all types of society (Northern Europe, Mediterranean and East Central Europe). So, there seems to be a life-cycle effect, but no generational effect. For example, in relation to turnout across each nation, 'although there is a large age gap in turnout, nevertheless this can be attributed more to life-cycle patterns, so that the younger groups can be gradually expected to vote more often as they enter middle age' (2003, p. 13). It is also worth pointing out here that Franklin (2004) identifies a gradually extended decline in turnout across all democracies as a result of lowering the voting age. He consequently argues that the decline in turnout which has occurred in Western Europe will cease and may be reversed as the generations affected by these changes mature.

The pattern in relation to the cause-orientated repertoire is different however; here 'older cohorts are least engaged in these ways, (but) there is a linear rise in activism until it peaks among the younger cohorts, and this rise is most marked in Scandinavia and, to a lesser extent, Northern Europe' (2003, pp. 13–14), which 'suggests that younger people are more likely than their parents to engage in cause-orientated political action, contrary to the thesis of youth apathy' (2003, p. 14).

Norris has also undertaken, with two colleagues, Walgrave and Van Aelst, a study of activism (2005), which pays significant attention to age as an explanatory variable. As they argue, 'Perhaps the most common explanation for the growth of protest politics, and the main reason for popular concern, claims that growing political disaffection and alienation has generated this phenomenon' (Norris *et al.*, 2005, p. 3). This position has been criticised by those who argue that viewing radicals as disaffected is a stereotype that ignores the broader sociological changes that underpin the rise of protest politics. Thus, authors like Inglehart (1997, 2005) and Dalton (2004) advocate modernisation theory, which emphasises that the shift from industrial to post-industrial society has been associated with higher levels of education, increased leisure time and more sophisticated communication systems and has produced more informed and demanding citizens. Finally, some authors (see McAdam *et al.*, 1996) argue that context is crucial; the extent and nature of protest depend on the context set by particular events, issues, actors, mobilisation frames and so on. Norris *et al.* attempt to adjudicate between these positions by posing the following question: are protest politics replacing (see Bennett, 1998) or supplementing (Norris, 2002) traditional forms of participation? To address this, they use two data sources. First, they used the 1973–76 Barnes and Kaase (1979) Political Action Survey, updated with material from World Values Study, for eight nations: the UK, West Germany, Netherlands, Austria, the USA, Italy, Switzerland and Finland. Secondly, they drew on a case study of Belgium, the country with the highest proportion of demonstrators in the comparative data and with sharpest rise in demonstration activism from the early 1980s. These data are taken from Van Aelst and Walgrave's (2001) study of demonstration participants in seven demonstrations in Belgium between 1998 and 2001, in which they conducted 2448 face-to-face interviews and postal surveys. Aelst and Walgrave identified four categories of demonstrations reflecting the type of organiser and the location of the issue involved on an ideological spectrum: 'new-left', 'old-left', 'new-mixed' and 'new-right'. These data were supplemented with data from the 1999 Belgian General Election Survey.

The main findings were that protest politics has increased, especially in Belgium, the Netherlands and Sweden (Norris *et al.*, 2005, Table 2). They argue (2005, p. 92),

> Estimates based on the World Values survey suggest that demonstrating (experienced by 16% of the public overall) has become more widespread today than many traditional forms of participation such as active party membership (5%), or active trade union membership (5%).

In predicting party participation or civic activism in Belgium, age continues to be important – participation increases in middle age before falling among the elderly. In contrast, as regards demonstration activism, 'protest activity remains more popular among the younger generation than for their parents or grandparents' (Norris *et al.*, 2005, p. 15). Their data tend to dispute the perspective that it is the disaffected who protest, since the people who take to the streets in Belgium are not particularly critical of the political system: 'Not only are demonstrators as a group generally not disaffected about government and democracy [. . .] but none of the seven specific demonstrations was crowded with anti-state radicals, not even the anti-globalisation protest' (2003, p. 18). They found some limited ideological effects, in the sense that demonstrators are drawn disproportionately from the left, but not from the far-left, but that tendencies to become members of political and civic associations were correlated, so that people who demonstrate are more likely to be civic joiners, party members and TU members. They suggest that indeed context matters a lot. 'New-left' demonstrators are usually young, well educated, middle class, more politically interested and 'left-wing'. 'Old-left' demonstrators are more usually working class, less interested and more satisfied with democracy. 'New-right' demonstrators are older, less politically interested, less satisfied with democracy and more 'right-wing'. Furthermore, event organisers played a role in mobilising protestors. Unions mobilised supporters for 'old-left' events, but there were fewer union members in 'new-left' and 'new-right' events. Parties mobilised for the 'new-right' and civic associations for the 'new-left'. Overall, they conclude, 'the popular concern that demonstrations are undermining representative democracy, by displacing conventional channels with radical and extremist politics, even violent tactics, due to political disaffection, seems misplaced' (2005, p. 20).

Norris' comparative data certainly suggest that the UK is not an exceptional case. Any comparison between the results of Pattie *et al.* (2003) and those of Norris (2003) indicates that young people do participate in politics, but their participation takes different forms. They are less interested in, and knowledgeable about, politics and feel limited levels of political efficacy. They are less likely to vote or join political parties. However, in contrast, they are more likely to demonstrate or protest. It is hard not to agree with Norris *et al.* (2005) that: 'the political energies among the younger generation in post-industrial societies have diversified and flowed through cause-orientated activism, rather than simply ebbed away through apathy'. This applies to Britain, as Pattie *et al.* show, as much as to the other countries in Norris *et al.*'s (2005) analysis.

1.2   Beyond the mainstream studies

Norris (2003) develops three arguments which can serve as a starting point for our own position. First, she argues that many people are now involved in 'consumer' or 'life-style' politics, and that these are areas in which the distinction between the 'social' and the 'political' breaks down. Secondly, she suggests that issues of identity politics, particularly centred around questions of ethnicity and sexuality, which also commonly blur that distinction, are becoming increasingly important (for a brief discussion of identity politics, see below). Finally, she contends that cause-orientated political activity is directed more towards diverse actors in the public, voluntary and private sectors, than towards politicians and bureaucrats.

So, there is growing evidence that young people are less involved in formal political activity, but more involved in cause-orientated activism. We endorse Norris' arguments, but wish to go much further because she, like Pattie *et al.*, fails to engage fully with the issues of identity and lived experience that she introduces. Indeed, as we indicated earlier, Norris' studies fail to address empirically any of these issues.

In our view, there are four flaws in the mainstream literature, although we acknowledge that Pattie *et al.* (2004) go some way to addressing them. First, although Pattie *et al.*'s study moves beyond the narrow conception of politics and 'the political' that exemplified early studies (such as Parry *et al.*, 1992), there is little engagement with how young people themselves conceive of the political and there remains a tendency in their work to impose a view of the 'political' on their respondents. Secondly, there is a lack of serious study of non-participation. As we have noted previously, many studies equate non-participation, defined in the researcher's own terms, with political apathy. Put simply, it is frequently assumed that if individuals do not engage in the activities that researchers take to represent political participation, they are politically apathetic. In our view, this is an unsustainable proposition because political participation, defined in this way, has a number of 'others', including apathy, alienation/disaffection and other types of participation. Third, and perhaps this is unsurprising given the behaviouralist/intentionalist approach of researchers like Pattie *et al.* (2004), age, class, ethnicity and gender are viewed merely as independent variables, rather than as 'lived experience' and, hence, the relationship between these and political engagement is poorly understood. Finally, as Bang (2004) argues, most researchers pay insufficient attention to the broader context of patterns of governance and citizenship, the ways in which they are changing and the consequences of these for political participation.

In the sections below, we develop the first three of these arguments, returning to the fourth in the next chapter.

1.2.1 A narrow conception of the political

Parry et al.'s (1992) influential study of political participation defined it as 'taking part in the processes of formulation, passage and implementation of public policies'; or 'action which seeks to shape the attitudes of decision-makers to matters yet to be decided, or... action in protest against the outcome of some decision' (1992, p. 16). They focused on particular types of political participation: voting; party membership; joining an interest group; contacting MPs or councillors; signing petitions; and taking part in a demonstration. Individuals were then asked which of these activities they engaged in and how frequently.[3] This definition of participation repertoires proved highly stable for subsequent studies of participation; however, the activities that Parry et al. considered to be political participation were focussed around a rather narrow list of what might be termed 'mainstream' or 'citizen-orientated activities' (see Norris, 2003).

Studies of participation, such as those by Norris (2003) and Pattie et al. (2004), have begun to move beyond this narrow definition of politics. Thus, Pattie et al.'s view of participation extends to a focus on consumer boycotts and what they call 'micro-politics'. So, Pattie et al. (2004, p. 23) accept that people interact with the state in all aspects of their lives. In order to tap into this 'micro-politics', they investigate their respondents' attempts to influence the education their children receive, the medical treatment their family receive and their own job conditions. As such, their focus on micro-politics is a significant step forward in the quantitative literature, particularly when compared to the work of Parry et al. (1992). Even so, it is easy to think of other dimensions of 'micro-politics' that could, and perhaps should, be investigated. Here, two examples from our data, which we shall return to when we present our results, should suffice to make our point: first, our group of hostel residents saw all aspects of their interaction with the social security system as 'political'; secondly, a number of the women we interviewed saw the whole issue of sex education, birth control and treatment of single parents as highly political issues at the level of their lived experiences. Furthermore, although Pattie et al. expand their view of the repertoires of political participation to include voluntary and civic activities, such engagement is essentially seen as auxiliary to the main acts of political participation that are still conceived of in somewhat narrow terms.

In our view, Pattie *et al.* (2004) still operate with too narrow a conception of 'the political' because they use an arena, rather than a process, definition of politics and focus, particularly, on formal political arenas.[4] The problem here is that arena-based definitions of politics do not allow a full investigation of the political processes that affect young people's lives, such as racism, the effects of unemployment or limited access to welfare benefits, because they assume that politics operates within arenas with reasonably porous, but stable, boundaries (such as the public sphere, Westminster, local Government, etc.). As such, they overlook processes of inclusion or exclusion, which may preclude, or facilitate, entry into those arenas, a point we return to below.

It follows that, for us, a key problem with political participation research is that little effort is made to investigate what we would identify as a central question, namely how individuals themselves conceive of politics. Yet, there is evidence that people do not always view politics in the same way as the researcher. Parry *et al.*, for example, assume that the activities they list are also seen as political participation by their respondents. Yet, their own study found that only 18 per cent of those respondents identified the list of activities that they drew up as 'political'. Parry *et al.* observe that this reflects something of a disparity between academic and everyday conceptions of politics, but do not investigate the implications of this finding (1992, p. 476). We would argue that the imposition of a conception of 'the political' which people may not themselves accept, at best, reflects a poor research design and, at worst, risks seriously misunderstanding political participation. By imposing a view of 'the political' on people that they may not share, one is blind to the fact that there are many different forms of political participation.

Here, in our view, Pattie *et al.* do not move much beyond the existing literature. It is true that they pre-tested their questions, conducting interviews with a sample that broadly shared the characteristics of their later respondents and they did ask this sample about their understanding of politics. However, they do not report the results of this pre-testing, there are no transcripts available and the main aim of the pre-testing was to test questions for their final questionnaire. As such, this approach fails to address the real problem; we do not know enough about how people conceptualise or understand politics.[5]

We would argue that to move to a broader conception of 'the political', it is important to allow individuals themselves to say how they conceive of politics, what it means to them and how they relate to it. In this sense, 'the political' is conceived of less as an arena or set of arenas, but rather as a lived experience, in which, for example, individuals who experience differing levels of inequalities may conceive of, and experience, politics differently. If this is the case, and we would argue strongly that it is, then it is a very limited research design to impose a conception of 'the political' that is focussed around one or more arenas. Instead, the conception of 'the political' must be broadened out by focussing on how individuals themselves conceive of politics.

As we saw above, Norris (2003) implicitly critiques the narrowness of most of the literature's definition and understanding of politics when she suggests we should take identity politics more seriously, although she does not use that insight in her own empirical work. More specific-ally, she suggests that we should pay much more attention to the politics associated with questions of ethnicity and sexuality. To an extent we agree, as is made clear later in this chapter. Certainly, we would argue that not only ethnicity and sexuality (not considered in our empirical material), but also age, class and gender, are political lived experiences. However, first we need briefly to consider the literature on 'identity politics'.

The identity politics literature is both strongly associated with the rise of social movements and deeply contested. Certainly, we would reject some of the arguments associated with that position. A core claim of identity politics is that certain groups are oppressed as a consequence of the lack of recognition of their social and cultural differences (see Young, 1990). The political implications of this have centred on consciousness-raising around issues of identity and difference (often involving a valor-ising of those differences to re-write dominant negative discourses) and the demand that public and political institutions recognise and respond to difference. Identity politics focus on the subjectivity of public insti-tutions and social practices, exposing the ways in which these (often subconsciously) normalise particular identity categories. It also interrog-ates the unequal power relations that underpin such practices. Drawing on these insights, feminist, gay rights and black power movements have successfully opened up the political terrain on which inequalities may be challenged. Nevertheless, a key challenge to identity politics has been directed at the tendency to adopt a standpoint epistemological position that isolates and privileges particular aspects of identity in ways that have sometimes verged on essentialism (for a sensitive critique of the theoretical and political implications of this, see Gilroy, 1993).

Whilst we would agree with the argument that societies are characterised by structured equality based on differences of ethnicity, gender,
class, age and so on, we do not accept the essentialist claims in much of
the identity politics literature, that identity is simply a reflection of one's
gender, age, 'race' or sexuality. At the same time, as will be clear below,
we also reject the standpoint epistemology inherent in much of the
identity politics literature, which isolates and privileges certain aspects
of identity in order to build claims about how social scientists can (or
cannot) achieve an understanding of how particular group identities
shape individuals' experiences.

1.2.2   The various 'others' of political participation

As we have already suggested, the (mostly unstated) implication in the
mainstream literature is that there is, at worst, a simple dualism or, at
best, a continuum between participation and apathy. This relates to the
argument made above that much of the literature imposes a narrow
conception of politics upon respondents. For example, an individual
who does not vote, or engage in other conventional activities, but who
is active informally in the local community campaigning against racism,
might be characterised by mainstream research as politically apathetic.
In our view, such an approach is likely to wrongly classify a range of
individuals.[6]

This critique of the mainstream approach has a number of other
implications. First, non-participation is rarely, if ever, seen as a conscious
choice. Yet, some, perhaps many, people do not vote because no political party satisfies them; their mantra is, 'a plague on all your houses'.
Similarly, many young people may avoid formal politics because they
feel it has nothing to offer them; a point confirmed empirically in the
work of White *et al.* (2000) and Henn *et al.* (2002). Certainly, to suggest
that those individuals who do not participate in the formal political
arena are politically apathetic is too simplistic and sweeping a statement.

Secondly, and relatedly, the concentration on fairly conventional
forms of participation (as exemplified in Pirie and Worcester's (1998;
2000) studies, for example, that conclude that young people are an
'apolitical generation') can come close to implying that only political
activity sanctioned by the state, or other authorities, is regarded as
legitimate. The point is easily made if we consider the anti-capitalist
demonstrations associated with WTO and G8 meetings in the UK and
internationally. Much of the contemporary media coverage of these
demonstrations focussed on the extent to which such demonstrations,
and the spate of violence associated with them, were, at best, the

posturing of a bored youth, biting the hand that feeds them, or, at worst, criminal. This argument echoes the views of politicians like Tony Blair who asserted: 'The people responsible for the damage are an absolute disgrace. Their actions have got nothing to do with convictions or beliefs and everything to do with mindless thuggery' (*The Daily Telegraph*, 2 May 2000). In contrast, the protestors viewed their actions as political and the violence as necessary to attract the publicity that would sensitise the public to the broader issues. As one protestor put it:

The trouble is that non-violent protests are just completely ignored. I remember just last year there was not one word about [a previous protest] in any of the media despite a massive turnout and no trouble. Sadly, I think a certain amount of trouble is the only way to get the media to cover a protest like this. (Urban 75,2001)

This point is made not to justify violence, but to suggest that what is political is in the eye of the beholder and what is regarded as legitimately political is policed by the state. To analyse politics and political participation, we need to rethink the claim that individuals who do not participate in politics in conventional, orthodox, ways are politically apathetic.[7]

In our view, we should distinguish between political participation and political non-participation. This leaves open the question of why individuals do not participate in formal politics. We would argue that the reasons for non-participation are varied and go beyond simple lack of interest in politics. Indeed, in our view lack of interest in politics, or political apathy, is not necessarily the most significant factor in young people's non-participation in formal politics; some young people are politically motivated and engaged, although in ways orthodox research does not explore. Indeed, we can see instances where groups may specifically reject the description of activities they are involved in as being political, for a variety of reasons – often predicated on how they conceive of politics. Spence's (1998) study of the activism of miners' wives, for instance, found that the women she interviewed who were working to support strike action refused to see their activities as political, preferring to describe them as community work, in order to differentiate themselves from those they saw as being ideologically motivated. Another such example arose in an interview with one of our young South Asian men, who gave a positive account of engagement in a local community action, which had involved residents and parents from different ethnic backgrounds lobbying the local Council. For him, this issue had permitted a transcendence of the racism that he associated with politics, because it had forced the Council to be accountable to all the community. Summarising the significance of this participation, he observed, 'and the Council does not get racist – not like politics at all'. The distinction drawn here by our respondent between politics as imbued with racism and 'apolitical' community action as racism-free tells us a great deal about why this respondent did not actively engage with many mainstream political institutions.

The key point here is that there are many 'others' of participation and many different understandings of politics that may be highly significant for understanding how, and whether, individuals choose to engage with political institutions and processes. As researchers, we need to ensure that we are sensitive to how respondents themselves conceive of the political, and this means avoiding making easy assumptions about non-participation.

1.2.3   Towards structured lived experience

Consequently, we want to move beyond arena-based conceptions in order to understand politics as lived experience. Our key point here is that if we treat politics as something outside people's experience, that is, in a sense, as merely something that is 'done unto' them, then we negate how people view, experience and live politics. Indeed, this is almost inevitable if we start from the understanding of politics advocated by Parry *et al.* or Pattie *et al.* Rather, we treat politics as a lived experience, more specifically as a structured lived experience.

We need to be clear about how we are using the idea of 'lived experience', as it is a term which can have a number of meanings. We shall set out our position by initially returning to the work of Pattie *et al.* (2004) in order to make it clear how our work differs. We start by quoting their comment on our previous work (Pattie *et al.*, 2004, p. 76, footnote 1):

> Critics of our methodology often claim that it imposes a narrow and normative definition of politics. A research team studying young people's attitudes and behaviour by using qualitative research suggest that the young define politics as 'anything to do with government, including the running of schools, hospitals and the police', and that their political behaviour is broader than an activity engaged in periodically, but is rather a 'lived experience'. While we do not disagree

with the point that politics to most people is broadly defined [. . .], nevertheless Marsh and his colleagues do not suggest any new, alternative forms of political participation which were excluded from our methodology.

We shall engage directly with this quote, not just because we want to defend our own work (although of course we do), but mainly because we want to explore more fully the differences between their work and our own. The best way to do that is to start by reiterating the areas of agreement between us and then moving beyond that to consider areas of contention. In particular, we want to focus on what we mean when we talk about 'age', 'class', 'ethnicity' or 'gender', as lived experience. More generally, we shall also suggest that our differences, in large part, reflect different ontological and epistemological positions.

Pattie *et al.*'s position is positivist and this is the dominant position in political participation research, but it is not our position. The positivists' aim is to produce generalisable causal statements about the relationship between social phenomena; in their view objectivity is possible. As such, they do not acknowledge the double hermeneutic. To almost all non-positivists, the most social science can achieve is our (the social scientists') understanding – the first level of the hermeneutic – of their (those we study) understanding of their actions and the social world more generally – the second level of the hermeneutic (for an introduction to these issues, see Marsh and Furlong, 2002). We do recognise that most modern positivists acknowledge the critiques of their position and positivism has consequently changed significantly, although much remains the same.

To take one UK example, David Sanders (2002), who is an excellent representative of the modern positivist position, acknowledges his debt to the positivist position, but recognises the 'ferocious philosophical criticism' to which it has been subjected. He argues that 'post-behaviouralists', who might also be called 'post-positivists': 'acknowledge the interdependence of theory and observation; recognise that normative questions are important and not always easy to separate from empirical questions; and accept that other traditions have a key role to play in political and social analysis' (Sanders, 2002, pp. 51–55). However, the ontological and epistemological issues which divided positivism from other positions have not gone away, rather they have been elided. Two quotes from Sanders illustrate this point. First, he argues (2002, p. 51):

Modern behaviouralists – 'post-behaviouralists' – simply prefer to subject their own theoretical claims to empirical tests. They also suspect that scholars working in non-empirical traditions are never able to provide a satisfactory answer to the crucial questions: 'How would you know if you were wrong?'

Later, he continues (2002, p. 54):

For modern behaviouralists, the ultimate test of a good theory is still whether or not it is consistent with observation – with the available empirical evidence. Modern behaviouralists are perfectly prepared to accept that different theoretical positions are likely to produce different observations. They insist however, that, whatever 'observations' are implied by a particular theoretical perspective, those observations must be used in order to conduct a systematic empirical test of the theory that is being posited.

This is a sophisticated statement of a positivist epistemological position, but it is still essentially positivist. The aim is to use observation (of whatever type) to test hypothesised relationships between the social phenomena studied. Research from within other traditions must still be judged against the positivists' criteria: 'observation must be used in order to conduct a systemic empirical test of the theory that is being posited'. Yet, that is not a standard most researchers from within a realist, let alone an interpretivist, tradition could accept (see Marsh and Furlong, 2002). Epistemological realists would see some of the key social relationships in the world as unobservable; so there is a disjuncture between appearance and reality. Interpretivists go further; to them observation is not 'objective' and thus cannot be used as a test of 'reality'.

One other aspect of Sanders' position is important here. He accepts that interpretation and meaning are important, which might suggest that the differences between positivist and interpretivist traditions are beginning to dissolve. So, Sanders (2002, p. 53), in criticising prior studies of voting behaviour, formulates an argument that would equally hold for many mainstream studies of participation: 'There are other areas – relating to the way in which individuals reflect, to a greater or lesser degree, upon themselves – where behavioural research has simply not dared to tread.' He recognises that such factors might, or might not, be important, but emphasises that they would be difficult to study empirically. However, the crucial point is that Sanders wants to treat interpretation and meaning as intervening variables. In this view, how a voter understands the parties and his/her own position may affect his/her voting behaviour. At best, this acknowledges only one element of one aspect of the double hermeneutic; in contrast, the interpretivist tradition would argue that we also need to acknowledge the subjectivity of the observer.

So, positivism has changed in response to criticism. Post-positivism is somewhat less assertive than was earlier positivism that there is only one way of doing social science. However, it still emphasises explanation, rather than understanding, and the primacy of direct observation. In our view, it is still foundationalist in ontological terms and located in the scientific tradition. Pattie *et al.*, and indeed Norris, are firmly within the positivist camp and their studies reflect that position. Their work has great value and represents an advance on previous work within the positivist tradition. But, there are other issues about how people understand politics and how that understanding affects their actions or inactions and those are the issues that we explore.

So, let us return to our view that politics can be seen as 'lived experience' in the light of this brief discussion of epistemology. What does that mean? The idea of lived experience would seem inevitably to privilege the view of the actor. Yet, the interpretation of the observer, in this case the social scientist, is always involved. We need to bear this in mind when we consider the four positions we can identify on 'lived experience', in part because these positions reflect broadly different ontological and epistemological stances.

1.2.3.1 Lived experience as a possession

Some sociologists and cultural analysts see experiences as something we can gain or possess. So, we can access the experience of others, perhaps those whose voices have not been heard in political science, sociology or the study of history, in order to question dominant accounts. In criticising this position many have suggested that this view remains foundationalist as the experience of those without voice is appealed to as being 'true'. In addition, the suggestion is that we, as observers, can discover the 'real' understandings of those we observe.

1.2.3.2 Lived experience as belonging

A second position sees experience both as a thing that is possessed by the individual and also as involving a process which defines the group to which the individual belongs; here we return to the idea of identity politics discussed previously. This position rests on what is usually known as standpoint epistemology. Here, the view is that the only people who can understand an experience are the people who are experiencing, or have experienced, it. So, the only people who can understand the experience of women are women (not men), and the only people who can understand the experience of black women are black women (not white women or black men). Understanding is possible, but only for those privileged because they share the same experience as those they observe.

1.2.3.3   Lived experience as a process

Here, the argument is that individuals, or subjects, have experiences; they are constituted through experience. In this view it would be claimed that experience is at once an interpretation and something to be interpreted. As such, experience is neither 'self-evident', nor uncontested. This is based upon an anti-foundationalist ontological position. Here, we are involved in interpreting those subjects' interpretations of the world; the double hermeneutic is at the core of this position. From this position, it is also crucial that we are reflexive about our interpretations as observers; we, as observers, are partial, in both senses of the term, and we must, as far as possible, acknowledge those partialities.

1.2.3.4   Lived experience as a structured process

This position shares much in common with the previous one, but we spend more time discussing it, because it is the position adopted here. We acknowledge the central importance of the double hermeneutic. So, an agent's understanding of the world, of meanings and actions, crucially shapes her/his behaviour. At the same time, there is no objective, non-fallible, knowledge; although there is a 'real' world independent of our knowledge of it, the way we, as social scientists, interpret the world is theory-dependent. As Cruickshank (2002, pp. 1–2) puts it:

> This (realist) view of knowledge holds that there is an objective reality, and instead of hoping one day we will somehow have absolute knowledge, the expectation is that knowledge claims will continue to be better interpretations of reality. As knowledge claims are fallible, the best we can do is improve our interpretations of reality, rather than seek a definitive, finished 'Truth'.

Nevertheless, our theories do make claims both about how this 'real' world impacts upon our understandings of it and about our behaviour.

As such, experiences are structured by 'real' world processes. Thus, a society like the UK is characterised by structured inequalities that effect, but by no means determine, the lived experience of citizens. In ontological terms, this position is foundationalist and in epistemological terms realist, more specifically critical realist.

In our view then age, gender, ethnicity and class are not independent variables to be used to predict participation; rather, they are 'lived experience' or identities which shape our respondents' political experiences and how they understand politics. This returns us to epistemological issues. In treating age, class, ethnicity and gender as independent variables, positivists like Pattie *et al.* see these as relatively fixed categories that have a consistent affect across time and space. So, they are not interested in what age, class, ethnicity or gender 'mean' to their respondents or, in our terms, how they live it, and how these meanings affect their actions, including the extent and the form of their political participation. As such, in our view their approach has significant limitations and, consequently, we will focus on our respondents' understanding of age (specifically youth), class, gender and ethnicity to see how that understanding shapes their understanding of politics and their 'political' activity.

There is another key point here which returns us to the issue of identity politics raised earlier. The literature on identity politics claims that people share an acknowledged identity, but, in our view, this is problematic for two reasons. First, we do not agree that identities can simply be read off from a person's ethnicity or gender. Nor do we accept that, if it cannot be read off where individuals are not conscious of their real 'identity', it is because their identities have been manipulated by the dominant culture or discourse. However, at the same time, we also do not accept the anti-foundationalist or post-structuralist view of identity, that it is complex and fluid, with the subject always a product of discourse. In contrast, as throughout, we hold to a critical realist position and suggest that we need to acknowledge the structural as well as the discursive constraints on how individuals construct and indeed live their identity, or what Butler (1999) calls their 'performativity'.

1.3 Conclusion

In this chapter, we have presented and then critiqued what we see as the best contemporary mainstream literature on political participation, especially in the UK. We did that in order to establish the parameters of our research. Consequently, our critique of the existing literature informs the methodology we adopted for our research and we outline this in Chapter 3. However, we have also argued strongly that debates about political participation need to be viewed in the broader context of arguments about citizenship and governance and these issues provide the focus of the next chapter.

2
The Context and Consequence of Political Participation: Citizenship and Governance in the UK

In the UK, and many other advanced democracies, the study of declining electoral engagement and the rise of other forms of political and civic participation has been conducted alongside increased public and academic interest in the nature and scope of citizenship and governance. In this chapter we address issues of citizenship and governance because they provide a key part of the context within which debates about the political participation of young people, and thus our study, are conducted. As such, this chapter is divided into four substantive sections.

Section 2.1 looks briefly at the reasons for the renewed interest in ideas of citizenship. It is important to note that debates about citizenship revolve around some well-established positions and that normative conceptions of what it means to be a 'good' or 'active' citizen vary considerably. In section 2.2, we set out the various conceptions of citizenship that underpin public and academic debates, highlighting the very different views on the proper nature and extent of participation that these express.

Debates about citizenship in the UK, as in many other countries, occur in the context of discussions of changing governance and democratic renewal. Section 2.3 discusses the relationship between governance and participation, examining existing explanations of both the cause and the consequences of the shift from government to governance, with a particular focus upon Henrik Bang's (2004) argument that the move towards governance has been associated with the development of changing forms of political participation. A number of researchers and commentators suggest that changes in governance practices, based on networks, rather than hierarchy or markets, have led to more participatory governance and the emergence of 'new citizens' who relate to politics in a different way and whose activism has shifted onto a rather different set of issues, terrains and levels (see, for example, the 2006 UK 'Power Inquiry').

However, section 2.4 takes issue with the idea that there has been a move towards participatory governance in the UK. We argue that, historically, a dominant, thin, conception of democracy and citizenship has underpinned both the institutions and the practices of British Government and is a key aspect of the framework within which contemporary politics occurs. Recently, this dominant conception of democracy and citizenship has been challenged by arguments for more active forms of citizenship associated with the perceived move to governance. In the UK context, New Labour has been particularly concerned with promoting active citizenship and participatory and devolved forms of decision-making. We argue, however, that New Labour's concern with active citizenship and participatory governance is less concerned with democratising the processes and practices of government than with issues of securing governmental legitimacy and enhanced policy efficiency.

2.1   A renewed interest in citizenship

Questions of citizenship have received considerable attention in public and policy spheres. Consequently, Pattie *et al.* (2004, p. 1) argue that:

> The meaning of citizenship, the relationship between citizens and government and problems of representation and accountability in the modern state have all become the focus of research in recent years.

It is possible to identify a number of reasons for this increased interest. In the first place, the consequences of globalisation since the late twentieth century have profoundly affected the relationship between states and citizens. In particular, there has been a 'hollowing out' of the state. As such, the loci of political power have relocated upwards to supranational bodies, downwards through processes of devolution or regionalisation, or outwards to non-state actors such as transnational corporations and non-governmental organisations. Such trends have altered the relationship between the state and its citizens in terms of: the location of decision-making processes; who is included within these processes; and the foci or targets of citizen's political action. Furthermore, with the globalisation of political economy and conflicts around the world (Castles, 2003) and the growth of environmentalism, political issues and movements have become increasingly globally interconnected and this has been facilitated by the development of new Information and Communication Technologies (ICTs). These trends have occurred alongside massive migration movements, intensifying both the transnational dimensions of political campaigns and diasporic political activity. These patterns of migration have also produced increasingly multicultural societies, prompting a reassessment of citizenship identities in many states, as well as the sense that a key political problem for contemporary states is the ability to govern culturally diverse societies. Finally, the increased pressure on the welfare state has challenged conceptions about the role and ability of the state to ensure, or create, the conditions for social equity or even well-being among its citizens.

In addition to these contextual changes, there has also been an increased interest in the potential of civil society to provide solutions to a variety of problems of governance, whether by harnessing social capital and social trust within civil society to enhance the effectiveness of governance, or by promoting civil society to directly provide public goods and services. So, within the UK, where our study is located, there have been government initiatives and cross-party interest in fostering 'active citizens' – as 'social entrepreneurs', agents of neighbourhood renewal and urban regeneration or partners in governance networks; developments we return to below. However, the normative conceptions of what it means to be a 'good' or 'active' citizen differ considerably. In section 2.2, we set out the very different conceptions of citizenship that inform public and academic debates.

2.2 Debates about citizenship[1]

We do not follow Pattie *et al.*'s treatment of the literature on citizenship (2003, pp. 5–22), which appears to us to be too narrow, suggesting a very thin, procedural, notion of citizenship rooted in rational choice theory. In our view, this notion misses many, especially normative, aspects of citizenship which other positions see as important, particularly its intrinsic value, relationship to identity and expressive and symbolic importance. Instead, we identify some of the key distinctions within the literature in relation to the normative aspects of citizenship.

Normative debates about citizenship revolve around three main issues: the *extent* of citizenship; the *content* of citizenship; and the *depth* of citizenship (see, for example, Turner, 1993, p. 3; Faulks, 2000, p. 7; Islin and Turner, 2002, p. 2).

The concern with the extent of citizenship refers to the appropriate criteria for the inclusion and exclusion of individuals as citizens. Whilst young people, formally at least, are citizens, this is complicated by confused and often contradictory policies on young people's legal, political and social rights (Newman, 1996). As we show in Chapter 4, this has clear implications for young people's conceptions of themselves as political participants. Questions regarding the extent of citizenship are also key issues in contemporary Britain in other respects, as witnessed by media coverage of refugees and asylum seekers and the rights of new migrants.

As regards the content of citizenship, two issues are important. First, there is the balance between rights and responsibilities, which is a key question that divides liberals from others. In essence, some theorists, classical liberals and neo-liberals particularly, privilege individual rights[2] and downplay both the role of the state and the responsibilities/duties that individuals have to the state. In contrast, others, like communitarians, civic republicans and neo-conservatives, albeit to different extents and in different ways, see the state as crucial to preserving order and emphasise the duties that individuals have to the state. Secondly, and relatedly, there is a dispute over the balance that should be struck between the individual and society; where liberals emphasise the individual, while communitarians and civic republicans put strong emphasis on community and society.

Finally, in relation to the depth of citizenship, the issue concerns whether we should have a thin or thick conceptualisation of citizenship; that is how active a conceptualisation of citizenship is appropriate or possible in contemporary advanced liberal democracies. To put it another way, we can distinguish between positions that see citizens as subjects, who have rights and duties conferred upon them by the state, and citizens as sovereign, who are the authors of those rights and duties. Liberals tend to have a limited, thin, view of citizenship, so citizens are subjects, whereas participatory democracy theorists particularly have a very thick view, with a strong emphasis on active participation and citizens as sovereign.

These preliminary distinctions in thinking about citizenship open up three broad approaches to citizenship: those that focus upon the *rights* that individuals have as citizens; those that stress the *responsibilities* of citizenship; and those that see citizenship in terms of *active participation*. Below, we outline these differing approaches in order to clarify our view of the relationship between political participation and citizenship.

2.2.1 Rights-based conceptions of citizenship

Here, we identify two related positions: liberalism, which includes contemporary neo-liberalism, and social liberalism, especially associated with the work of T. H. Marshall (1950). There is no doubt, as Janoski and Gran (2002, p. 17) argue, that 'liberalism is by far the dominant theory in philosophy and political theory in Anglo-Saxon democracies'.

Liberalism places very strong emphasis on individual and negative rights and argues that the individual should be free to pursue her/his preferences, subject to limited state interference. To the classical liberal, and in modern neo-liberal thought, legal and political rights come first, especially civil liberties and political rights, with the consequence that social and economic rights are downplayed. At the same time, there is little emphasis on obligations or duties; for most liberals even obeying the law is a matter of incentive and calculation, not obligation.

All this means that liberals have a very restricted conception of politics and make a clear distinction between the public and the private spheres. More specifically, they operate with an arena-based definition of politics,[3] so, for the liberal, 'the political' is equated with the public sphere and civil society with the private sphere. In this view, the state should confine its activities to the public sphere, while in civil society the individual should be free to pursue personal goals with minimal constraint from the state. As such, people should have the opportunity to participate, which necessitates civil and political rights, but if they do not participate that is their choice. Since participation is regarded as an individual choice, non-participation is usually seen as reflecting a lack of interest, or as an expression of apathy. Because of the tendency to see participation as taking place within particular public arenas, liberal studies of political participation generally operate with a narrow definition of political participation that is focused on voting, party membership or interest group activity.[4]

While classical liberalism remained dominant after the Second World War in the US, and experienced a resurgence in the guise of neo-liberalism for periods after 1980 in countries like the UK, New Zealand and Australia, the key strand of liberalism in most of Europe has been, and to a large extent remains, social liberalism. Social liberalism is strongly associated with the work of T.H. Marshall (1950), who famously distinguished between civil, political and social rights. This distinction was rooted in his identification of the three chronological stages in the development of citizenship in the UK: civil rights, basically property rights, were established by the end of the eighteenth century; political rights, particularly voting (although initially not for women), were established in the nineteenth century;[5] and social rights were established in the twentieth century. His focus was upon the formal political, legal and social rights that underpin citizenship. So, Marshall was much more concerned with social rights than were the classical liberals. At the same time, he recognised the importance of the social and political conditions under which those rights are exercised.

Indeed, as Turner (1993, p. 6) argues, 'placing Marshall within a wider context, we can see his work as the legacy of the liberal political response to the problem of the relationship between democracy and capitalism'. Consequently, Marshall, unlike classical liberals, recognised both that it was impossible to exercise political rights without social rights and that inequalities prevented the exercise of full citizenship. He also had a broader, if still limited, notion of the duties of citizenship than classical liberals and saw the state as having a key role to play in ensuring a more equal playing field. Marshall's ideas significantly influenced the thinking behind the establishment of the welfare state in the UK; indeed to him the welfare state represented the institutionalisation of social rights. His ideas also had an important influence on the growth of social democracy in Europe.

However, Marshall, like classical liberals, still operates with an arena-based definition of politics and thus a limited idea of political participation. Relatedly, while he recognised the relationship between the public and the private, he retained the distinction to the extent that he saw state and politics as part of the public realm and the family as part of the private realm, and hence apolitical, a position later strongly criticised by feminists.

2.2.2   Responsibility-based conceptions of citizenship

Here, we consider three positions which share a focus on the responsibilities of citizenship and the key role of the state in the preservation of social order, although they differ in other senses: communitarianism; civic republicanism; and neo-conservatism.

Communitarianism has a strong emphasis on community membership and takes a more holistic view of society, concerned above all with stability, integration and order. Communitarians are critical of the excessively rights-centred approach of liberals and, instead, place a strong emphasis on the responsibilities of citizenship. Their aim is to ensure a cohesive society with a strong common identity; here, collectivities, both the society in general and the groups within it, are more important than individuals and their rights. The state plays a pivotal role in ensuring order and, if necessary, constraining individual freedoms.

Citizens are expected to fulfil obligations and one of those involves participation in the political process. Like rights-based views, communitarians operate with an arena-based definition of politics and a separation between the public/state and the private/civil society. However, this separation is not as pronounced as in liberalism, because communitarians, unlike liberals, do not see the state as threatening individual freedom and, as such, individuals do not need rights to protect a private realm from the state.

Another variation of those approaches that are primarily concerned with the responsibilities of citizenship is expressed by civic republicanism, which has a long history stretching back to ancient Greece and Rome. Here, the emphasis is upon 'civic virtues' as the qualities necessary for responsible citizenship; citizenship is not based on self-interest as it is for liberals. As such, the focus of civic republicanism is upon civic virtue and duty and the need to foster this civic virtue.

Here, there is a narrow arena definition of politics and a clear distinction between the public and the private, although there is much more emphasis on the role of civil society than in communitarianism or neo-conservatism. In particular, political participation is seen, not as a means to affect government and pursue one's interest, as it is for liberals or communitarians, but as an end in itself; a proof of civic virtue and an indicator of a healthy society.

More recently, we see the emergence of a neo-conservative concern with the responsibilities of citizenship. As Lister (2003, p. 17) argues, at the turn of the twenty-first century, 'an increasingly influential "duties discourse" (has been), in various guises, supplanting the dominant postwar social rights paradigm'. As we saw, the duties discourse is a crucial aspect of communitarianism, but neo-conservatism has become an increasingly important perspective, especially in the US. It emphasises citizens' obligations and, to a limited extent, the role of the state in preserving order. However, the main emphasis is upon responsibilities in the workplace and particularly the 'duty to work'. So, while both neo-liberals and neo-conservatives would emphasise work, the former would rely on financial incentives to encourage it, while the latter would see coercion as an option. One can see how neo-conservatism and neo-liberalism can be reconciled; the state's main job is to ensure that people work, so that they are not a drain on society and, particularly, on business.

Once again, this articulates an arena-based definition of politics and a clear distinction between the public and the private, where the primary duty of citizens is to participate in the workplace and exercise responsibility for themselves and their families.

2.2.3   Participatory-based conceptions of citizenship

Here, we look first at what we call 'radical conceptions', before turning to the postmodern or post-structuralist position. These receive more attention than the other positions in this chapter because our own perspective is informed by the debate between radical and postmodern/post-structuralist positions.

There are a variety of radical views. All, however, emphasise the need for more participation and a more active, thicker, citizenship. Barber (1998), for example, advocates a 'strong democracy' that seeks to maximise citizen participation. Here, civil society is seen as an inclusive, mediating, civil domain made of voluntary groups, in which the public and the private realms are fused. Government must be more responsive and active in encouraging civic life.

At the same time, most radicals also emphasise the presence of structured inequality in society. So, Barber (1998) argues that corporations dominate government and therefore contemporary capitalist democracies. As such, if government does not act to ensure that they relinquish much of their power, then that will be the end of democracy. In a similar vein, Marxists and materialist, or second-wave (for a brief discussion of second-wave feminism, see Chapter 6), feminists and anti-racists contend that liberals place too much emphasis on individual agency and insufficient focus on the structural constraints that particular groups face. They emphasise that inequalities, based upon class, gender and 'race', constrain the individual's access to citizenship. In essence, they argue that liberals ignore the power structures in society which facilitate the participation and influence of some, while constraining the participation and influence of others.

There are differences of focus between radicals as to how groups disadvantaged, with Marxists (and to an extent Barber) focusing on economic or class inequalities, while feminists privilege gender inequalities and anti-racists focus on inequalities that follow from racism and racialisation. However, here we are more concerned with what unites them and that is a criticism of the liberal view that politics occurs on a level playing field and that individual choices are open and not structurally constrained. Faulks (2000, pp. 9–10) effectively summarises this position and its putative solution to the problem of citizenship: 'The key to rendering citizenship more inclusive is to recognise the inherently racialised, patriarchal and class-based nature of the state and the corrosive effects of the free market upon rights and responsibilities.' In this view, as Faulks (2000, p. 10) again argues, 'the citizenship liberals advocate has been too thin and has been subordinated to market principles and the interests of political and economic elites'.

Such a radical perspective would emphasise the rights of, and the need for increased participation by, excluded groups (such as the working class, women, ethnic minorities, etc.). However, rights are not prioritised at the expense of duties. Indeed, on this issue, many radicals take an intermediary position between liberalism and communitarianism. So, in contrast to communitarianism, this position sees empowerment and participation as rights, not duties, but, in contrast to liberalism, it believes that individuals need more equal access to resources in order to exercise those rights. Overall, rights and obligations are seen as symbiotically related. As Janoski and Gran (2002, p. 19) argue, political participation results in the growth of a self-identity that: 'fuses individual interests through participation in community activities, whether they are work, neighbourhood, or welfare-related needs, but at the same time it protects individual rights'.

For the radical then, politics extends well beyond the formal political arena; politics is a lived experience (the idea of politics as a lived experience was discussed at more length in Chapter 1) and individuals' experiences in all aspects of their lives can have a political dimension. At the same time, the ways in which rights and duties are experienced or lived are classed, gendered and raced. More broadly, most radicals wish to subvert the distinction between the public and the private.[6] This argument is most associated with feminism, particularly second-wave feminism. These feminists saw the clear demarcation between the public and the private sphere as meaning that women's concerns, for example domestic violence, were ignored by the state and the gendered hierarchy that existed in the family was thereby rendered non-political. In addition, they also saw this distinction as often accompanied by a view that while the public sphere was male, the private, domestic, sphere was female.

From this perspective, the failure of individuals to participate in the formal political arena, by voting, joining a political party or demonstrating, is not usually a sign of apathy. Rather, it may reflect alienation from a political system which is biased against them. At the same time, although they may not be involved in formal political activity, they may be involved in community groups or local action that plays a crucial role in shaping their identity and also, perhaps, empowers them. In addition, if the 'personal is political', then formal political activity is not necessarily the most important dimension of political engagement. Nevertheless, to the radical, the depth of citizenship will only really improve if (see Barber, 1998) citizens have the time, resources and opportunity to gain education and participate.

Another perspective on the participatory aspects of citizenship is expressed by postmodern/post-structuralist theorists. A key difference between this perspective and the radical perspective just examined, perhaps unsurprisingly, is that it privileges agency over structure. Indeed, some postmodern theories claim citizenship is dead, rather in the way, as we shall see in Chapter 5, that they see class is dead, because they take an anti-foundationalist ontological stance. Here, citizenship is seen as a static idea in a multi-facetted, ever-changing world in which difference is the only defensible absolute value.

However, the radical pluralism of Laclau and Mouffe engages directly with issues of citizenship, while seeing it as an ever-changing, contested idea. Mouffe (1993) uses the term 'agonistic pluralism' to characterise her conception of politics. It involves: 'confrontation between adversaries who agree on [. . .] the rules of the game while disagreeing not only about substantial, political and moral issues but also about precise interpretation of the rules of the game' (1993, p. 502). The aim is to advocate an open, continually contested, democracy where difference is axiomatic and there is a thick citizenship.

In this view, the distinction between the public and the private is false, but it is also a construct which reflects existing power relations. As Rasmussen and Brown (2000, p. 177) put it, 'The category of citizen drove a wedge between the public political citizen and the private self within civil society, hiding the real sources of power within the sphere of the private.'

At the same time, this approach calls into question the limited, and limiting, concept of the political in liberal thought. As Laclau (1990, p. 185) argues:

> the terrain of the political must be expanded to consider a wider range of potentially political activities and locations because power operate[s] at a range of sites and the definition of politics [is] the chief site of politics: the distinctions public/private, civil society/political society are only the result of a certain type of hegemonic articulation, and their limits vary in accordance with the existing relations of forces at a given moment.

Indeed, Mouffe suggests that the conflict between the liberal concern for individual autonomy and the communitarian concern with unity and community is actually the location of the political. In a similar vein, Rasmussen and Brown (2000, p. 178) argue: 'The subject of politics and the terrain of politics [are] mutually constitutive and engaged in constant struggle.'

So, to these theorists, the idea of citizenship needs to be rethought: 'Radicalising the site of democracy require[s] a rethinking of the place of citizenship within politics. Politicising social relations and resisting the privileging of any particular positions, citizenship [can] not be defined as a fixed identity in relation to a state or a community' (Rasmussen and Brown, 2000, p. 178). They also suggest (2000, p. 178) that citizenship is no longer an identity, but, rather, a 'political activity involving a struggle for hegemony'. Consequently, it is a struggle which can occur on many sites, involving 'engagement with the state, in the economy, or in the everyday practices of identity formation'.

To sum up, Rasmussen and Brown (2000, p. 179) emphasise that the radical democracy perspective identifies three features of the way individuals understand their position in contemporary politics: first, all political struggle is temporary and contextual; second, political agency, that is citizenship, involves a continual process of struggle; third, the location of that struggle is identity formation.

As such, identity is a crucial concept in this approach: it is the site of politics and is multi-facetted, contested and ever-changing. As Rasmussen and Brown (2000, p. 182) put it:

> identity [can] not be understood as pre-political, either as an authentic essence or the private construction of the subject, but nor [can] it be fully determined by the essence of the social structure – the Marxist version. Rather, identity must become the ultimate site of politics, determined neither by the agent nor by the structure but in the process of struggle.

They continue (Rasmussen and Brown, 2000, p. 182): 'The agency of citizenship is the act of identification, of seeking identity in familiar forms of representation – ethnicity, nationality, race, gender, and sexuality – that shape but do not determine the subject'.

All this means that politics and citizenship is seen as involving a search for, and expression of, identity. As Lister (2003, p. 24) puts it:

> The case for acknowledging less formal expressions of citizen-ship responsibility has also been made in relation to mutual aid and self-help activities. These provide an example of more radical

and collectivist conceptions of active citizenship, as embodied in Ray Pahl's alternative definition: 'local people working together to improve their own quality of life and to provide the conditions for others to enjoy the fruits of a more affluent society' (Pahl, 1990, 8). This is a form of active citizenship that disadvantaged people, often women, do for themselves, for instance through community groups, rather than a paternalistic top-down relationship; one that creates them as subjects rather than objects.

Most classic studies of political participation operate with a liberal view of citizenship. In this view, young people have the opportunity to participate, and if they do not, that is their choice. So, non-participation reflects apathy: an idea we are critical of throughout this book. At the same time, many, more recent, studies of political participation operate with a social liberal or, perhaps more often, a radical view. Here, citizenship and political participation are seen, in the social liberal view, as constrained by access to resources, or, in the radical view, as classed, raced and gendered.

Our position is influenced by both the radical and the post-structuralist views of citizenship, although more by the former than the latter, as should be clear from our discussion of ontology and epistemology in the previous chapter. We do acknowledge, like post-structuralists, that politics involves a contested struggle about identity and that, in contemporary society, identity is complex. However, post-structuralists see this struggle as more open than we would. In our view, young people's struggles for a political identity occur on a terrain that reflects age, class, gender and ethnic inequalities, that is on a structured terrain.

2.3   Governance and changing political participation

It is almost a commonplace in contemporary analyses of liberal democracies to identify a move from government to governance. In this section we look first at the reasons given for that change, then focus on the supposed characteristics of contemporary governance, before finally addressing the link between governance and participation.

2.3.1   Rapid change and the move towards governance

Many authors have made sweeping claims about the extent of changes in the economy, culture and politics in recent times. So, in relation to the economy, authors identify the rise of post-Fordism and/or of globalisation (see Held *et al.*, 1999 among many others) or the replacement of production location by consumption location (see Pakulski and Waters, 1996) as the key feature of change. In relation to culture, some authors argue that lifestyle has replaced class, and even gender, as the key social force shaping society and politics (see, for example, Pakulski and Waters, 1996), while others emphasise the rise of celebrity culture (see, for example, Rojek, 2001) or the increased globalisation of the media and of culture (see, for example, Held *et al.*, 1999, Chapter 7) – often seen as Americanisation. In politics, several authors have emphasised variously: the decline of the nation state (see, for example, Held *et al.*, 1999, Chapter 1); the decline of the welfare state; the replacement of hierarchy by markets, and especially networks, as a mode of governance (see, for example, Rhodes, 1997); and the growth of different forms of politics (Bang, 2004).

Some of the theorising of contemporary changes in governance has been broader and a number of authors have talked of a shift to 'late-modernity', 'post-modernity', 'reflexive-modernity' (Beck, 1994a), 'institutional reflexivity' (Giddens, 1994)[7] or 'liquid modernity' (Bauman, 2000). We are particularly interested here in the debates about reflexive modernity and, particularly, the arguments of Beck and Giddens which have particular resonance with Bang's analysis which we set out below.

Beck (1994, p. 2) argues against the view that there is a simple linear process of modernity, suggesting that 'high-speed industrial dynamism' undercuts the structures and processes of modernity and leads to a new, 'reflexive modernity' (1994, p. 3). This process happens without revolution or even policy change and the process is unintended, unpolitical and unplanned. To Beck (1994, pp. 4–5), this change to a period of reflexive modernity results, in large part, from increased 'risk' and resultant changes in the way risk is managed. So, in the past there was a consensus that social, economic and political risks could be addressed through the Enlightenment project; that is by utilising increased knowledge, particularly scientific knowledge, to propose solutions to social, economic and political problems and ensure 'progress'. However, now risk is at the centre of people's concerns: uncertainty and risk are key aspects of their lived experience and they are increasingly aware that the old institutional system cannot deal with those risks.[8] Consequently, reflexive modernisation is the way in which people face the effects of risk.

To Beck, politics has also changed. The nation state has metamorphised; it has 'hollowed out', although he does not use the term. So, he suggests (1994, p. 39) that 'the authoritarian decision and action state' has disappeared. In its place, a new 'sub-politics' has emerged (1994, pp. 42–44). This politics is based on communities and localities and involves activities outside the traditional sphere of government.[9] This discussion has clear resonance with Rhodes' argument, discussed below, about the move from governance based on hierarchy to governance based on networks. The key aspect of this new political activity to Beck is reflexive self-organisation and, although that process often involves professional experts, it is crucial to Beck that it occurs outside the old political arenas. As we shall see, there is a clear overlap here with Bang's 'Expert Citizens'.

In contrast, Giddens is concerned to see how the notion of tradition has changed in reflexive modernity. He suggests that, in the past, tradition was a way of managing risk. According to Giddens (1994, p. 63), tradition involves collective memory, ritual and 'formulaic truth'; it has 'guardians' to promote, protect and perpetuate it. It binds people symbolically, both in terms of identity and emotionally. In Giddens' view, tradition 'remained central' in early modernism and science, to an extent, had formulaic power. However, subsequently, new traditions developed, especially associated with the rise of feminism (1994, p. 94). At the same time, tradition was undermined by 'the evacuations of most traditional contexts of action' (1994, p. 96). For Giddens, in the period of 'high modernity' which preceded reflexive modernity, or institutional reflexivity, the 'core aspects of social life' were the family and sexual identity (1994, p. 56). It is when these core aspects began to be undermined that the move to reflexive modernity occurred.

To Giddens, unlike Beck, the role of trust is as important as that of risk. In reflexive modernity, 'active trust' is supplanting older traditions of personal trust. In high modernity, trust was linked to social status, now people have to win trust and actively sustain it. Now, he suggests: 'Active trust depends on more institutional 'opening out' (1994, p. 187). In some ways as a response to this problem, new forms of democracy have developed in reflexive modernisation (1994, pp. 190–194). More specifically, the following are emerging: (i) increased emotional democracy among families and friends (1994, p. 192); (ii) more 'flexible and decentralised systems of authority' which are replacing bureaucracies and hierarchies, although not uniformly; and (iii) new modes of social association, such as self-help groups, are challenging existing authorities. Again, this idea has resonance with Bang's work, but this time with the idea of 'Expert Citizens' and 'Everyday Makers', who Bang sees as civil society actors engaged in horizontal, reflexive and networked forms of participation. Overall, according to Giddens, the post-traditional society of reflexive modernity is (1994, p. 193):

> a global society, not in the sense of a world society but as one of 'indefinite space.' It is one where social bonds have effectively to be made, rather than inherited from the past [...] It is decentred in the terms of authorities, but recentred in terms of opportunities and dilemmas, because focused upon new forms of independence.

As we shall explore in later chapters (and particularly Chapter 7), these developments are seen as particularly important in politicising identity, since identities are no longer seen in terms of traditional norms, practices and roles; rather they are seen as reflexively constituted, where identity itself becomes a political project – in large part due to the rise of social movements such as feminism, gay rights and civil rights. As a consequence, identity and difference become key terrains on which political struggles occur – reflecting what Giddens refers to as 'Life Politics' or a 'politics of identity as well as of choice' (1994, p. 91).

2.3.2 Governance

As we already indicated, over the last decade or so, the move from a focus on government to a focus on governance has been one of the most noticeable developments in political science generally, and in the study of public policy particularly. It is also an idea which, indirectly but not directly, is referred to in Beck's discussion of reflexive modernity.

As Rhodes (1997, p. 15) argues: 'The term "governance" refers to a change in the meaning of government, referring to a new process of governing.' He defines governance as involving (1997, p. 15) 'self-organising, interorganizational networks characterised by interdependence, resource exchange, rules of the game and significant autonomy from the state'. In a similar vein, Pierre (2000) asserts that modern governance is no longer state-centred with government steering; rather it involves more hybrid, informal and co-operative processes. Rhodes (1997) sees this change as involving the replacement of hierarchy and markets by networks as the dominant mode of modern governance. In effect, he argues that such change results, in large part, from the increased complexity, dynamism and diversity in what Beck and Giddens term 'reflexive modernity'. This complexity, dynamism and diversity result from a variety of processes, including globalisation, devolution and the growth of non-governmental organisations and lead in this view to a 'hollowing out' of the state.[10]

More broadly, Newman (2005b, p. 8) identifies four processes involved in remaking governance:

1. A shift from government to networked, multi-level processes of governance
2. Welfare-state transformation in response to globalising pressures
3. The development of new technologies of power through which subjects are constituted
4. The emergence of collaborative or participatory governance associated with the replacement of hierarchy by networks.

Here, it is easy to see how the emphasis on governance links to discussions of participation. So, Newman (2005c, p. 119) defines 'participatory governance' as: 'a *decentred* form of governance in which the role of the state – and the institutions of representative democracy on which it rests – is viewed as unable to deal with the complexity of policy problems and to the differentiated needs and identities of citizens' (see also Kooiman, 2000). This argument has probably been most fully, and certainly most interestingly, addressed by Henrik Bang (2003, 2004) and it is to his argument that we turn next.

2.3.3   Governance and participation: Bang on

Bang builds upon these arguments about reflexive modernity and governance and, in our view, offers a very interesting interpretation of the so-called 'participation problem' in Western democracies. We consider his work at some length here, and return to it again in Chapter 4, for three main reasons. First, Bang offers an empirically grounded justification of why we need to conceptualise politics as a lived experience. Secondly, we can use our data to reflect on Bang's argument, although our research was not devised to address his work. Third, Bang raises very important issues about what is happening in developed democracies, which we shall return to in the conclusion of this book.

Bang, like Rhodes, focuses on the importance of networks, seeing governance as a process of social and political communication. He argues (2003, p. 242): 'Governance forges partnership, joint ventures and team building between elites and sub-elites from public, private and voluntary organisations.' He acknowledges the individualisation of politics and the decline of formal participation, and points, in particular, to the rise of lifestyle politics, consumer politics and celebrity politics (2003, p. 1). In his view, many observers see these developments as indicating that we are witnessing a 'thinning' of social and political community, a perspective we suggest that is evident in Pattie *et al.*'s work (2004, p. 1).

Bang identifies two versions of this argument. First, there is Putnam's view that there has been a 'mysterious disengagement'; a growth of defection, distrust, disorder and stagnation across developed liberal democracies. Overall, Putnam's argument is that this weaker civil engagement will lead to less effective and less responsive government. Secondly, there is the view to be found in the work of Norris and Pattie *et al.*, which we examined in the last chapter, which highlights the growth of new forms of participation, such as what Norris calls 'cause-orientated' participation. So, Pattie *et al.*, argue that atomisation is reflected, not in broad disengagement, but rather in a decline in collective participation and a rise in individualised or micro-political participation.

To Bang, these approaches share two assumptions: first, that citizen participation is aimed at influencing the decisions of public authorities; and, secondly, that the core of citizen identity revolves around 'the creation of strong, affective moral ties, committing citizens to act normatively, responsibly and in the name of the common good' (Bang, 2004, p. 3). In Bang's view, this inevitably means that, from this perspective, the key problem that an atomised citizenry raises for liberal democracies is a free-riding problem. As Pattie *et al.* (2004, p. 18) put it:

> The core problem to be addressed by a theory of citizenship is to explain why a group of people are willing to cooperate with each other to solve common problems when there are real incentives not to do so and to free-ride on the efforts of others.

Bang does not doubt that free-riding is a problem, but he disputes that it is the *key* political problem. In his view, individualisation does not lead only to atomisation. More broadly, there is not just one core political problem for democracy, rather ever-changing problems and challenges that stem from diversity, which is the key to understanding democracy. To Bang (2004, p. 3), participation involves 'the matching of political power and values in the situated interaction between political authorities and laypeople'. He argues, and this is absolutely crucial to his position, that 'a democratic political relationship of authority [. . .] is one where everybody has the right and the possibility to make a difference to the constitution of politics and policy'. This leads him to make a distinction between political and social solidarity: political solidarity is thinner and, crucially, not based on any conception of the common good. All you need for political solidarity is that 'each and everybody in a political authority relationship holds the general political value that democracy requires the mutual acceptance and recognition of difference' (2004, p. 4).

Given this view, Bang argues that the crucial problem of contemporary politics is political exclusion, rather than 'free-riding'. What is occurring is the uncoupling of the political authorities from what he terms the 'lay-people' and a consequent undermining of political capital. The increased complexity in reflexive modernity – particularly as a consequence of globalisation, the decline in the power of Parliaments and the growth of expert systems and policy networks – makes governing much more difficult. In addition, the reaction of politicians, bureaucrats and corporatist interests is to exclude some groups/individuals, that is lay-people, from the process of deliberation. This process is also influenced by both the increased professionalisation of political participation and the growing role of the media in politics.

Bang argues that contemporary governance networks operate in three arenas: parliamentary, corporatist and discursive. He contends that the discursive arena is becoming more important, because it is crucial for attempting to resolve the tension between the complexities of 'high modernity' and the imperative to produce effective public policy. The idea here is that, because states are under more pressure to deal with increased complexity, they both incorporate more interests in the policy-making process and engage more directly in the discursive arena; it is for this reason that they turn increasingly to 'Expert Citizens'.

In part, Bang's argument, like ours, is a normative one; he certainly embraces a participatory view of citizenship. In his view, the weakest and the most vulnerable are the most excluded from the local, national and global levels. Yet, political authorities 'cannot make and implement authoritative decisions for a society unless lay-people accept them and recognise themselves as bounded by them' (2004, p. 4). In his view, hierarchy is no longer a workable form of governance.

In Bang's view (2004), citizens, particularly young people, have reacted to these changes in innovative ways; they are certainly not apathetic. Rather, many have become involved in very different arenas. In this context, Bang sees two new political identities emerging: the 'Expert Citizen' and the 'Everyday Maker'. Crucially, Expert Citizens and Everyday Makers do not have a legitimating or an oppositional role *vis a vis* political authorities. Their participation is not focussed upon the state, so they do not engage in state-driven or society-driven activity, but rather they engage in building and running governance networks and reflexive political communities, either as full-time Expert Citizens or as part-time Everyday Makers.

2.3.3.1 The Expert Citizen

These are most often new professionals, particularly in voluntary organisations, who feel they can do politics and make and implement policy as well as old authorities. They deal with all types of elites and sub-elites; both political and corporatist. Many Expert Citizens were previously grassroots activists. Expert Citizens demonstrate:

- a wide conception of the political as a discursive construct;
- a full-time, overlapping, project identity reflecting their overall lifestyle;
- the necessary expertise for exercising influence in elite networks;
- negotiation and dialogue before antagonism and opposition;
- a view of themselves as part of the system, rather than external and oppositional to it (see Bang, 2005, p. 164).

To Expert Citizens, politics is a fusion between representation and participation; where they use knowledge, skills and strategic judgement to influence others. Expert Citizens build networks of negotiation and cooperation with politicians, administrators, interest groups and the media; they develop 'network consciousness'. As compared to more traditional activists, Expert Citizens have a weakening antagonism to the system; their aim is to make it an effective partner. Consequently, Expert Citizens are also a resource or political capital for democracy. In particular, they have a fund of everyday experience about how to deal with problems of exclusion based on 'race', gender, poverty and so on.

2.3.3.2 The Everyday Maker

As we saw, Bang argues that, in many ways, the Everyday Maker is a response to the Expert Citizen. Everyday Makers do not feel defined by the state; they are neither apathetic nor opposed to it. They do not want to waste time getting involved with the state; they prefer to be involved at the lowest possible, local, level. Everyday Makers typically think globally, but act locally. They have no interest in producing a new form of interest representation and have minimal interest in party politics. They are also sceptical of new Expert Citizens; in their view Expert Citizens pursue their own interests: 'They [Everyday Makers] draw a clear distinction within the realm of politics between elite networks and their own politics of the ordinary in the locality' (2004, p. 24). Similarly, they are not driven by a sense of duty, nor are they interested in gaining influence; rather they wish to feel involved and develop themselves. They aim to encourage what Bang terms 'small local narratives' (2004). Unlike Expert Citizens, they do not want to mould the identity of others; this, in particular, leads to conflict between Expert Citizens and Everyday Makers on the ground. Bang argues that Everyday Makers live by a credo of everyday experience, which argues (2004, p. 28):

- Do it Yourself.
- Do it where you are.
- Do it for fun, but also because you find it necessary.
- Do it ad hoc or part-time.
- Do it concretely, instead of ideologically.
- Do it self-confidential and show trust in yourself.
- Do it with the system, if need be.

Like Expert Citizens, Everyday Makers do not believe that representative democracy can be rescued, either by steering from above or by accumulating social capital from below. They present a practical alternative to Putnam's notion of 'strong government' and 'thick community'. Everyday Makers vote and are informed about 'high politics', but they do not get their political identities from being citizens of the state or members of an interest group or a social movement. They, like Expert Citizens, are concerned to enhance their personal capacities for self-governance and co-governance. In Bang's view: 'They prefer a "thin" form of democratic political community that allows for the reciprocal acceptance and recognition of difference. They also consider "strong", effective and responsive government from above as a permanent threat to their self-governance and co-governance' (2004, p. 26). They react against 'network politics' in which experts from private, voluntary and public organisations impose their views, rather than against the state.

In Bang's view, the advent of Expert Citizens reflects a demoelitist ethos in which the key meta-principle of democracy is the need to rationalise, and gain legitimacy for, the discourses of the experts who are controlling a complex negotiated economy. Everyday Makers challenge this by showing that democracy is not merely about strategic articulation of interests within expert networks. In contrast, they argue that their narratives of everyday experience are equally valid.

To both Expert Citizens and Everyday Makers, elite and mass attitudes are two sides of the same coin. Disagreement does not automatically signal a culture of distrust, as it does for most democratic theorists. Rather, to Expert Citizens and Everyday Makers, trust must be rooted in the acceptance of disagreement and diversity, which are at the core of democracy. Bang also argues that, while Expert Citizens and political authorities see Everyday Makers as a threat, they are in fact a potential source of political capital who can be drawn on.

We shall examine Bang's views empirically in Chapter 4, in large part to see whether we can identify any evidence of Everyday Makers among our respondents. However, if Bang is right, these are important developments for political participation and for the nature of governance. As far as participation is concerned, Bang's work suggests, in common with our own view, that mainstream studies have been ignoring important developments in participation, in large part because they have operated with a liberal conceptualisation of citizenship and imposed a narrow definition of politics on their respondents. As far as governance is concerned, Bang's work suggests that networks, especially discourse networks, are a key feature of modern governance, which both social scientists, and more importantly political authorities, need to acknowledge.

We have included a lengthy summary of Bang because we think his work is interesting and important. In particular, we want to focus on how our research can build on Bang's approach and examine its utility as a framework for understanding what is happening to youth participation in the UK. We return to Bang's work in Chapter 4, where we attempt to identify Everyday Makers among our respondents, and in the conclusion. In the next section however, we focus on a key issue in the interface between governance and citizenship and participation: the elitist nature of British democracy, or what we call the 'British political tradition', and the extent to which New Labour's putative move towards participatory governance challenges that dominant tradition.

2.4   New Labour and the British political tradition

We start here with a brief discussion about the nature of the British political tradition (for a more detailed discussion, see Marsh and Hall, 2006), which is here taken to mean the dominant ideas about democracy that underpin the institutions and processes of British Government. Our argument is that debates about citizenship and participation occur within the context of this tradition. This dominant view is not unchallenged. Indeed, those who argue that we have entered a period of 'reflexive modernity' (see Beck *et al.*, 1994) and/or stress the move to participatory governance taken by New Labour would suggest that there has been a move away from the mode of governance based on hierarchy that the British political tradition underpins, to governance based on networks. Consequently, the second part of this section critically analyses New Labour's move towards participatory governance.

2.4.1   The British political tradition

There are a number of discussions of the British political tradition and here we can only briefly outline our argument which is rooted in Beer's (1965) and Birch's (1964) analyses of the development of British democracy (see Marsh and Hall, 2006 for a fuller discussion). In our view, despite continuing contestation, a dominant political tradition underpins the institutions and processes of British Government. The British political system is based on a conservative notion of responsibility, which emphasises the need for strong government, and a limited liberal notion of representation, which stresses the need for free and fair elections, but places relatively little emphasis on the government's responsiveness to the electorate. As Birch (1964, p. 245) himself argues, the British political tradition emphasises, 'first consistency, second accountability to Parliament and, third, responsiveness to public opinions and demands'. We would agree with that assessment, but characterise it slightly differently. The stress in the British political system is on strong government, rather than responsive government, on elite, or leadership, democracy, rather than participatory democracy.

It is also crucial to our argument here that this dominant political tradition, which stresses a limited notion of representation and a conservative notion of responsibility, has underpinned UK political institutions and processes. This is evident if we look at one key aspect of the British political system, the simple plurality system (SPS) for elections to the House of Commons. The main attraction of the system to its advocates is that it, almost invariably, produces majority, and thus strong, government. As such, this is always the crucial argument used by supporters of the SPS in the UK, in contrast to a proportional system (PS) which would produce minority or coalition, and thus weak, government, incapable of providing strong, consistent, even if unpopular, government. Supporters of a PS, however, base their advocacy on a different view of democracy and a different political tradition; they argue that a PS would produce a government that is more responsive to the wishes of the electorate. Three points are important here. First, debates about the nature of the electoral system, and thus of possible electoral reform, in the UK have almost always been conducted between proponents of different models of democracy. Secondly, the proponents of the British political tradition have always won this argument; so the electoral system is underpinned by that view. Third, debates about electoral reform take place within a political system shaped by that British political tradition; that is it sets the parameters within which contestation occurs.

Overall then, we argue that the British political system tends to reify strong, rather than responsive, government, and elite/leadership, rather than participatory, democracy. If there is an epithet which sums up the British political system it is, 'government knows best'.

2.4.2 New Labour, citizenship and the British political tradition

New Labour claims that its approach to the British political system is different: emphasising active citizenship, partnership between state and civil society and the devolution of decision-making to localities, neighbourhoods and communities.[11] Indeed, Dean (2002) argues that the language of citizenship is a key element of New Labour's 'project'. He also contends that, while New Labour's discourse links rights and responsibilities, its key focus is upon responsibility, rather than rights (see also Dwyer, 2000). There is certainly evidence to support this interpretation and, indeed, Tony Blair (1998) identified responsibility as one of the four key values of the Third Way, while there is a similar emphasis in the work of Giddens (1998).

In the light of this, some have argued that New Labour have been influenced by either civic republican (see especially the contributions to Newman (ed.), 2005a) or communitarian ideas (see Standing, 2002; Orton, 2004a). We do not have space here to unpack the relative influences of those two strands; rather our concern is to flag up the emphasis on duty and responsibility in New Labour's discourse of citizenship. As Newman (2005b, p. 4) puts it, 'citizenship is undergoing a transformation from a supposedly passive (rights-bearing) to a more active (performing) subject, taking on new responsibilities as the public/private/personal boundaries are reconfigured'.

Newman subsequently argues that (civic) republican ideas are particularly associated with New Labour's focus on social exclusion and the concomitant emphasis on the need to encourage the socially excluded to become more active citizens. In her view (2005c, p. 129): 'Citizen, user and stakeholder engagement has become a taken-for-granted norm of economic development, poverty reduction, health improvement and social inclusion strategies' (see also Leach and Wingfield, 1999; Wilson, 1999). More specifically, she identifies (2005c, pp. 128–129) a variety of New Labour initiatives that reflect these ideas, including: deliberative forums; citizen panels; user empowerment; consumer consultation; user or citizen involvement on the governing boards of public institutions; and participatory evaluation (and see also Barnes, Newman and Sullivan, 2007, for a detailed and critical study of the types of participatory initiatives that have been developed by New Labour in relation to neighbourhood renewal, health, regeneration and family support services).[12] All of these initiatives appear to involve a more participatory form of governance; an issue we return to below.

At the same time, a number of authors have argued that this emphasis on responsibilities and duties is clear in particular policy areas such as: unemployment and welfare benefits (Hewitt, 1999; King and Wickham-Jones, 1999); education and housing (Deacon, 2002); the family (Orton, 2004b); and urban regeneration.

While it is evident that New Labour has been influenced by elements of a civic republican/communitarian critique of social liberalism, it seems equally clear that the liberal critique of social liberalism has also played a role in their thinking on citizenship. As Johansson and Vinden (2005, p. 115) put it:

> Marshallian [socio-liberal] citizenship has been complemented by more emphasis on some aspects of libertarian [liberal/neo-liberal in our terms] and republican citizenship. In other words, recent reforms have not only involved a stronger emphasis on obligations, but also upon notions of individual responsibility, freedom of choice and contract as well as the participation, dialogue and self-activity of citizens. (our comment in brackets)

Liberal, or neo-liberal, ideas of citizenship are most obviously associated with public sector reform generally and welfare reform particularly, where citizens are viewed as consumers; indeed, some authors have even talked of citizen-consumers (Clark, 2004; Clark and Newman, 2005; Newman, 2005b, p. 4). So, Clark and Newman (2005, p. 1) argue:

> The reform of the public services in the UK has been driven – in part – by a conception of citizens as consumers of public services, a conception which is lodged in narratives about the wider social transition to a consumer society and a consumer culture.

Similarly Marquand (2004, p. 118) asserts:

New Labour has pushed marketisation and privatisation forward [. . .] narrowing the frontiers of the public domain in the process [. . .] Ministerial rhetoric is saturated with the language of consumerism. The public services are to be 'customer focused'; schools and colleges are to ensure that what is on offer responds to the needs of the consumer.

This focus on the market and citizen-consumers is rooted in liberal/neo-liberal ideas of citizenship. The idea is that the market is the best way to allocate resources and consumer decisions should play a key role in shaping government policy. As Clark (2004, p. 6) puts it:

The starting point for New Labour's articulation of the citizen consumer is the critique of the 'old' formation of the public services – and its anachronistic character in the 'modern' world of consumer culture. [. . .] the New Labour project juxtaposes old and new in the distinction between a 'rationing culture' and a consumer culture.

In this view, choice is regarded as open in a way that social liberals would reject (see Clark, 2004 and Chapter 5, which revisits some of these issues in relation to class).

In our view, New Labour's conceptualisation of citizenship contains a residue of social liberalism which has been shaped, and in certain aspects undermined, by elements of communitarianism and civic republicanism and liberalism/neo-liberalism. However, there is significant doubt about the depth of New Labour's commitment to the idea of participatory governance, in large part because it conflicts with the dominant British political tradition, and it is to that issue that we now turn.

The key question here is to what extent New Labour has a commitment to more participation and empowerment relative to previous conceptions of the relationship between governors and governed within the British political tradition. We are very sceptical for two major reasons. First, there is little evidence that they are committed to the type of constitutional reform that would mark a move from an elitist to a more participatory democracy. Second, their emphasis on active citizenship and participatory governance seems more concerned with legitimacy problems associated with falling turnout, than with a commitment to empowering citizens, and more with control, than empowerment.

New Labour came to power seemingly committed to an agenda of constitutional reform (see Marsh, 2005). However, as Gamble (2003, 2006) implies, particular reforms were not underpinned by a broader commitment to a more participatory idea of democracy (2003, p. 101): '(the government) has been reluctant to present its reforms in the language of democratic renewal and citizenship, and to connect its constitutional reforms with reform of the public services'. Rather, their constitutional proposals represented a series of particular responses to perceived political problems. For example, Scottish devolution, in large part, was a response to the perceived threat from the Scottish National Party to New Labour's electoral hegemony in Scotland. Similarly, the commitment to consider electoral reform for Westminster was made at a time when New Labour felt that it might need to rely on the Liberal Democrats for an overall majority. Unsurprisingly in this context, New Labour failed to deliver broad constitutional reform when it came to power. Of its main proposals, only Scottish devolution was delivered, while electoral reform was sidelined and Freedom of Information emasculated (for a more detailed discussion, see Marsh, 2005). In our view, this reflects the continued resonance of the British political tradition identified above. More importantly here, it indicates that New Labour is not committed to a coherent and significant move towards a more active citizenry, at least in the area of 'high politics'.[13]

In contrast, in areas of low politics New Labour has embraced participatory governance, although we suggest that this does not reflect a desire for a more participatory democracy. Rather, we agree with Newman (2005c, p. 122) who argues that 'underpinning the normative statements about the importance of public involvement and dialogue [. . .] is a set of government concerns about policy legitimacy and effectiveness' (p. 122).

At the same time, in our view, most of New Labour's policy initiatives in the area of 'low politics' reflect a concern with control, rather than empowerment. As Rose (1999) emphasises, new forms of governance (or 'governmentalities' as he terms them following Foucault) are designed to incorporate citizens into new fields of power which appear to grant autonomy, but demand greater responsibility. Newman (2005c, p. 128) makes a similar point:

> new governmental strategies may involve calling into being particular conceptions of the public realm and may define – or constitute – the public in particular ways. Here, participatory governance can

be understood as a new political rationality through which citizens, users or communities are constituted as governable subjects.

Indeed, it is easy to find analysts who are sceptical of New Labour's commitment to participatory governance. So, Newman (2005c, p. 130) argues: 'Participatory initiatives may fall short of the ideals of empowerment or co-production and become part of a fundamentally managed rationality' (see also Newman, 2001). She also contends (2005c, p. 133) that 'power imbalances mean that public officials' 'claims to truth' tend to prevail over the experiences and knowledge that the collaborating publics bring to those interactions'. In a similar vein, Sterling (2005) argues that:

> like other elements of new governance practice, partnerships largely tend to by-pass traditional mechanisms of representative democracy, and some authors have argued that partnerships thus represent a form of elite, non-accountable governance (see also Elander and Blanc, 2001).

Perhaps Somerville (2005) makes this point most forcibly. He argues that we need to make a distinction between empowered citizens, who are given a say in all key decision-making processes, and disciplinary citizens, who are signed up, but not listened to, and thus used to legitimise elite decisions. In his view, New Labour's participatory governance involves disciplinary citizens.

Sterling focuses upon how partnerships work under New Labour arguing that (2005, p. 148) 'research consistently finds that most partnerships involve participation by only a small number of people and, with a few isolated exceptions, issues of community diversity, "race", gender, disability and class still receive little attention in partnership practice'. As such, participatory governance often creates '(a) veneer of consensus (which) can mask power relations between the "partners" that could work to silence some voices and bolster others' (Sterling, 2005, p. 149; see also Saward, 2005, p. 190). So, participatory governance in areas of low politics can often be exclusionary.[14] This is particularly crucial given our concerns in relation to young people, and Chapter 4 highlights that young people are very conscious of such exclusions, in relation to both mainstream political institutions and local and community political engagement.

2.5   Conclusion

We turn now to our empirical work. The next chapter reviews our methodology and the subsequent four chapters present our findings about age (Chapter 4), class (Chapter 5), gender (Chapter 6) and ethnicity (Chapter 7). The issues examined in this chapter have set out the broader context for this empirical research and we return to many of them in the concluding chapter.

3
Methodology

Our methodological approach is strongly influenced by our critique of the existing literature. As we have argued, a key problem with much of the current research on political participation is its restricted conception of the 'political'; where the focus has been on an arena definition of politics and political participation has been equated with a narrow range of activities, centred on contacting public officials, voting and membership of parties and/or interest groups and so on – the inclusion of 'micro-political' activities by Pattie *et al.* (2004) notwithstanding. As we noted, few studies explore how respondents themselves conceive of the political, or when they do, these conceptions are not applied to the analysis of how people participate. Furthermore, failure to participate in the repertoires specified by researchers has often been equated with political apathy. Yet, as we argued, political participation has many others, not just apathy.

As such, the literature on political participation needs to establish a much clearer idea of how young people understand and relate to politics. Only then can we assess whether young people are apathetic, because it is perfectly possible that many young people are politically engaged, but in ways that differ from the definition of most politicians and indeed social scientists. From such a perspective, many young people may not be apathetic; rather they may be alienated from the social and political system they experience. Consequently, the key aim of our research was to explore more fully how young people understand and experience politics. In particular, we were anxious to avoid, as far as possible, two problems in the existing literature: imposing a view of what is political on our respondents; and equating non-participation in the formal political arena with apathy.

This position has methodological implications. It pointed us towards a qualitative, rather than a quantitative, approach,[1] which involved both focus groups and individual interviews, for reasons we explain below. In order to reduce the extent to which we imposed our own view of 'politics' on our respondents, we needed a less directive way of questioning respondents about their understanding of politics. Consequently, we used images to stimulate discussion in the focus groups. In this chapter we outline, justify and discuss in more detail our methods.

3.1   Research design

As we discussed in Chapter 1, we are not positivists and, thus, we are not seeking a methodology which uncovers generalisable 'truths' about young people's understanding of politics. Consequently, we are not driven by the need to study a representative sample of young people from which we can make statistical generalisations; rather we set out to achieve a 'thick' understanding of young people's views and experiences through purposive sampling. More specifically, and given our concern to investigate young people's own conceptions of politics and the political, we needed a respondent-led methodology, in which our respondents were not merely responding to preset questions, of the sort inevitable in surveys or structured interviews, which reflect the researchers', rather than the respondents', understanding of politics. To obtain respondent-led data we needed to use open-ended techniques and, hence, qualitative methodologies.

There are a variety of reasons why researchers use qualitative interviews, in particular the concern to achieve an understanding of respondents' views, understandings and experiences in their own terms underpins the rationale for much qualitative research. Through the reflexive and flexible process of qualitative interviewing, researchers are able to interact with respondents to probe their views and under-standings. In our case, this method permitted exploration of how our respondents viewed politics; how this shaped their conceptions of polit-ical participation or non-participation; their experiences of political participation and their understanding of its significance; their views on these experiences of involvement; and the extent to which, if at all, their experiences of participation underpin their view of politics. In other words, such qualitative interviewing permitted 'thick description' (Geertz, 1993; Rubin and Rubin, 1995).

3.2 Choosing a sample

As we emphasised earlier, we were not interested in selecting, and indeed, given our resources, would have been unable to select, a representative sample of young people. However, we were concerned to ensure that our sample was varied; in particular that we had young people drawn from different demographic groups, as such, we used a purposive, rather than a representative, sample. Overall, we conducted 12 focus groups (including one pilot), involving 65 respondents and 54 follow-up individual interviews. All our respondents were aged between 16 and 25 and our aim was to ensure diversity within our sample across five variables: gender, ethnicity, class/socio-economic status, education and contact with the state. We drew our sample from six sites across the city of Birmingham: one Further Education (FE) college; two secondary schools (one comprehensive and one selective); one organisation working with young homeless people providing 'foyer' type accommodation (which is medium-term accommodation offered to young homeless people on condition that they engage in some programme of formal or informal education or training); one organisation which offers training and support for young offenders and those on the government-sponsored New Deal scheme; and the University of Birmingham, where we recruited a sample of undergraduates from outside the School of Social Sciences (where the research team was based). We also piloted the focus group design with a friendship group.

Four issues need brief discussion here: how we conceptualise youth; how we deployed our variables and our strategy for accessing respondents across them; our relationship with 'gatekeepers', who played a key role in allowing us access to many of the sites at which we worked; and the profile of Birmingham as the context in which our research took place.

3.2.1 Conceptualising 'youth'

Our research is concerned with youth, although its significance and the age range that is connoted by the term 'youth' are frequently disputed. Our perspective on these issues was informed by the concept of 'youth transitions'. Much youth studies research references the concept of 'transitions' in order to theoretically frame the status of young people as neither dependent nor independent, but in a state of transition between childhood and adulthood. The literature on youth transitions has a number of weaknesses, however. As Wyn and White (1997) point out, although in theoretical terms researchers see young people's transition as a fluid, changing process, in empirical research they often use a narrow, static, categorical notion of youth. As such, research into 'transitions' has tended to impose a particular conception of what it means to be a young person, focusing *either* on young people's experience of employment and education *or* on consumption patterns and youth subculture(s).

In this way, researchers often divide young people's lives into discrete, well-defined, elements; it is almost as though one minute young people deal with issues to do with employment, training and the future, while in the next they deal with cultural matters to do with consumption and identity. As such, it can appear that young people's lives are 'divvied up' among researchers; an over-simplification that can limit our perspective on young people's lives. What we needed was an approach that allowed young people to speak for themselves and which did not see politics as a discrete area, but rather as part of young people's lives; something they lived.

This critique of the youth literature reinforced the need for a more qualitative approach. However, it still left open the question of what age range our sample should cover. The age of 16 is often used as a threshold by youth researchers and organisations as a definition of the starting point for youth, because, for statutory purposes, it signals a key moment in young people's transitions from childhood to adulthood. It is at this age that they are no longer subject to compulsory schooling and, therefore, may move into the world of work, government-supported-training, further education and so on. This is seen to trigger many of the processes involved in the transition to adulthood – such as increasing autonomy and economic independence – and this may entail a move away from the parental home (although young people may also experience significant barriers during these transitions experiences). In other words, the acquisition of some legal autonomy, and the advent of career trajectories, is taken by many as a starting point for youth, because of its legal and social significance.

We chose a relatively large age range with a cut-off point of 25, guided by recent youth research which stresses that the period of transition from childhood to adulthood has become longer and more fragmented in the last few decades, due in large part to changes in policies on young people's entitlement to, and opportunities to access, education, housing and employment (Coles, 1995; Bynner *et al.*, 2002). This endpoint was selected then to acknowledge that for many young people the acquisition of economic and social independence may begin or continue while they are in their twenties.

3.2.2 Use of variables

As already emphasised, we set out to include respondents who reflected differences of gender, ethnicity, class/socio-economic status' education and contact with the state. We employed a site-based approach in order to obtain a sample which allowed for variance across these variables.

The representation of gender across the sites was relatively easy to achieve, as all the sites were accessed by men and women. Most of our focus groups were mixed gender groups and, where they were not, we returned to the site to conduct another focus group to achieve representation of men and women from each site.

Similarly, our range of sites gave us access to respondents from different ethnic groups, although there was a clear link between ethnicity and individual sites, given the ethnicised geographies that pertain in Birmingham, which we discuss at greater length in Chapter 7. The distinctive aspects of participants' ethnic identities (which were self-defined) were explored in the follow-up individual interviews, such as how they chose to describe themselves, how they negotiated their identities, their conception of themselves as holding multiple identities and the aspects of their identity where they felt strong affiliations, conflicts or confusion. We discuss these issues throughout and in Chapters 4 and 7 particularly, but generally the way we report differences of ethnicity in relation to particular data extracts is by using less highly identifying categories than the very specific and multiple categories elucidated by our respondents. We have employed a broad categorisation of our respondents' ethnicity when we indicate ethnicity in reporting our data, where 'black' refers to participants of black African or Caribbean origin; 'white' refers to participants of white Irish, Scottish, Welsh or English origin; and 'South Asian' refers to participants of Pakistani, Afghan, Bangladeshi or Indian origin. The more nuanced and specific perspectives of our respondents on ethnicity and identity (their own and others') are discussed contextually.

Utilising class as a variable presented us with the greatest problem for a number of reasons. There is a particular problem establishing the class position of young people who are not yet in the labour market. Most research uses the young respondent's report of their parent's, normally their father's, occupation/employment location as a proxy for the young person's own class position. Unsurprisingly, some researchers have argued that this is problematic. More importantly, however, as we argue at length in Chapter 5, we are critical of approaches which treat class as an independent variable measured in terms of employment location. Instead, we argue for a Bourdieusian approach to class. Given our position then, we saw little point in asking our respondents to identify their father's/parents' occupation/employment location.

After some thought, we decided to use our sites as proxies for class. Of course, this approach has limitations, particularly to positivists, because it might seem that we are assuming that everyone in the same site shares a similar class position. In fact, we are merely assuming that the sites are 'classed', that in Bourdieu's terms they are institutional embodiments of fields,[2] and particular sites are likely to be closely associated with our respondents' access to economic, social and cultural capital (for a more detailed discussion see Chapter 5). So, all our educational sites are part of an education field which clearly reflects and leads to differential access to economic, social and cultural capital. However, the views and actions of individuals in these 'classed' sites are not determined, although they are constrained or facilitated, by the classed nature of that site. As such, we are interested in the extent to which the classed nature of the site influenced the views of politics in both the focus groups and the individual interviews from those sites.

We divided our sites into three class categories. The hostel and the New Deal sites were treated as underprivileged sites in class terms, because if we see them both as part of the economic field then the respondents from these sites have less access to economic, social and cultural capital; an assertion amply demonstrated in Chapter 5. The FE college and the comprehensive school sites were viewed as intermediary sites in which there was greater diversity of access to economic, social and cultural capital. Finally, the University and selective secondary school sites were viewed as privileged sites.

These sites reflected different educational structures and experiences and these were also explored in our follow-up individual interviews. Our sample, then, included respondents with varying educational histories and trajectories, such as those who had pursued or were pursuing progression through formal academic and vocational courses or work-based and government-supported training programmes as well as those who had left the formal educational system altogether or were accessing more discrete life skills training programmes.

Our final variable, contact with the state, was selected as a variable for two reasons. First, there is considerable variance in the contact that different young people have with the state. So, while many young people have little contact with the state, other than in relation to education and health, others have much more contact through the social security system or welfare-to-work programmes. In our view these differing levels of contact that young people have with the state may affect their experiences of, and views on, politics. As such, those young people reliant on social security or on welfare-to-work schemes have a much more direct relationship with the state; a relationship which may underpin their conceptions of politics. We recognise that there is a close relationship between class/socio-economic status and contact with the state.

This variable was a key factor in determining our selection of sites. In other words, we considered the structure and purpose of organisations working with young people as a means of accessing young people with varying levels of contact with the state. In this respect, we anticipated that young people at the New Deal training centre and the homeless hostel would have a high degree of contact with the state, because of their experience of the Social Security or Criminal Justice Systems. This certainly proved to be the case and, in addition, our sites included respondents who had been 'looked after children', having grown up, or spent periods, in the care of a Local Authority. Our sites were not always wholly predictive of such contact. A number of respondents from across our sites, not just at the site that specifically worked with young offenders, had experienced contact with the Criminal Justice System. In addition, even those respondents who were not reliant on the state for funding, benefits, care or support, or who had not experienced policing, probationary or courts procedures, had had some level of contact with the state (for example, in relation to issues involving housing or health). However, the more intense contact with the state which arose from the provision/withdrawal of benefits or funding, or from disciplinary experiences, had a significant effect on the ways in which our respondents conceived of the political, as is clear in the more detailed discussion of our data in the following chapters.

3.2.3 The role of 'gatekeepers'

Our decision to work through sites involved working with 'gatekeepers', who were contacts at the sites from whom we needed permission to invite people to participate in the research and who provided introductions and access to young people at the sites (in some cases playing a selection role). Although in some ways we would have preferred all our respondents to have been self-selected, this might have introduced its own biases, perhaps producing more respondents who were particularly interested in politics. Generally, we were dependent (as many researchers are) on gatekeepers, to varying degrees, to achieve access to respondents. The initial contact with representatives of the sites where we wanted to interview made us immediately aware of the role that gatekeepers would play in our fieldwork. We had expected this when we were working within schools, but other sites required numerous visits and phone calls to establish an understanding of the purpose and validity of the research and the credentials of the researchers. Increasing demand on curriculum time meant that some schools were unwilling to let their students take part, while, in contrast, other schools saw co-operation with a university as good for students and the school in general. Some gatekeepers were happy to facilitate us meeting people at the sites, by providing inform-ation on where and when young people gathered without playing a role in introducing us or the research, whereas others played a more interventionist role by selecting, and explaining our research to, poten-tial respondents. In all cases, we began contact by explaining ourselves, the research and the voluntary nature of participation. But, even when agreement from gatekeepers was achieved and interviews undertaken, gatekeeping did not cease. Indeed, in one site a member of staff took part in the focus group, posing as a respondent, unbeknown to the interviewers.

Our access negotiations also indicated two other difficulties that researchers may experience in conducting similar research. So, it was not always easy to get the cooperation of sites. One or two of the sites we approached were regularly asked to participate in research projects or programmes. Consequently, there was some 'screening' by gatekeepers to establish the purpose and kudos of the research project. In addition, one or two potential sites were concerned that the published research would reflect negatively on the particular organisation involved.

We overcame these challenges in part through negotiation. These negotiations usually involved discussion of our ethical framework, the fact that our project was focused on the respondents' conceptions of politics rather than on evaluating the particular structure and practices of the site and a discussion of the benefits to the respondents from their participation in the project (which included the opportunity to commu-nicate their views as well as financial remuneration for their time).

By and large, respondents found the interviews engaging and inter-esting. Young people were quite willing and able to talk about their perceptions of politics. The impression we got was that they welcomed the chance to talk about their views. The response of one female FE student was typical:

> That's cool I find this really interesting y'know. I'm just getting more knowledge and then I don't normally talk about politics . . . you're

probably thinking: O.K, this girl doesn't know what the hell she's talking about, or rabbiting on, or O.K she's just talking, but I'm thinking while I'm talking to you. There's so many things that are going on in my head that I didn't realise.

Female, FE college student, 18, South Asian, individual interview

3.2.4 The context of Birmingham

All of the sites in which we worked were located in Birmingham, UK, and there were some significant contextual features relating to the city that had an impact on our data. In this section, we set out some pertinent features of Birmingham and indicate some examples of where it was apparent to us that these shaped our respondents' perspectives on particular issues.

Birmingham is a large city with a population of almost a million (Census, 2001). It is also an ethnically diverse city. According to the 2001 Census, Black, South Asian and mixed/dual heritage groups constituted 29.6 per cent of the population. Birmingham's black and minority ethnic population is a diverse one, comprising significant numbers of people of Pakistani, Indian and African Caribbean origin, as well as emergent groups of recent migrants, notably from Somali, Turkey and Iraq. It is anticipated that by 2011, non-white groups will form over 50 per cent of the city's population (Birmingham Race Action Partnership, 2004), making Birmingham perhaps Britain's first black majority city (although this status might be reached first by Leicester in the East Midlands). As Chapter 7 discusses, Birmingham's outward profile as a thriving multicultural city sits alongside patterns of marked and persistent inequalities between ethnic groups – which are both economically and spatially expressed. In Chapter 7, we explore in some detail how Birmingham's ethnicised geographies are woven into our respondents' political consciousness.

Additionally, Birmingham is a city that has been experiencing significant de-industrialisation and, consequently, it is a city that has been reinventing itself. As Henry *et al.* (2002) argue, Birmingham City Council's response to the de-industrialisation of the 1970s and 1980s has been massive investment in service industries and it has taken a highly entrepreneurial approach to regeneration. Thus, between 1986 and 1992 it spent around £276 million on flagship projects aimed at regenerating the local economy (Henry *et al.*, 2002). In this way, Henry *et al.* suggest, Birmingham City Council has sought to project Birmingham as a global city, which has reinvented itself as the 'Meeting Place of Europe'. Nevertheless, they argue that:

In Birmingham, prestige development has failed to provide enough well-paid jobs, city finances have been diverted from other sectors (such as education and housing) to pay for these projects, and the exclusivity of the spaces created has been questioned. Moreover the formulaic nature of such redevelopment [fails] to reflect the full diversity and difference to be found amongst the residential population. (2002, pp. 117–118; also see Bhattacharrya, 1998).

Certainly, some of the areas in which our sites were located have acutely felt the impact of de-industrialisation, without attendant benefits from the prestige model of development. For instance, the decommissioning of a major car manufacturing plant that had operated as the dominant employer and economic pulse in south Birmingham had a particular impact on working-class young men in sites in that area. For these young men, the prospect of secure, well-paid jobs as skilled manual workers was one that had existed in their lifetimes, but was currently receding and they were in the process of reconsidering their career trajectories. A key theme of the focus group that we held with some of these young men was a pronounced sense of a 'generation gap' – reflecting perhaps the felt impact of such economic transitions on their own lived experiences. This sense of change was also expressed by another male respondent on the New Deal programme, particularly in relation to the collapse of manufacturing jobs and how that translated into young men's aspirations:

[Birmingham has] changed a lot, you know, back in the days and all that, people had physical jobs, and what everyone wants today is pure computers. You know, at the end of the day, computers can't get up off its own desk and build a house. It can design them, but you need someone to design them for them. People ain't into the physical work no more, they're getting lazy, they wanna sit on their bums and do computers, design games, and get into entertainments or become a footballer. There's loads of lads hooked on being footballers so they can earn millions and that. I can understand why, you know what I mean? I would love to put on an England shirt, and I would have loved to play at Wembley, but there's no chance of that now. But that's . . . things like that should be kept as dreams, you know, there's only the minority that's gonna make it.

Male, New Dealer, 23, white, individual interview

3.3 The use of focus groups

Perceptions of the political influence notions of political participation
and we identified these as two separate, but linked, research areas. It
was crucial for us to adopt an approach that avoided, first, predic-
ating the definition of political participation on the researcher's definition of politics rather than the respondents' and, secondly, equating
non-participation in a set of activities specified by the researcher with
political apathy. As such, in our focus groups we set out to explore
young people's conceptions of the political, whilst respondents' perceptions and experiences of political participation were investigated in a
follow-up individual interview, in the light of the data generated by the
focus group.

3.3.1 The use of focus groups in social science research

Focus groups are now a widely used tool in marketing research, as well
as in social science. Wilkinson (1997, p. 187) argues that they are used to
'elicit people's understandings, opinions and views, or to explore how
these are advanced, elaborated and negotiated in a social context'. The
idea is that participants are encouraged to interact, thus exploring, and
to an extent justifying, their views and beliefs.

The method was developed during the Second World War and some
of the first academic focus groups were undertaken by Morton *et al.*
(1956) in the early 1950s, although the method was slow to catch on
in social science, because of the dominance of positivism and quantitative methods (Munday, 2006). Indeed, the use of focus groups in
social research has continued to be heavily criticised by positivists who
doubt the method's usefulness, validity, reliability and reproducability
(for example, see McDonald, 1994; Carey, 1995; Smith, 1995). So, in a
manner typical of this positivist critique, Langford *et al.* (2002, p. 60)
argue that there is 'no research that empirically demonstrates reliability,
much less validity, in focus group research'. However, the method has
been used increasingly by business, particularly for product development and marketing. Here, the argument was that it allowed companies
to keep in touch with consumers, to ensure they responded to consumer
demand. They were also useful because they provided believable results
at a low cost (see Krueger and Casey, 2000, p. 6). It has also been increasingly used in the political field, to market both parties and policies (see
Lees-Marshment, 2001, 2004; Gould, 2002; Wring, 2002; Savigny, 2004).

Krueger and Casey (2000, p. 10) argue that focus groups generally
have five characteristics: (i) they involve people, (ii) who possess certain

characteristics and (iii) provide qualitative data, (iv) in a focussed discussion, (v) in order to help the researcher to understand the topic under consideration. All this seems straightforward, but the method has been broadly applied and there are very significant differences between the way it is used in marketing, including political marketing, and in other types of related social research, and the way it is used as an ethnographic technique.

In marketing, focus groups are used to produce 'answers' on which decisions about product development or, increasingly, brand development can be based. They are also used to show customers that the company is listening; thus they have a symbolic role (see Strother, 2003, p. 16). Furthermore, market researchers generally attempt to make focus groups 'more scientific'. Here, the emphasis is upon systematic procedures and researcher neutrality. The aim is to produce credible results, which, at least in some sense, can be generalised. Kreuger and Casey (2000, p. 203), for example, emphasise 'transferability', by which they mean the ability to produce broad conclusions which can be generalised to a different environment or situation, even if the specific conclusions cannot.

This approach to focus groups, and indeed more broadly to qualitative research, extends well beyond the marketing literature. King *et al.*'s (1994) attempt to establish basic rules for what they term 'scientific qualitative research' is indicative of this approach. They suggest that qualitative research can, and should, adopt the standards of scientific research by constructing falsifiable theories (1994, p. 100) that are internally consistent (p. 105); choosing observable, rather than unobservable, concepts/variables whenever possible (p. 109) so that the theory can be tested and falsified (p. 24); and ensuring, as far as possible, that all data and analysis are replicable or reproducible (p. 26).

This is not the place to critique King *et al.* However, their approach is positivist; there is little appreciation of the first level of the hermeneutic and none at all of the second level; objectivity is the goal and can be achieved, even with qualitative data, if appropriate methods are properly, that is scientifically, used. The use of focus groups in marketing, and in some social research, adopts this approach, aping the scientific method.

Ethnographic researchers, by contrast, set out to use a 'respondent-led' methodology to explore and access people's own experience. Here, the first level of the hermeneutic is at the centre of the analysis. Focus groups enable researchers to do this and also allow the researcher to appreciate how contextual factors, such as the group composition and group dynamic, affect the individual's experience. At the same time, ethnographers recognise the second level of the hermeneutic; so the researcher's understanding of the respondent's understanding is partial, in both senses of the word. As such, if an ethnographer uses focus groups, she attempts to acknowledge, and to an extent reduce, those partialities in two ways. First, she attempts to make the method as respondent-led as possible by reducing the researcher's intervention in the research process. When using focus groups, this means restricting the focus group facilitator's intervention; in our case, as we explain below, by using photographic images as a stimulus to discussion in the group. Secondly, reflexivity is crucial in this approach. The researcher needs to acknowledge, both during the focus group sessions and, particularly, when analysing the data, how her own experiences, views and theories affect her understandings of the respondent's understandings. These cannot be exorcised from the research or the analysis, but they can, to a greater or lesser extent, be acknowledged.

It is clear then that different researchers use focus groups in very different ways. We are firmly located in the ethnographic camp. Our aim was to produce respondent-led data and our understandings of how our respondents understood and experienced politics also formed part of the analysis.

Even if we acknowledge, and take a position on, different ontological and epistemological approaches to the use of focus groups, there are still other methodological issues involved in conducting them, some of which inevitably reflect these ontological and epistemological differences. The debate focuses mainly on two issues. First, and this follows from our earlier discussion, there is considerable debate about the nature of the questions' stimulus that should be used in the focus groups. Market researchers, given their positivist credentials and concern with generalisable results, favour structured sessions in which a tight set of questions are asked and then discussed in the group; these questions can then be asked in other focus groups, with different demographic characteristics, so that comparisons can be made. In contrast, other researchers favour a semi-structured format, in which a series of themes are addressed, thus allowing the group greater opportunity to develop and elaborate their views. We took this last point even more seriously, using photographic images, discussed below, in order to allow the respondents the maximum amount of space to express their own views in the focus groups.

Secondly, a key criticism of focus groups is that they can change the beliefs and attitudes of participants through the process of interaction.

Such change can result from over-intervention, or agenda setting, by the focus group facilitator(s). This is almost inevitable with marketing research when the focus group leader wishes to discuss a particular product or brand. A particular issue arises when one, or a small number, of the group's participants dominates discussion and changes views (see McDonald, 1994; and, especially, Bristol and Fenn, 2003, p. 433). Indeed, Bristol and Fenn (2003, p. 450) argue that such attitude change is much greater than with individual surveys or interviews. We attempted to deal with this issue in four ways.

First, we aimed to minimise the role of the focus group facilitator, as emphasised above. Secondly, we took the view that the tendency for views to be shaped by interaction within the focus group should be methodologically embedded rather than viewed as a limitation; since participation is a social activity, the appropriation of the social dynamics of a focus group in many ways is closer to the context in which participation takes place. Group membership is a fundamental aspect of how social actors situate themselves within the social world and social roles, norms and values are learned through, and maintained within, membership of a group (Bourdieu, 1977). As such, this gives us an important insight into a key aspect of participation that cannot be captured by survey techniques – that is the nature of participation as an activity that is shaped by membership of groups and social interaction. Where survey techniques tend to capture a snapshot of attitudes, group work, by contrast, allows the processes of argumentation, consensus-building and dissent to be observed and explored (Smithson, 2000, p. 116; Munday, 2006). It allows the researcher, to an extent, to appropriate the socially constructed features of participation into the research process, by enabling an examination of people's different perspectives as they operate within a social network, and to examine how these accounts are articulated, censored, opposed and changed through social interaction (Smithson, 2000, p. 112; Munday, 2006). Thus the opportunity to witness agenda formation, disputation and consensus building is itself an interesting aspect of how people form their conceptions of the political. In addition, the processes of group discussion more closely reflect the dynamic nature of political participation, because political beliefs and attitudes are formed and determined in a social context; this approach is also underpinned by our realist epistemology.

Third, we took account of this issue of the ways in which the focus group setting intervenes in respondents' understanding and discussions of politics in the process of analysis, by acknowledging, as Smithson (2000) emphasises, that focus groups should not be analysed as if they were natural conversations, but as 'discussions occurring in a specific, controlled setting'.

Finally, we conducted follow-up individual interviews with as many of the focus group participants as were willing, in order to explore their own views in the light of the focus group's discussion. This allowed us to draw out anyone who had been more reticent, and to explore any differences that had emerged, in the focus group. This gave us an opportunity to explore whether views expressed in a focus group might be different to those expressed outside that setting. In other words, this method provided us with an opportunity to see the ways that views may be shaped by the cultural and social context, by following these up in individual interviews.

Kitzinger and Barbour (1999) suggest that focus groups and group interviews are ideal for eliciting views from people who might initially state that they do not have much to say on the topic in question, as they allow participants to be guided by, and to respond to, views of other group members. Thus, this method was particularly useful for us in exploring non-participation, as it provided cues on issues and activities in which people were not necessarily engaged, thus helping to alleviate the problem that it is enormously difficult to ask people to be discursive about non-activity.

Furthermore, group interviews, including focus groups, can help to orientate the researchers to a field of inquiry, providing contextual details and familiarising researchers with the idioms employed by the research sample (Gaskill, 2000). This was particularly important in facilitating research across a variety of social and cultural groups, which in this study included male and female sixth-formers, college students, undergraduates, homeless and unemployed young people from different ethnic groups. The use of focus groups also allowed participants to frame their own questions and concepts and to pursue these in their own terms and vocabulary, in dialogue with one another rather than in a dialogue dominated by the researcher (Kitzinger and Barbour, 1999). Given our critique of the existing literature, this was a very important advantage of the focus-group method for us.

Finally, we saw in the focus group method a key advantage in addressing the issue of an unequal power relationship between researchers and researched. In non-elite interviews there are frequently issues resulting from unequal power relations in the interview, which can mean that researchers implicitly frame the data. In particular, interviewers can often be deferred to by respondents as 'experts'. This is especially an issue in youth research where it has been suggested that the nature

of adolescence/childhood inevitably leads to unequal power relationships between young respondents and adult researchers, in which the
researcher imposes her definitions on the respondent and the respondent
defers to, or resists, the researcher. (France, 2000; Harden *et al.*, 2000).

Focus groups can help to overcome this power imbalance between
the researcher and the researched by encouraging the development
of the collective voice, or the collectively powerful 'we' (Smithson,
2000, pp. 111–112). In this context, the researcher can acknowledge the
collective voice and shared knowledge of the group, so that the group is
recognised as expert and the researcher as the listener/learner. Furthermore, where the participants form part of a peer-group, the researcher
is automatically the outsider.

We did see elements of the power imbalance issue in our encounter
with some of the groups. So, for example, a feature of the interviewing
which reflected such power imbalance was respondents asking if their
interpretation of the image was 'right':

> *Respondent 1*: Is there a clear meaning to these pictures, 'cos I, you
> know what I mean, I think hard on them and I try and work it out.
> Is there meaning to each one?
> *Interviewer*: You mean like one meaning?
> *Respondent 1*: No, like each one like/
> *Respondent 2*: /You need to try and work them out
> *Interviewer*: I mean we haven't got a sheet with y'know what the
> answer is on it.
>> Males, FE college students, ages and ethnicity
>> unknown, focus group

As such, we had to acknowledge that the age and status of the interviewers conducting this research was an issue. In addition, we had to
recognise this problem might be heightened by the nature of the sites in
which we were interviewing, as well as by people's experiences of interviews or group working. In some sites respondents wanted to establish
our relationship with the institution/authority. This was particularly a
concern with the hostel and the New Deal groups. In all sites respondents were keen to understand the 'ground rules', if any, of the discussion.
In particular, respondents asked if they could say certain things or swear
or joke. Here, it seemed they wanted to know if we would establish adult
control of the discussion or whether they could set the rules.

Bearing these issues in mind, we aimed to conduct the focus groups in
as open a way as possible. Although our research concerns may have set

the group's agenda, we did not control the discussion. We distributed the images that we used in the focus group in a random order which was different for each group. We also let any discussion run its course rather than distributing the images to any fixed timetable. There was an overall time restriction on our discussions, although this varied from group to group, and meant that we were not always able to distribute every image. However, we were not aiming to assess each group's response to every image; rather we wanted to understand the group's understanding of politics. For this reason, at the end of each session, even if we had not circulated all the images, we asked the group to sort the images they had discussed into two piles: those they considered to be political, and those that they did not (taking care to open the possibility that they may all be one or the other).

3.4 The use of images

In the focus groups, our aim was not to ask direct questions about politics or political activity because we did not want to set the agenda for the discussion, thus predisposing our respondents to talk about politics. In addition, previous research (White *et al.*, 2000) suggested that young people are resistant to discussing politics directly. As such, we considered a number of alternative methods before deciding to use images.

Initially, we considered task-orientated methods such as Participatory Rural Appraisal (Thomas-Slater, 1995) and requesting respondents to draw pictures as a means of exploring their perspectives on politics (Punch, 1998). These methods were rejected because they are time-consuming to analyse and require skills in interpreting meanings that none of our research team possessed (see Backett-Milburn and McKie, 1999). In addition, it was not easy to see how we could use these methodologies to tap into respondent's understanding of politics (for instance, we were not sure what we would ask respondents to draw that might reflect their understandings of politics). Subsequently, we looked at sentence completion, a method commonly used in youth research (Morrow, 1998), but again could not see how this could be used to elicit understanding of politics. In addition, we felt that, because politics is often perceived as a difficult topic to 'discuss', this could encourage the respondent to rely on the researcher for confirmation of her understanding and interpretation of, and response to, the sentence that needed completion, thus exacerbating the problems of unequal power relations involved in youth research.

Consequently, after considering a number of alternatives, we decided to use what might be called a vignette method, using photographic images to get people talking, narrating their response(s) to the image in the light of their own understandings and experiences. The use of vignettes has become increasingly popular with social researchers (for one review, see Wilks, 2004). The strength of the method as far as our research was concerned was that it allowed respondents to interpret the image and the subject matter of the interview, in this case politics, according to their own experiences and priorities (Gaskill, 2000). In addition, some of our respondents had lower levels of literacy and texts were not a commonly used medium for all of them, whereas images were and so were more easily accepted and discussed.

We presented a series of images to each group and asked our interviewees to discuss what they thought about each one (i.e. we asked them to 'free-associate'). Given that the subject of politics is perceived as, at best, delicate or, at worst, boring, the images allowed interviewees to explore political ideas less directly through constructing a story about an image. By presenting a series of images, we were able to explore the complexity of young people's understanding and experiences of the political (Finch, 1985). In this vein, this technique enabled us to explore situational contexts and influential variables, which reflected differences of gender, ethnicity, class and so on, through the narrations developed in the focus groups across the various sites.

The use of images within the focus group to stimulate discussion of the political allowed us as researchers to avoid imposing a definition of the political on the respondents because images, more so than text or direct questions, are multi-dimensional and allowed respondents to interpret topics according to their own values and beliefs (Gaskill, 2000). It is important to recognise, however, that the images themselves were not neutral with regard to conceptions of the political. This meant that some definition of the political was inevitably embedded within the images. We decided to draw on ideas and associations with very broad political content (the themes of which are set out below). By asking respondents to free-associate with the images, we were able to prompt discussion about the political, without requiring them to rigidly adhere to narrowly defined conceptions. Furthermore, by asking the respondents to conduct a simple sort of the images at the end of the session into those they considered political and those they did not, we avoided obliging respondents to agree that all, or indeed any, of the images were political. The process of sorting as a group also allowed respondents to express and debate their own conceptions and definitions.

Using images proved to be an effective way of both gaining young people's attention and taking the focus off us as the researchers, and thus as supposed experts. We realised when pre-testing the form of the focus groups and, particularly, the use of the images that holding up, or indeed projecting, pictures for people to look at focused attention on us, as if we were teachers. As such, we used two identical sets of images and they were passed, one at a time, around the group. In this way, the images became a tool; being able to handle images helped people to relax and reinforced group discussions. For example, people would pass the image to each other and point to parts of the image to reinforce what they were saying; perhaps pointing to the clothing worn by someone in an image to identify that individual's social status (see Chapter 5). By using the image as evidence to reinforce their argument or speculate about the image, the participant was freer to develop his or her interpretation using the image without being influenced by the researcher.

3.4.1 Choosing the images

Even when we had decided to use images, the choice of particular images was crucial as this decision was obviously a critical part of the process. We were very conscious that we needed to avoid as much as possible choosing images that represented our interpretation of politics, yet aware that any such choice would be partial, in both senses of the word. Consequently, while we recognised that the images could not be neutral, we made an initial broad selection that included images that were overtly political, for example, a political candidate wearing a party badge and images which were social, for example, a woman pushing a pram, or sporting, for example, cricket fans celebrating. We originally piloted 20 images, before choosing the 17 images that provoked most discussion about political themes among the pilot group. We are unable to reproduce these images in this book due to our inability to achieve copyright clearance for a substantial number of them. Whilst the images which are described below were selected and piloted for their value as research tools, the process of selection unfortunately did not take sufficient account of their potential use in future publications. We can respond to personal requests to view the images, but we can only offer here our experience as a cautionary tale to other researchers considering using this method. The final images covered four broad themes:

1. Socio-economic inequality: Here we used images which to us, and here our own partialities are immediately in play, suggested poverty, homelessness and single parenthood, for example, images of a

woman with two children standing outside a tenement block (*Women and Children*), which we used as a warm-up image; a young woman holding a baby (*Mom and Baby*); a man pushing a pram past a row of boarded-up council houses (*Empty Houses*); a homeless hostel (*Hostel*) and a group of refugees (*Refugees*).

2. Political inclusion/exclusion: Here we used images of political candidates, (*Male Candidate* and *Female Candidate*), campaigners (*Polls Apart*) and protesters (*Facing Police*).

3. Identity: Here we used images which evoked national identity, patriotism, ethnic diversity and conflict, for example, images of a group of people sitting in Trafalgar Square, wearing and waving Union flags (*Trafalgar Square*); a man with the George cross painted on his face (*St George*); cricket fans wearing team shirts and with the Pakistani flag painted on their faces (*Cricket Fans*); and the Oldham disturbances (*Oldham*).

4. Citizenship and public services: Here we used images which suggested social diversity, public space and public services, for example, images of school pupils in a classroom (*School*); a hospital scene with an elderly male patient and two hospital staff (*Patient*); a public park with 'No Skating' marked on the path and two older people walking into the park (*No Skating*); and three women police officers wearing police-issue hijabs (*Police*).

Although we identified these themes, we did not impose this classification on the respondents. We distributed the images in random order, so the images we saw as associated with a particular theme were not necessarily together, and we let the interviewees tell us what they thought was going on in each image. The images were not neutral or objective and so could be interpreted in a variety of ways. Respondents, in discussing the images, constructed and, to an extent, negotiated the meanings they attached to the images. As such, in discussing the images, respondents invoked their own experiences and mapped them onto the image.

The way in which a group negotiated 'meaning' through experience was evident in one focus group's response to an image of a school room (*School*):

Respondent 1: No, but you can tell, you can tell [repetition is common when a speaker wishes to emphasise of point and also establishes that it is the speaker's turn] because of the backgrounds, right do ya get me? If they was to take the picture, and say ah you're all

studying, then, but you get kids messing about and you get the two
concentrating on their sums.

Respondent 2: It's like they choose some people though innit?

Respondent 3: But, they all look natural.

Respondent 4: And again and again, there's lots of Asians in the class
there's a lot more a lot more and it's true though innit?

Respondent 3: Well why should there be more white people in the
class?

Respondent 4: No, I'm just saying.

Respondent 3: It's got to be the area where the picture was taken.

Respondent 4: No, but again it brings the whole thing into scope
dunnit? It's about England.

Males, FE college students, 17–20, South Asian,
black and mixed ethnicity, focus group

Our respondents' responses to the images were rarely simple, because,
as we emphasised, the images were capable of many interpretations.
However, there were some interesting patterns in the way our respondents related to the images. For example, it was common for respondents
to associate elements of the image with something or someone that/who
was familiar to them. For example, with the image *Cricket Fans*, one
respondent, part of a mixed gender South Asian group in the FE college,
laughingly, emphasised, 'Ali, Ali, it's Ali'. Similarly, when looking at
image *St George*, a member of an all-white, male group from a sixth-form
centre, asserted, 'Steve, ha hah ha, it's Steve'. In such cases, the respondents went on to broaden the discussion, talking more generally about
ideas of nationalism and sport.

The image *Oldham* offered a similar example, but one that showed
how personal experience affected how an image was viewed. Here, the
image was invariably discussed by the groups as an image of a 'race
riot', but the respondents then proceeded to discuss why the people
were fighting and, in doing so, drew on their own experiences. Various
themes emerged in the 'explanations' respondents offered of the 'riots',
but some of the variation reflected different personal experiences (these
issues are discussed at more length in Chapter 7). So, South Asian
group members were more likely to see the 'riots' as a consequence of
poor, and they argued, racist, policing, or of inadequate local council
provision of housing and community services, and to see 'rioters' as
protecting their homes and communities. Some white respondents
agreed, particularly those in mixed ethnic groups, but others focused
on inadequate, or soft, responses to the disturbances. In the individual

interviews, it was common for South Asian respondents to discuss this image very much in terms of their personal experiences or the experiences of family or friends. So, one male, South Asian, FE college student argued:

> There is quite a lot of racism in Bradford, and most of the businesses there, restaurants and that, they're all full with English people, you know, white people, who eat all the food and that, but now that the riots have happened, and I've been there just there after the riots, and it's all completely dead. It's like a no-go area now.
>
> Male, FE college student, 18, South Asian, individual interview

The image showing protestors confronting police, *Facing Police*, provoked an interesting response. A number of groups discussed whether the image was 'posed', because many of the respondents felt that the people in the picture would not 'in reality' get away with shouting in a police officer's face in this way.

In most of the focus groups respondents asked where the image came from and who created it, as well as who the people in the picture were (a point made earlier). However, what is interesting here is how, within the focus group, these situations could be resolved by the groups themselves:

> *Respondent 1*: Her name's not Julie by any chance?
> *Interviewer*: I don't know what her name is.
> *Respondent 2*: They didn't take 'em.
>
> Male and female, homeless hostel, 16–23,
> white and mixed ethnicity, focus group

Here, Respondent 1 asks for confirmation from the researcher, but is assured by Respondent 2 that the researchers had not taken the images and, as such, had as little knowledge of who, or even where, the image represents as they do.

3.5   Individual interviews

The data generated in the focus groups were followed up in individual in-depth interviews, where the individual respondent's understanding of politics and experiences of participation were explored in the light of the previous discussion. The antecedent focus group then provided an important context for the individual interview.

3.5.1 Development of concourses

The focus group was linked to the individual interview through the generation of a 'concourse' (Dryzek and Berejikian, 1993) of the dominant themes that emerged in each focus group for the researcher and respondents to reflect on. The concourses differed across the groups, revealing the significant concerns and preoccupations within groups with differing demographic profiles, which were then explored in greater detail with individual participants.

The following quotes provide an example of how these concourses developed from the respondents' understandings of what the image signified and how these understandings formed around a number of politically current themes. The image is a monochrome photograph of a woman holding an infant (*Mom and Baby*). In this first example, the two respondents are a white male aged 23 and a black woman aged 19, both living in the homeless hostel:

> *Respondent 1*: A baby and a mother a nice picture actually if it was my wife I'd put it on the wall.
> *Respondent 2*: That one, the young mother and child, that would be it the fact that she is alone probably. That would be it. This would be, not refugees, you can't but they look like refugees. And like they've been in the news and so that one.

In another group, the respondents were male and female students at a FE college, South Asian and aged between 18 and 20 years. A snapshot of their discussion of this image reveals somewhat different analyses:

> *Respondent 1*: Teenagers, she looks like yeah, teenage pregnancy . . .
> *Respondent 2*: Yeah, she's obviously unhappy. She's got problems.
> *Respondent 1*: Yeah, she doesn't look very happy either.
> *Respondent 3*: Maybe she has to give it up for adoption.
> *Respondent 1*: She can't support the baby.
> *Respondent 3*: Or maybe her parents have like disowned her for it . . . Obviously she's not educated. . . . Well she's young.
> *Respondent 1*: Lack of sex education.

Here we can identify the following themes: (i) motherhood, (ii) single parenthood, (iii) teenage pregnancies, (iv) sadness, (v) adoption, (vi) alienation from parents, (vii) poverty, (viii) youth, (ix) lack of education, and (x) lack of sex education.

Each one of these elements is centrally positioned in three overlapping and society-wide discourses, namely (i) a discourse on the place of women in society; (ii) a discourse on the place of children/youth in society; and (iii) a discourse on motherhood and childcare.

Drawing on the formulations of these political themes which were developed in the focus group and expressed our respondents' understanding of politics, we were then able to investigate the respondents' experiences of political participation. As such, the concourse of dominant themes generated from the focus groups were a key organising principle of the individual interviews. Table 3.1 summarises the

Table 3.1   Concourses of political themes from the focus groups

Site	Respondent profile	Dominant themes
Pilot (friendship group)	Men White and mixed ethnicity 16–17	Coercive interventions from police, schools and state. Exclusion from public spaces. Politics as connected to all aspects of government and as everyday experience.
FE college	Men and women South Asian 18–20	'Race' as a political issue. Mixing in of ethnic groups (as aspiration). Nature of patriotism (exclusiveness of Britishness). Policing practices. Politics as the ability to change things.
FE college	Men Black, South Asian and mixed ethnicity 17–20	Ethnic diversity in society and public services (as incomplete). Policing practices and (lack of) representativeness and accountability. Disempowered neighbourhoods (and need for spokesperson).
New Deal training centre	Men and women White, black and South Asian 17–23	Equal rights and opportunities. Prevalence of racism. Single parenthood (constraints and responsibility debate). Unfair policing practices. Remoteness of political institutions.
Comprehensive school XI form	Men White 17–18	Patriotism and Englishness/Britishness. Neighbourhood patriotism. Exclusion of the English within multiculturalist discourses. Generation gap. Remoteness of politicians.

Comprehensive school XI form	Women White 17–18	Importance of education. Lack of consultation in education policy. Exclusion of women from political institutions. Condemnation of violence and street disturbances.
Comprehensive school XI form	Women White 16–17	Responsiveness and accountability of City Council to its tenants and residents. Mixing of ethnic groups (expressed as aspiration and conflict). Declining public services. Resources for refugees.
Selective school XI form	Men and women White, black and South Asian 16–18	Unresponsiveness of state and police to communities. Tension between goals of equal opportunities and meritocracy. Condemnation of violence (in relation to street disturbances and football hooliganism).
Homeless hostel	Men and women White and mixed ethnicity 16–23	Multiculturalism as everyday experience. Neglect by the state. Importance of achieving self-reliance. Remoteness of politicians. Women's independence. Remoteness of royalty.
Homeless hostel	Women Black and mixed ethnicity 18–22	Mixing in of different faith and ethnic groups (conflictual and convivial). Resources for refugees. Lack of neighbourhood resources/spaces. Ability of women to achieve independence. Faith in politicians.
Homeless hostel	Men White 18–19	Importance of self-reliance. Multiculturalism as everyday experience. Lack of accountability of state.
University	Men and women White 21–22	Ethnic conflict in Birmingham/Britain. Efficacy of demonstrations and political violence. Britishness (as contested, fluctuating). Partiality of media. Limits of representative politics to address youth issues.

key concourses from each focus group, which structured a section of the individual interviews.

These concourses are discussed in further detail in Chapter 4, where we set out how these related to our focus group respondents' conceptions of the political.

3.5.2   Autobiographical data

In addition, we included a section on autobiographical discussion within the individual interviews to provide information on the demographic background, identity and the life transitions experienced by each individual interviewee, so as to investigate how these affected their notions of the political. As we highlighted earlier, youth research suggests that the transition to adulthood has become more extended and our research design allowed us to examine both whether the changing social conditions such research has emphasised had any implications for how young people understand and experience politics (Jones and Wallace, 1992) and whether such conditions produce different experiences of the political for young people (Du-Bois-Reymond, 1998; Thomson *et al.*, 2000). We tapped into respondents' sense of themselves and how they located themselves in the world in part by inquiring about their 'future selves'. This device is used not so much to explore respondents' predictions, but rather to establish how, through projecting themselves into the future, they understand their own social locations.

Experiences of political participation and conceptions of the political were discussed throughout these sections of the interview.

3.6   Analysing the data

In setting out to analyse the data, the issue of hermeneutics became relevant. If the respondents were articulating their interpretations/ understandings of the images, we were interpreting/understanding their interpretations/understandings; as such, there was a double hermeneutic involved. Our interpretations were affected by our experiences and, to an extent, we have dealt with this issue earlier. At the same time, our interpretations reflected our academic concerns and our epistemological and theoretical positions.

The first of these issues is perhaps particularly important given our research interests. We wanted to understand young people's understandings of politics and, although we developed a research design that, in our view, reduced the problem of imposing our conception of politics on the respondent, nevertheless, for ethical reasons, we told the sites and the interviewees at the outset that what we were interested in was 'young people's political opinions'. Consequently, we had to acknowledge that this may have led respondents to be more likely to view the images as political than they would have done if they had seen the image in a book or newspaper. Unfortunately, there was no way of avoiding this problem, except perhaps by being less than truthful about our concerns, which would have undermined our ethical relationship with our respondents. However, we attempted to reduce the problem by avoiding raising politics as an issue in the focus group, until the 'sort' at the end. In our view, the fact there was a great deal of variation in the number of images different groups regarded as political in that 'sort' suggests that the problem was not overly determining.

As we said, our interpretation is also influenced by our ontological, epistemological and theoretical positions. We acknowledge that politics is a 'lived experience', and, in particular, that whether an image was seen as political was a question of understanding and interpretation. We accept that there was a double hermeneutic involved, so that we are offering our understanding and interpretation of our respondent's understanding and interpretation of politics. However, as we emphasised in Chapter 1, we also argue that lived experience is structured; so, individual's experiences were gendered, 'raced' and 'classed'. As such, our analysis looks at both how class, 'race' and gender were experienced as political experience, and how class, 'race' and gender structure lived experience. Not all our readers will share that position. In fact, there is a third level of the hermeneutic involved: our reader's understanding and interpretation of our understanding and interpretation of our respondent's understanding and interpretation. However, the key point is that we make our position clear and allow the readers to judge our understanding and interpretation.

3.6.1 The importance of context

There were also more mundane, but still important, issues involved in interpreting group discussions that we must acknowledge. As we already emphasised, the views explored in the focus group were reported within a social context and these may well have differed if the context had been changed. The dynamics of any particular group may also have obscured controversial perspectives (for example, racist discourses) or produced a consensus driven by one or two members. Thus, we needed to consider the composition of the group, identifying the shared and differing characteristics of the participants and the extent to which group members were known to one another. There were also ways in which we as researchers could reflect on the socially constructed character of the group responses, for example, by paying attention to whether consensus was imposed by dominant members; looking for contradictions between responses to differing images and considering their significance; paying attention to silences – especially where people appeared to retreat rather than voice dissent; and reconsidering the arguments, views and themes in follow-up individual interviews. As Smithson argues, the discussions generated by group interviews should not be analysed as if they were natural conversations, but rather as 'discussions occurring in a specific, controlled setting' (Smithson, 2000); thus the dynamics of group interaction needed to be taken into account within the analytical framework.

3.6.2   The differing standpoints of researchers and respondents

We have to acknowledge that the different experiences of researchers and respondents were bound to have an effect on the interviews. Most of the interviews were conducted by two white, thirty something, women researchers interviewing people, all of whom all differed from them in age, and many of whom differed from them in class, gender and ethnicity. In addition, their life experiences were very different from most, if not all, of their respondents. We are not developing a standpoint epistemological position here. Rather, we are emphasising that such different experiences shaped our understandings and interpretations of both politics and the interview situation, but we do not think this disqualified us from interpreting these young people's experiences because we did not share those experiences. Indeed, in our view such a position makes social science research almost impossible. Rather, the point we are making here is that many of our respondents were aware of some of the issues which resulted from the different experiences of the researchers. For example, one male, FE college student with Pakistani heritage commented,

> *Respondent*: Like my dad says, the longer we live in a mixed society, the more diluted people culturally are becoming. Every time we make our religion flexible, we're losing a part of it. Every time we make our culture flexible, we are losing a very large part of being Pakistani . . . and he goes you can't do that.
> *Interviewer*: And what do you think to that?
> *Respondent*: What do I think? That I'm sitting here talking to you puts a question mark over my culture, not my religion of course, but my

culture, it puts a slight question mark over it, but it's flexible as I see it.

Male, FE college student, 19, South Asian,
individual interview

Here, the respondent is suggesting that even talking about these issues with a white female researcher changed his identity, albeit in a small way.

When asking individuals to reflect on the concourse generated from a focus group, it was common for people to check if the interviewer understood details of the discussion. To an extent, this is a common practice in daily discourses, and sometimes respondents doubted the interviewer's knowledge, and thus understanding, of their experiences. An excerpt from the individual interview with a male, South Asian, FE college student illustrates this point:

Respondent: In the news recently there's meant to be a march in Birmingham on Saturday, I don't whether you've heard? At Alum Rock? [an area in Birmingham].
Interviewer: Yeah right.

The narration continues,

Respondent: Yeah, I mean there may be one or two riots over this and that between whites, like recently, I'll give you an example, do you know Balsall Heath [an area of Birmingham]? There was a stabbing there, an Asian youth, he got stabbed by a black youth and died. Did you hear about that?
Interviewer: I didn't hear about that.
Respondent: In Balsall Heath, and at the time they explained that the race issues were going off, and then the media played a big part in the story, so that they could say, oh maybe relations between blacks and Asians aren't very good either. Because I think one paper I was reading . . . generally race relations, you know they are good in that area, it's just one of those things . . .

Male, FE college student, 18, South Asian,
individual interview

Respondents did have a level of control during the interviewing process. One focus group was uncertain if there was another underlying reason for the interview other than our initial statement about our interest in young people's political opinions. The group started to break into smaller groups each grabbing one image and talking about it. Two people were particularly nervous about what was happening and one decided to question one of the researchers:

Respondent 1: Is it like Psychology, is it like Psychology?
Interviewer: No. I mean, no it's not like a psychological test where we are trying to find, discover, secret things about you.
Respondent 2: Yeah, yeah.
Interviewer: Y'know by interpreting your answers. I mean it's really about what your opinions are about things; for some people these things y'know mean one thing, for some people they mean something else.

At this point, two of the other respondents were whispering to each other.

Respondent 1: That's why it is difficult.
Interviewer: Exactly, yeah, so what we want to find out is what...
Respondent 2: Right, let's show them each one. No, stop messing them all up and show them individually... one at a time and then we can have a debate about them.

Males, FE college students, 17–20, South Asian, black and mixed ethnicity, focus group

3.6.3 The use of NVIVO

Both the focus groups and the individual interviews were recorded and transcribed so that we could analyse the data using a computer-assisted qualitative data analysis software programme – NVIVO.

We used NVIVO to analyse the data at one level as a sophisticated storage and retrieval tool. But, using the capabilities of NVIVO, we were able to conduct fairly complex and layered analyses of the interview data, by: examining common themes that emerged across the interviews; comparing views about the images expressed in the free-association exercises across groups and individuals; analysing and comparing the sorts; and analysing and comparing data according to class, gender, ethnicity and contact with the state. Furthermore, we used NVIVO to test our methodology and our selection of the images, by analysing our respondents' analyses of the images, reactions to the interview structure and to us as researchers and the impact these had on their responses to the images and formulations of the political. Below we set out an outline schema of the way we built 'trees' of coding (Richards, 2005) within the NVIVO programme:

1. *Responses to the research process* (including ways of 'reading' photographs – such as looking through, at and behind the images (Banks, 2001); references to researchers; deliberation and questioning of the interview formats).
2. *Interpretations of the images* (considering recurring and dissonant responses and analysed across groups and in relation to group profiles).
3. *Particular group themes* (coding dominant themes within a focus group to build view of 'concourses').
4. *Common/recurring themes* (coding recurrent themes across the focus group and individual interviews, such as 'race', representation of young people, locality, etc.).
5. *Particular issues across respondents* (including references to September 11th, the role of the media, the monarchy, the NHS, etc.).
6. *Comparison of responses to themes across gender, ethnicity and site.*
7. *Conceptions of the political* (coding discussions relating to politics, the political, politicians, political institutions and processes; community politics; and political participation across focus groups and individual interviews).
8. *Coding of sorting exercises* (coding allocation of images to political and non-political categories, justifications and definitions of political deployed in this process).

The building of this coding structure was developed through an iterative process of reading the data, shaping the coding and looking back again at the data. This method brought some issues to our attention that we had not discerned prior to reading the NVIVO coding results, such as the prevalence of the term and idea of 'mixing in' across age, class and ethnic groups and sites (which we discuss in Chapter 7). A limitation that became evident in using NVIVO was the tendency sometimes to lose a contextual sense of the data, due to the extraction method of the coding function of the programme (and to overcome this we needed to frequently refer back to the interviews). The use of NVIVO did provide, nevertheless, a useful and systematic scoping and handling tool with which to explore our data.

3.7   Conclusion

Overall then, our methodology reflected our theoretical concerns. In particular, we wanted to avoid imposing our definition of the political, whilst finding a way to open discussion about political issues and concerns, which necessitated the use of methods that allowed us to gather respondent-led data. In other words, our research questions required us to use qualitative methods. Our feedback from talking with other researchers working with young people suggested that simply asking young people what they thought constituted 'politics' or 'the political' would be met with hostility, incomprehension or indifference (White *et al.*, 2000). This meant that we needed to think creatively about how we would open discussion on a topic regarded as potentially dry, obscure or alienating by our respondents. Furthermore, we were constrained in our choice of research tools by varying levels of literacy amongst our respondents (so word games or cards which entailed a lot of text were inappropriate). These issues underpinned our decision to use images in our focus group work. Although we wanted to use less directive methods, we were obliged to acknowledge that our research tools would not be neutral with regard to the scope and dimensions of the political. Thus, our images carried within them a set of political thematics. Nevertheless, the variety of opinions expressed in the focus groups about the images suggests that their political content was open to different interpretations across the groups.

We also wished to acknowledge that young people are active social agents and to explore how their conceptions of the political operated at the level of lived experience. To this end, we linked our data on their views of the political with in-depth individual interviews that explored their personal biographies and experiences.

These methods allowed us to explore how young people conceived of and experienced the political, and the results are discussed in detail in Chapters 4–7 that follow.

4
The Politics of Youth

4.1 A crisis of youth participation?

As we have discussed in Chapter 1, there has been a great deal of
attention paid to the issue of youth political participation in Britain
(as in many other countries) – prompted, particularly, by low youth
turnouts in recent elections. In addition, there has been a dominant
media narrative that portrays young people in Britain as politically
inactive, with commentators talking of the growth of an 'apathy generation' or 'Thatcher's airheads' (Toynbee, 1997; Hiscock, 2001). It is
routinely observed that young people are more likely to vote in the
reality TV show *Big Brother* than in local, European or general elections
(news.bbc.co.uk, 2002; Coleman, 2003; Mulvey, 2003).

As we saw, the notion that British young people's interest and participation in formal politics is declining is supported by several survey
studies. Pirie and Worcester (1998), for instance, claim that the 'Millennial Generation' of young people who reached the age of 21 just before
or just after the turn of the millennium are less involved in politics
than the equivalent age group were 30 years ago, less likely to vote
in national or local elections than older people now or young people
30 years ago and have little knowledge of politics at local, national
or European levels. They conclude that this generation is an 'apolitical generation'. Similarly, Park's (1998) survey data of social attitudes
among British youth indicate that teenagers and young adults are less
likely to be involved in conventional politics, be knowledgeable about
politics, have an attachment to any political party, or view voting as a
civic responsibility.

91

4.2   Questioning the youth apathy myth

There are a number of in-depth research studies of young people that question this view of them as politically apathetic or inactive (Eden and Roker, 2000; White *et al.*, 2000; Henn *et al.*, 2002). These studies, often drawing on qualitative methodologies rather than quantitative survey techniques, take a broader view of the ways in which young people engage in political and civic life. They suggest that young people are indeed turning away from formal, mainstream politics, but this does not mean that they are necessarily politically apathetic. Rather young people are reasonably interested in politics and political issues, but cynical about politicians and formal mechanisms for political participation. Eden and Roker (2000) argue, furthermore, that debates about young people and politics habitually fail to consider areas where young people *are* active. Their research suggests that certain types of youth civic participation are in fact increasing, particularly peer education, youth councils, youth run and managed projects and peer support groups. These findings are supported by more recent survey research, including that of Pattie *et al.* (2004) and Norris (2003), that we discussed in Chapter 1, which suggest that young people's patterns of political participation are *different* to that of adults.

More recently, a revaluation of the myth of youth political apathy was prompted by the anti-war demonstrations of 2003, when we saw classrooms empty and young people (many below voting age) take to the streets to engage in political protest. Since then, there has been a questioning among media and political commentators of the consensus that young people are necessarily politically apathetic (Brooks, 2003; Turner, 2004).

Whilst there is perhaps rather less certainty now that young people are an 'apolitical generation', the gap between falling participation in formal politics on the one hand and higher levels of political interest on the other requires further investigation. It is not clear in the literature *why* young people's participation is different to that of other age groups. Most explanations of why young people appear to be 'tuning out' of formal mainstream politics – such as cynicism regarding the integrity of politicians, perceived lack of choices between parties, dissatisfaction with local government procedures – might equally apply to adults. Yet, not only do young people tend to participate less than adults, but their levels of participation are generally declining at a faster rate (Phelps, 2004). Furthermore, the nineteenth British Social Attitudes Survey (Park *et al.*, 2002) suggests that young people are actually no more distrustful of government than other age groups. At the same time, within many studies (for example, see, Parry *et al.*, 1992), age is treated merely as a variable and consequently there are insufficient youth-specific explanations for declining political engagement among young people. Overall then, there is, a lack of clarity about how, or why, young people approach politics differently: nor do we have satisfactory data to explain why young people are increasingly less likely than adults to vote, write to politicians, join a political party and so on.

4.3 Why are young people different?

In order to understand why young people's political engagement seems to be different to that of other age groups, we argue that there are four issues that need to be addressed.

First, we need to understand politics as a 'lived experience' for young people (Bhavnani, 1991), rather than as a set of arenas into which they do, or do not, enter. This entails taking a broader view of the political. Given the arguments introduced in Chapter 1, that much of the research on political participation operates with a rather narrow conception of 'the political', which is generally arena-based and imposed upon the respondents, we suggest here that this tendency compounds the problem of the lack of youth-specific explanations. We argue that, by listening to how young people themselves conceive of, and experience, politics, we can begin to theorise about the distinctive issues and experiences that have an impact on young people's political engagement.

Secondly, and relatedly, there is a tendency within much survey research to treat age merely as a variable and this does not allow for the exploration of the specific factors that affect young people, such as changes in the political environment, which may give rise to generation effects. Generation effects arise when successive generations face new challenges or experiences that make them different to previous generations. Thus, the political issues and arenas familiar to older generations as foci and sites of political activity may well have little relevance to young people (Jowell and Park, 1998). Indeed, Phelps' analysis of electoral turnout data by age suggests that there is a generation effect at work. He argues, however, that we need a better understanding of *why* this is taking place and he raises the question that 'if there has been a profound shift in political engagement, what has caused this and what participatory norms can we expect to emerge as a generation that is not apathetic but is distinct matures?' (Phelps, 2004, p. 245). In this chapter, we argue that Henrik Bang's (2003) theory, that new modes of political participation are developing as a consequence of the emergence of new forms of governance, is particularly relevant to these kinds of questions. As we saw in Chapter 2, Bang implicitly builds upon ideas of 'reflexive modernity' and argues that, within the new 'culture governance' environment, new types of political participants have emerged: the 'Expert Citizens' and the 'Everyday Makers', for whom political engagement is about being involved in concrete issues at local levels within social networks rather than in formal groups that are focused on the state. Young people, he suggests, are very likely to exhibit the characteristics of Everyday Makers. Clearly, longitudinal data are needed to establish whether the changes Bang identifies are indeed underpinning generational change. But, Bang's work is helpful in allowing us to theorise about how structural, political, environmental changes may explain why young people's engagement is somewhat different to that of adults.

Thirdly, we argue that we need a better understanding of life-cycle effects. Life-cycle effects arise from the similar constraints, choices and expectations that young people experience, which differ from other age groups and which are likely to change when they themselves are no longer young. Such differences may arise from differential legal and policy status with regard to the age of responsibility, assumption of voting rights, welfare entitlements and so on. They may also arise as a consequence of processes of transition, such as from education to employment or from dependency to partial dependency to independence (Coles, 1995). In many studies of the differences between youth and adult political participation, life-cycle effects are invoked to explain why young people appear to participate less than older cohorts, but there is little systematic investigation or analysis of any specific life-cycle effects or the ways in which these may shape young people's political engagement. Parry *et al.* (1992), for instance, suggest that young people are politically inactive simply because they have other things to do, but their data do not offer any evidence to support this interpretation. We argue here that there are particular life-cycle factors and constraints that shape young people's everyday lived experiences and that these have a strong bearing on their political engagement.

Finally, there is a need to view young people as political agents, rather than political apprentices. Within many studies of, and policies designed to increase, youth participation, there is a tendency to view young people's political engagement as a means of inducting them into adult politics, rather than a means of including or engaging young people in political processes so that they may have a say about issues that affect or concern them. The tendency to see young people as apprentices

(or as *future* citizens), rather than political agents, incurs specific problems of political exclusion for young people and this is something which
our data clearly show.

4.3.1 Politics as lived experience

The first issue relates to the need to move beyond seeing political engagement as a set of activities in a range of specified arenas, towards understanding it as lived experience. In particular, the way that age shapes
young people's lived experience often has strong political implications.
Political geographers, such as Philo and Smith (2003), argue that there
has been a lack of attention within mainstream political science to the
'personal politics of identity', defined as attempts by the individual to
gain a sense of themselves and their place in the world and to gain power
over their immediate conditions of existence. They contend that this
lack of a youth-centred approach has resulted in an inability to explain
why disengagement among young people is increasing or how these
groups can be engaged in politics. Consequently, they suggest that it is
necessary to develop a youth-centred understanding of young people's
politics, which takes account of the 'connections between knowledge,
meaning, agency and identity', or what they identify as the micro-
politics of 'everyday life'.

Philo and Smith warn, however, that 'the message is not that politics
should be redefined *solely* in terms of the personal and localised experiences of children and young people' (2003, p. 111). The development of
a youth-centred approach should not involve becoming blinkered to the
macro-politics of the (adult) public sphere of political action and institutions, since these fundamentally shape the environments in which
youth and child-centred politics are played out. Rather, they suggest we
should 'concentrate on connections between the micro and the macro'
(2003, p. 111). In other words, we need to develop a sense of how
young people's lived experiences shape their conceptions of the political, whilst maintaining an awareness of how macro institutions and
processes have an impact on young people's lived experiences (i.e. to
understand lived experience as a structured process, as we discussed in
Chapter 1).

In our interviews these connections emerge quite strongly in the
ways in which young people's everyday experiences shape their conceptions of the political. Drawing on the concourses of dominant themes
generated by the group interviews on the nature of the political (as we
described in Chapter 3), we gain extremely useful insights into the ways

in which lived experience shapes young people's sense of politics and, hence, their political engagement.

For instance, we conducted a focus group with seven 16-year-old males, who were of white, black and mixed ethnicity, and who had recently finished, or were coming to the end of, their school studies. Their responses produced a discourse on the nature of politics which was characterised by themes of authority, lack of autonomy and exclusion from public spaces. Their definition of politics included any activity in which they were affected by government. Thus, they suggested 'everything to do with government is political' and this was also heavily associated with authority relationships, such as with police and teachers, or coercive interventions. Their subsequent suggestions about types of political participation also reflected activities where one was affected by government or the police, rather than activities in which one participated in order to affect or influence government. So, for instance, the group had decided that an image of boarded-up houses used in the interview process had a campaigning purpose, which was to put pressure on the Council to address the problem of homelessness. However, when they were asked to differentiate between those images they considered to be related to politics, and those they did not, they placed this image in the *non-political* pile. Reflecting this disengagement, the group did not recognise two images of rosette-wearing parliamentary candidates, identifying them as winners of some kind of competition, such as a dog-show, despite the fact that the General Election had been held just four days earlier.

In another focus group composed of South Asian, 17–19-year old male and female FE college students, a narrative about the images that was much more focused on issues connected to 'race' emerged. This group tended to analyse all the images as 'all to do with ethnics [sic]' and related them to issues of racial inclusion or exclusion. The dominant themes that emerged from this group were racism; tensions between ethnic groups; the nature of patriotism and the importance of different ethnic groups 'mixing-in'. Among the definitions of politics which emerged from the sorting exercise was the suggestion that politics was about the capacity to change things, and this exercise also prompted a vigorous debate about 'race' as an inherently political issue. As one woman argued, 'It's all politics: 'race', racism and the fight and the NF.'

We also carried out a focus group with New Dealers composed of men and women aged 17–23, who were black, white and South Asian, some with children, and all, by virtue of their participation in the New Deal (welfare-to-work) scheme, in receipt of benefits. The views of the political among these participants were dominated by themes of neglect and exclusion; for example, they interpreted an image of a park, with the words 'No Skating' on the path as political, because of the Council's role in running the park and 'getting rid of the kids'. The themes which emerged were the sense that government failed in its duties and that politicians were remote, as one stated, 'It's basically people who've never lived in the shoes of people who are not well off. They've been born with a silver spoon in their gob.' They felt that their life-chances were very much dependent on their own resources or the support of family networks (or the lack of such support), whilst some groups were able to unfairly claim resources (including single mothers and asylum seekers). Interestingly, the group took a very wide-ranging definition of politics, which they related to either coercive interventions from the government or the withholding, or unfair distribution, of resources. For example, when showed an image of a football fan, they defined this as a political image for two reasons: first, due to the police presence at football matches and their role in controlling the crowds – 'that's sport and politics. You know, trying to control the crowd and all that'; and, secondly, due to the extremely high salaries paid to footballers – 'look at the footballers, man, they're earning millions and there's people on the street starving' and 'That's all politics, you know, there is a lot of politics in sport, especially how much the players are getting paid.'

In a focus group with some students from a comprehensive sixth form, aged 16–18, who were all male, white and predominantly working-class, the themes that emerged centred on issues of 'race', patriotism and identity. Their discussions revealed a strong concern with identity issues (manifested by a preoccupation with patriotism) and a sense that they were marginalised from, indeed threatened by, current debates on 'race' and identity. A second key theme to emerge from this discussion was the strong sense of generational differences – in particular they were highly conscious of their lack of status as young people and their exclusion from public spaces and decision-making processes. Like the first group of young men discussed above, they defined politics as anything to do with government, including the running of schools, hospitals and the police: 'Politics is mainly stuff to do with the government and everything that happens in the country affects the government, so probably everything's political innit?' In common with the first group, their view of politics was characterised by a sense that politics was something that affected them, but which they did not, or could not, affect themselves: 'I think it's like a cycle for us 'cos we haven't really been interested in it 'cos . . . we haven't been included in stuff except writing to your councillor and stuff and then it would have just been seen as kids messing around.'

Interestingly, a focus group held at the same site, this time with white, working-class, 16–18-year-old female sixth-formers, who lived in the same, mainly white, area, did not produce similar concerns with regard to 'race', patriotism or national identity. The young women in this group were much more concerned with issues concerning the opportunities for representation of women: 'Yeah, I'd like to see more women now. I think, generally, there needs to be more women in [parliament] because it's like they seem to be in a minority and women aren't a minority. So that needs to be more, that needs to be represented more in parliament, it needs to be shown more', whilst another commented that for this to happen 'You'd have to be very strong, because no doubt there might be quite a few men in parliament who would look down on you because you are a women, because it was mainly a male thing.' This group tended to view politics as a means of effecting change. An additional divergence between the men and the women at this site emerged in the subsequent individual interviews. During the interviews we asked the respondents for some autobiographical details, including their views about how they saw themselves in the future. All the men saw themselves staying very close to their present homes to work and bring up families, whereas all the women stated their intention to move away to pursue educational or career objectives.

A focus group with male and female, black and white, young homeless people living in a 'foyer' type of hostel[1] produced a discourse on the political that was characterised by neglect and exclusion. For this group, receipt of benefits and living in temporary accommodation created a situation where they felt they were self-reliant but without the means of achieving self-determination. As one respondent stated in a follow-up interview:

> To be honest, I can't see myself what I'm going to be in five years, I don't know where I'm gonna be. I don't even know where I'm going to be tomorrow. That's the chance you take when you move out at a young age and into hostels, you know, you really don't know where you're going to end up, or know what you're going to get out of it, or, you really don't know. You just have to take each day as it comes and just try and use whatever's there. You can plan, but it's very difficult to plan when you're in such an awkward position, because you're really not in control of where your life is going in a place like this. It's very easy to lose control.
>
> Male, homeless hostel, 23, white, individual interview

A strong theme of the responses across this group was that the government, or often 'the system', conspired against the achievement of self-determination. For example, one respondent related an image of a young mother to the lack of autonomy of mothers living in hostels and their experiences of being moved on: 'There's loads of mothers and that in hostels like this... you see loads of places like this, and it gets me, and nothing's been done... and then other people say look you've gorra move 'cos we want to do summat better on this site.' In another exchange, respondents discussed the limitations to self-expression and self-determination that they experienced:

> *Respondent 1*: We live in a very restricted world where we have to keep a lot of thoughts to ourselves.
>
> *Respondent 2*: Exactly, you know, you've got a job and that and they found out what record you had, or how you are, they're not gonna like it. Imagine if you really you did, when you was little, bad things and that, say when you come 16, but when you come older, you want to look after children and that, they're probably gonna say no, you'll beat the kids up or whatever, and they're thinking na na. So that's why, sometimes, you like, you just want to get rid of the past and come to the future, so I think some of the people should give you a chance as well. Like when you come out of prison and that, I know they've done bad things but they want to get over it now and do something but people don't give 'em a chance they don't give 'em a job or anything.

The group, nevertheless, placed a great deal of importance on the ability to achieve things for oneself without relying on others or the state. As one stated, 'from my position, I was always taught to believe and have faith in that y'know – the people who don't have much, start from the bottom, actually can become stronger people... than people who have had someone to support them and take them through stages of life'. They suggested that politics was about being able to express one's views and demands, but felt there were significant constraints on their opportunities to do so, not least because they viewed politicians as disconnected from their life experiences as one argued, 'They should have people like us y'know... they're just people that have come up and have got money and that, we need someone who's gone through like what we've gone through' and 'they probably look at us and thinking na. That's why we need someone from our own side to understand us.'

As these responses show, by examining how young people's lived experiences determine their conceptions of the political, we can achieve insights into the ways in which they politically engage. This perspective on politics as a lived experience – rather than a set of distinct arenas – helps us to contextualise young people's political concerns and understand why many seem to relate very weakly to mainstream political institutions.

4.3.2 A distinctive generation?

There are studies claiming that a generation shift in young people's political culture is taking place, which makes their views and expectations different to those of previous generations (Wilkinson and Mulgan, 1997; Pirie and Worcester, 2000). Inglehart (1997), for instance, identifies a postmaterialist generation, for whom increasing affluence, consumerism and individualism have led to a breakdown in the collectivist values of previous generations and, thus, a shift in their political orientations. As a consequence, we see greater participation in issue-led, rather than ideological, politics and a concern with issues such as the environment or animal rights, rather than industrial relations and so on. Furlong and Cartmel (1997) also point to increasing individualisation among young people in post-industrial society, whilst Putnam (1995) has famously argued that there has been a decline in social capital and associational membership, which many link to the decline of political participation in advanced democracies. These studies tend to see the origin of these trends in social change and pay rather little attention to the role that changes in the political environment may have on political engagement. Recent attempts to relate these social changes to the changing role of the state and to explore how these affect political attitudes and behaviour have been made by Pirie and Worcester (1998, 2000) and Henrik Bang (2003, 2004).

As stated above, Pirie and Worcester identify an apolitical 'Millennial Generation' (1998) of young people who they argue are less likely to be political participants than older people now, or young people 30 years ago. They claim that today's young people are increasingly unwilling to participate in social or community activism and that '[c]itizenship, insofar as it involves participation in the community, is the big turn-off' (2000, p. 24). They cite the increasing withdrawal of the state from people's lives as a reason for young people's declining civic and political participation. Consequently, they suggest, young people do not vote 'because they feel it does not meet their concerns or address their needs. They do not see its relevance, or think it will make any difference to them' (2000, p. 12). Pirie and Worcester argue then that there are generation effects at work, which have serious repercussions for young people's propensity to participate in political or community activities.

Yet, the notion that the state is withdrawing from people's lives, particularly in the case of young people, may be somewhat overplayed, as the state still figures very substantially in their lives, since, by virtue of their age, they tend to have very little economic autonomy and do not always enjoy full political, legal or social rights (Newman, 1996). In other words, young people may be rather less affected by the state's declining role in providing social or economic goods, as many experience compulsory vocational, education or training schemes (such as New Deal). Pirie and Worcester's analysis is premised on the view that there has been a contraction in political participation that is a corollary of a contraction of the political sphere. What they do not explore is the possibility that changes in the political sphere may have resulted in new repertoires or modes of political participation. This possibility is addressed by Henrik Bang, who suggests, contrary to Pirie and Worcester, that the political sphere has *not* contracted; rather the boundaries between the political (public) sphere and society are dissolving (Bang, 2004). In fact, he suggests, the scope of the political in late modern society is expanding and is much more expressed in and through people's everyday lives – in his phrase the 'political is now personal'. In this analysis, changes in the political sphere have altered the modes of political participation.

As we discussed in Chapter 2, Bang identifies the emergence of a new relationship between political authorities and lay people, 'in the shape of a highly politicised and culturally oriented new management and administration', which he terms 'culture governance', and a 'strongly individualised and consumption oriented new citizen', who he terms the 'Everyday Maker'. Culture governance is characterised by 'strategic communication oriented towards attaining influence and success by involving and partnering with individuals and groups in the political community' (2003, p. 241). Everyday making is characterised by 'tactical communication oriented towards the building of reflexive communities where individuals and groups can feel engaged and practice their freedoms in their mutual recognition of difference' (2003, p. 241).

According to Bang, Everyday Makers do not relate strongly to ideological politics, or to conventional types of participation such as inter-elite bargaining or outright opposition to the state. Rather, they engage in the building and running of governance networks and reflexive political communities – often in voluntary and social organisations and groups. This is, Bang suggests, because Everyday Makers are 'much more interested in enhancing their personal and common capacities for self-governance and co-governance, right where they are, than in submitting themselves to an abstract social norm or mode of state citizenship' (2004, p. 26). Everyday Makers 'want to decide what to do for themselves' and are engaged in 'a micropolitics of becoming' (2004, p. 14). Thus, he contends (2004, p. 26),

> To be an [Everyday Maker] is to be more individualistic, more project oriented, more 'on' than 'off' and 'hit and run' in one's engagement, more pleasure oriented and more fun-seeking, than is usually associated with being civilly engaged. Everyday makers do not primarily gain their political identities from being citizens of the state or of an autonomous civil society, but from being ordinarily engaged in the construction of networks and locales for the political governance of the social.

What is interesting from our point of view is that Bang sees the Everyday Maker mode of participation as being particularly evident among young people. As one of his respondents described (2004, p. 23),

> I've seen how young people over the course of the last decade organise and involve themselves very differently. The fact of the matter is that young people are actually very engaged. The thing is that they are engaged in ways that the older generations consider unconventional. It's often a matter of getting involved in a concrete project, and then engaging oneself 100% in it for a short period and then they stop. They don't participate in the long term.

There are a number of key features of Bang's Everyday Makers, which we will analyse now in relation to our own data on young people's conceptions of the political. First, Bang suggests that Everyday Makers are distinctive in their orientations towards elite politics, in the sense that they do not relate to concepts of right and left and are critical of politicians and parties. Secondly, they politically participate in distinctive ways: preferring to get involved on the lowest level, in concrete issues and on a short-term basis. Finally, they are disengaged from the state, neither seeking influence within it nor engaging in opposition to it.

In this section, we will examine how far our data support the notion that young people can be seen as (emergent) Everyday Makers.

4.3.2.1 *Young people as 'Everyday Makers': Attitudes towards elite politics*

Our respondents were highly sceptical about the credibility and integrity of politicians and political parties. In common with Bang's Everyday Makers, they were hostile towards the pursuit of political power and influence. There was a common perception, unsurprisingly perhaps, that politicians were self-interested, untrustworthy and power-hungry.

> I think young people particularly are very suspicious of MPs...
> I mean, we've grown up in the era of sleaze... This person's a crook, that person's a crook. And it doesn't even appear to be from one particular party, although they've made a big deal that it was about the Conservatives, it's just turned out that they're all involved... Credibility is a real problem for politicians.
>
> Female, university student, 20, white, individual interview

> the people that are attracted [to politics] aren't necessarily the people that are going to identify with ordinary people, because they are usually only going for the job because they're interested in power.
>
> Female, university student, 21, white, individual interview

> Politics to me is just the one with the biggest boot gets to kick ass... the one with the biggest sword on your side.
>
> Male, New Dealer, 22, white, individual interview

In addition, there was a recurring theme across our respondents that politicians and parties did not represent the views of young people, either because they were seen as remote and unrepresentative or because they lacked any real commitment to addressing their interests or concerns.

> I think people try to let them know, but they just choose not to listen, before they go out and even ask anybody, they've got their own ideas about what they're gonna do, even before they ask. And they go around asking, just asking people to see if they'll back up their ideas, and if they don't like it, then it's tough on the people that they've asked.
>
> Female, sixth-former, 17, white, focus group

The sense that politicians and government are unresponsive was expressed across our range of respondents:

> I don't think younger people are that interested. Yeah they're more interested in issues that affect them, I think, and I don't think they see politicians as kind of, you know, representing those and stuff.
>
>   Female, university student, 21, white, individual interview

> Basically, they go: oh yeah we'll do for ya, and then when it comes to it, when it comes to it, they're like, the way they say it, they're all mouth and no action . . . They should have people like us . . . they're just people that have come up and have got money and that, we need someone who's gone through like what we've gone through.
>
>   Female, homeless hostel, 18, black, focus group

There was a dominant perception that politicians were disconnected from the lives of ordinary, and especially young, people, which was exacerbated for most by inadequate numbers of black, Asian, female or young politicians:

> you get a youthful politician say in their early twenties, late twenties, yeah, she could help. But someone who's 40, 50, seeing themselves as having their own views, I mean, they don't like the kids nowadays, they just see them as just scallies or something.
>
>   Male, sixth-former, 18, white, individual interview

> There's a lot of older politicians, and I know that they've got the benefit of experience, but it's difficult to see them speaking on our behalf . . . because they do seem to be from one strain . . . it often seems to be the way, I think, to young people that we're not truly represented.
>
>   Female, university student, 21, white, individual interview

> most of them are just snobby white people to me, and I wouldn't give them the time of the day, I wouldn't, and I'm white myself. . . . they're always sitting in a room full of the same sort of people, not going out there talking to the people in the streets.
>
>   Male, homeless hostel, 23, white, individual interview

This was also reflected in a recurring critique of politicians' representativeness. One respondent suggested that problems of racism were exacerbated by the poor visibility of ethnic minorities at a national level and because politicians did not mix across ethnic groups. He suggested this was necessary for change to occur:

> If the politicians started mixing with different races, they might understand about what people actually need, and maybe they could make a difference.
>
> Male, FE college student, 19, South Asian, focus group

Several young women complained that there were too few women in politics, and perceived politics as dominated by men and a male culture that was not welcoming or accessible to women:

> because there are more men involved than there are women, I think generally, one: women are put off by that; and then secondly: the nature of the whole, of the whole government, that things happen behind closed doors, everything happens after hours, and you know late nights, and the whole sort of gentlemen's sort of idea of government... there is definitely a male culture, like you know, like I said this whole idea of a gentlemen thing, it's really, it's a really difficult thing for people, for women, to think about getting involved in.
>
> Female, sixth-former, 18, white, individual interview

The view that Parliament should be much more socially diverse was also shared by male respondents:

> I'd like to see more women representing the nation... I'd like to see more women in there, and I do think it's important to give a true reflection of Britain, and so they should take a wide range of people.
>
> Male, university student, 21, white, individual interview

In addition, many felt that politicians were not closely identified with the areas they sought to represent and this engendered a degree of cynicism about their ability to understand issues in those areas:

> then you hear them speak and they don't even have the accent of the area they live in that they are supposed to be representing. That's stupid, how can you represent somewhere if you probably do a fly-by visit in your car and then toddle off back to your nice little mansion?
>
> Female, New Dealer, 19, black, focus group

The sense that politicians are not demographically representative tended to have a negative impact on our respondents' views about their own abilities to participate meaningfully in politics or to have their opinions taken seriously. The expectation that politicians ought to be representative tends to confirm Bang's view that Everyday Makers see politics as being about the recognition of difference; the failure of political institutions to embody this is seen in deeply negative terms.

There was also a tendency not to identify with parties as organisations articulating distinct ideologies, but to see them as divisive and opposed to community interests:

> if there was no Conservative, there was no Labour, there was no BNP, but a United Kingdom party, it was the United Kingdom party, then everything would be fine.
>
> Male, FE college student, 19, South Asian, individual interview

The hostility among our respondents towards seeing politics as an expression of ideological differences also confirms what Bang describes as a preference for community organisation.

4.3.2.2   *Young people as Everyday Makers: Experiences of, and attitudes towards, political participation*

Very few of our respondents could be characterised as conventional participants: we found no party members; few were members of single-issue groups; and none could be described as activists in the conventional sense. A high proportion of our respondents stated they were unlikely to vote in either local, national or European elections. Many of the themes expressed in our respondents' attitudes towards elite politics were also expressed in their attitudes towards electoral participation:

> I didn't vote last time. I think it's a load of bull, that's what I say. I'm not into politics, it's just all like in a big circle . . . just goes round and round.
>
> Male, New Dealer, 22, white, individual interview

> I think a lot of young people feel like every party's going to be bad to them no matter what they do, so they see no point in even bothering.
>
> Male, university student, 21, white, individual interview

Those who had actual experience of political participation tended, overwhelmingly, to have participated in local community actions or campaigns. For example, one had been involved in a local campaign for the introduction of speed-bumps after a young child had been killed on a dangerous stretch of road:

> there was a road in Kingstanding [an area of Birmingham], it used to be a very dangerous road, my little cousin got killed on there, out posting his Christmas letters, the whole family done a sit-down protest until they got speed-ramps and ghost-islands and traffic lights and barriers all around the post boxes and telephone boxes and that to protect the kids. It took about a year to get all that done... everyone got involved, even all the family. All the family, the whole area.
>
> Male, New Dealer, 23, white, individual interview

One respondent had been involved in lobbying the Council to clean up a children's playground, whilst another had engaged in a community action to demolish a building used by injecting heroin-users located on a children's playground. Our respondents' views of such actions were highly positive, and such views were in sharp distinction to the negative views from many of our respondents towards national or mainstream politics.

> I would [politically participate] if it had some good for the community... I'd put my name on a petition, I'd go to a rally in the city centre or something. But that would be it. When it came down to mainstream politics – no – because in the community, when you campaign for something like a park, you would get parents who are black, white, Asian, everything. Then there is no racism, it's all about the kids. And, it doesn't matter how racist you are, your kids come first, or they should, and it doesn't matter. We are all doing good for the greater good of the community and it doesn't matter at all. But anything that goes into large-scale, I don't want to be a part of. I wouldn't like to be a part of it... when you get into mainstream politics, you're fighting against people...
>
> Male, FE college student, 19, South Asian, individual interview

During the course of a focus group of seven female sixth-formers, nearly all from the group indicated they would not vote in general elections, even if they were old enough, yet all of them stated that they would have voted in a local referendum on a proposal to transfer housing

stock from Birmingham City Council to Housing Association ownership, and all would have voted against the proposal. This group, at
least, were highly politicised by the campaign to block the transfer,
even though they were ineligible to vote. In particular, they argued
that the transfer would reduce the accountability of landlords to
tenants:

> Because you had the landlords, and that group, the Housing Associ-
> ation, actually picked 'em: you didn't get a say.
>
> Female, sixth-former, 17, white, focus group

> at least you know you've got 'em, with Birmingham City Council, if
> you need a repair done you go to them, you complain to them, but
> when you've just got one landlord, then you're just stuck with that
> one person.
>
> Female, sixth-former, 17, white, focus group

Similarly, respondents who had little interest in voting were considerably more interested in participating in initiatives to enhance activities
and resources for young people at a local level. Thus, when discussing
actions that they would be likely to get involved in, there was strong
interest in local community involvement:

> probably about my community or something, you know, I don't want
> my community run down, even though I don't like the place, I don't
> want to see it trashed . . . I'd do something about drugs as well . . . like
> give a session in the community centre . . .
>
> Male, New Dealer, 23, white, individual interview

Our respondents tended to express higher levels of political efficacy in
relation to local participation:

> Say, if you wanted to build like a youth centre or community centre
> and stuff like that, . . . then maybe you'd have to go through your
> local council, just to like, even just to get the planning permission,
> or whatever, or maybe money, but that's your main way. But, if you
> wanted to make a difference and you thought like the council is not
> gonna bother, so I'll do something myself then, yeah.
>
> Male, sixth-former, 18, white, individual interview

This stood in sharp contrast to their lack of political efficacy at other levels:

> You've got to be Prime Minister just to vote your views across . . . 'cos they listen to you, but not really, they're just looking at you, they don't really give a crap.
>
> Male, New Dealer, 22, white, individual interview

> I don't really think MPs, the Prime Minister, MPs, are gonna listen – not until something really happens.
>
> Female, FE college student, 17, South Asian, individual interview

For many of our respondents, then, political engagement was expressed in terms of self-help, community involvement at the local level and everyday self-actualisation.

> I think politics is basically helping others by helping themselves more in a way . . . 'Cos like they all, like, they do something for a reason, for the community and everyone else, but they'll be gaining something out of it as well themselves, it's not all for people, it's for themselves as well . . . I think people only do things like that, as in participating, when it's got something to do with them.
>
> Female, FE college student, 18, South Asian, individual interview

> I think it is an everyday life thing – politics.
>
> Female, FE college student, 20, South Asian, focus group

4.3.2.3 Young people as Everyday Makers: Attitudes towards the state

Bang's Everyday Makers are characterised by their focus on engagement in flat communities, rather than by direct negotiation with, or opposition to, the state. Indeed, what is distinctive about them, he suggests, is their lack of engagement with the state. Here, our data part company with Bang's Everyday Maker model. Our respondents' conceptions of the political tended to be intensely state-centred:

> I would say [politics] would be someone who worked for the government, or is associated with the government.
>
> Male, FE college student, 20, black, focus group

I still think all of [the images shown in the interview are political], you know, government and politics – it applies to everything nowadays. If you look at everything, and it's all government and they are involved.

Male, sixth-former, 18, white, individual interview

Many believed that their lives were constantly determined by the state – at one extreme, one respondent felt as though he were treated as a laboratory experiment by the state:

they [the government] look down on people's lives sort of thing, really – I'll stick you there, see what happens to you, stick you there, see what happens to you, like a lab experiment sort of thing. That's what it felt like.

Male, New Dealer, 22, white, individual interview

Whilst they tended to believe that the state had a big impact on their lives, they felt it was unresponsive and this was connected to very low levels of political efficacy expressed by our respondents – as will be made clear in section 4.3.4. In other words, the young people in our sample did not see the state as irrelevant to their everyday lives; rather they did not believe that they could have any impact on it.

4.3.3   Young people's political interests

As we argued, it is unclear what if anything is distinctive about young people's political concerns compared with other cohorts. Many issues that are traditionally seen as being of concern to young people, such as the environment or animal rights, do not seem to occupy a particularly prominent position in the data generated by recent research (Henn *et al.*, 1999); certainly, these issues were not mentioned by our respondents as issues of political interest or concern. However, a number of common concerns were expressed across our groups which were viewed by our respondents as political, such as concerns about racism, sexism (findings similar to those in Park's study), problems with public services, crime and so on. There were also a number of issues which concerned our respondents that seem to relate specifically to their experiences as young people in transition to adulthood, such as teenage sex, pregnancy and parenthood, problems in accessing employment, training or education, and a lack of resources within local communities for young people. Discussions during the sorting exercises and the follow-up interviews indicated they regarded these as political issues. In this respect, the relationship between young people's everyday making politics and the external structures that shape and constrain them is particularly important. As Philo and Smith (2003) argue, political institutions and processes at the macro-level (which have tended to be colonised by adults) shape the self-actualising micro-politics of young Everyday Makers. Thus, they caution *against* collapsing the political into the personal.

For example, many discussions about the political aspects of young people's experiences of, and views about, teenage sex, pregnancy and parenthood were prompted by an image of a young woman holding a baby (*Mom and Baby*). All of our respondents interpreted the image as that of a teenage single mother, and nearly all decided that this image portrayed a political issue, although for a variety of reasons. For some, this image reflected the lack of material support from the state for single mothers, with many commenting on hardship as a generalised aspect of teenage parenthood due to insufficient benefits, inadequate housing and the lack of support to pursue education or employment. Others felt this was a political issue because of the unwillingness of the state or schools to equip young people with the information and self-confidence to deal with, or avoid getting into, such a situation. In particular, many suggested that the government and the educational system failed to inform people of the practical or emotional aspects of sexual relationships and the responsibilities of parenthood:

there definitely needs to be something done about that. Education . . . you know, not enough education to do with sex. You get taught about your reproductive organs and stuff like . . . the fallopian tubes and the ovaries and the eggs and stuff like that: how do you like them – scrambled or fertilised? Yeah, but something definitely needs to be done about that, you know what I mean? And it's not just down to the parents, it's down to the government as well, the educational system.

Male, New Dealer, 23, white, parent, individual interview

sex education in school, it's too basic, what they tell you is, oh the sperm does this, the egg does that, it doesn't actually tell you the whole process of what can happen, will happen, if you have unprotected sex and all the rest of it, it's just mad.

Female, New Dealer, 19, black, individual interview

the government aren't addressing that as well as they should be. There are a lot of teenage pregnancies... I think there should be some more emotional help, like centres for young parents to go to, to actually find out the information they need, or if they're struggling for money, maybe there could be loans or grants for them. They could help to find them a safe place to stay in.

Female, 17, sixth-former, white, individual interview

A number of respondents felt there was a social resistance towards addressing this issue adequately, with an unwillingness on the part of adults generally to speak to young people about sex in a frank or relevant way. This is a view reflected in Dennison *et al.*'s (2002) research into young people's experiences of sex and relationship education and information:

the English prudence, the stiff-upper lip, try to ignore it, but you know it's an everyday thing. There's a baby born every minute... and then they start complaining when their kids get pregnant at 13, 14. .... They know it's going on, but they don't want to believe it's going on.

Male, New Dealer, 23, white, parent, individual interview

There was a very clearly gendered aspect to the views expressed about the politics of teenage parenthood.

the responsibilities are different for a man and a woman. You know, because at the end of the day if the woman gets pregnant, and the man does one, she's got the responsibility, or the decision to either keep the kid or get rid of it or have it aborted, which is a very difficult decision to put on a child, especially if they're under sixteen... This is still a child. They might be proud to have the baby, and love it to bits, but if they're still in school, they've buggered it up. You know, they've missed time from school because they're pregnant and the school won't have them in because it gives them a bad look and a bad reputation. Basically the lad can just walk off.

Male, New Dealer, 23, white, parent, individual interview

Women, particularly, tended to blame poor levels of general education for early pregnancies. So, a focus group of female, South Asian, FE college students agreed that the mom in the image was in her situation because 'Obviously she's not educated.' They also emphasised that early pregnancy acted as a major constraint on the mother's life chances:

> Yeah, looks like she's having to sacrifice her childhood and that, for the sake of this baby.
>
> Female, sixth-former, 17, white, focus group

Whilst many were critical of those women who had begun families at a young age, they also blamed the government for doing too little for women in this situation and felt that the government preferred to dump single mothers onto benefits, rather than do anything to cultivate their educational aspirations:

> They're just chucking money at people who've got kids and wondering why? You want them to get a job, you want them to better themselves, but basically saying oh have more kids and we'll give you more money and just stay at home, but they're not getting an education out of it.
>
> Female, New Dealer, 19, black, individual interview

The disproportionate responsibility borne by young women in this situation was a political issue for many, with both men and women commenting on the state's culpability for the negative impact that teenage pregnancy had on the life-chances of young women and the children of teenage or single parents.

With regard to problems in accessing employment, training or education, many felt that the state did not do enough to support young people. Government-supported youth employment schemes and government-supported employment opportunities, for instance, were regarded as very poorly paid and exploitative, with the types of employment options and training offered seen as too narrow and often acting as disincentives to come off benefit:

> get a training course, where you're gonna earn crap money, but you still work for your giro and you work 40 hours a week and you are only getting your giro, or get a job for £3.60, for your national minimum wage and you have to work a couple of years before you get experience, which is pants. It shouldn't be like that. There's always moaning that you need experience and that, but no-one's willing to take you on to give you the experience, unless you work on a Modern Apprenticeship, it's just no good. And you want a Modern Apprenticeship

and you're taking home £45 a week and you're doing 40 hours, you know, that's like £1.10 an hour, you know, that wouldn't encourage me to work, to be honest. I wouldn't wanna work 40 hours for 45, I'd just be thinking, I'd just be dossing to be honest . . . they're doing more apprenticeships and that, instead of just trying to claim dole and getting crappy jobs working in factories and then later on in life realising that they don't want it, and then having to go to college when they're 20, 30 and that. The government should definitely do something about that.

Male, New Dealer, 23, white, individual interview

Furthermore, where the outcomes were not successful, the costs of failure were very high:

then I lost my job and that's how it goes . . . And it's hard to pick yourself back up after that, because it was like I give it my all, you know, I got my flat, everything was nice . . . and your job's working out, your train is getting there, and then you fall ill, and then you've got no money because you get the sack and you're in arrears with housing benefit, I was in all that, normally had no food, everything just crashed down, it was like harder, I'd give it my all, I did my best and this is how it has ended up. It's the instability that I'm left with.

Male, homeless hostel, 23, white, individual interview

Whilst the young people participating in the New Deal scheme that we spoke to were positive about the centre that they attended, and generally of the New Deal Advisors, they tended to be quite critical of the framework of the scheme, as well as other government-supported training. Some New Dealers felt that the options available on the New Deal scheme, particularly with regard to the type and range of training on offer, were insufficient. Some felt that the scheme acted as a barrier to the career aspirations, and pigeon-holed them:

this New Deal thing that Tony Blair has come up with, it's not for everybody, it does not suit everybody's needs. It basically puts every-body in a little box and expects them to go either this way or that way. It doesn't work for everybody . . . You have to treat people as individuals, not just a little group, so that everybody does have the opportunity to do something.

Female, New Dealer, 19, black, individual interview

Many respondents in full-time education expressed concerns about opportunities for undertaking or continuing their education and about the ways in which decisions about education provision were taken:

> As far as the government overall, I think they haven't listened to young people in terms of the AS levels,[2] because from day one everyone was saying this is never going to work, and they haven't listened to us... And I think that the government didn't think it through at all, I don't think that enough young people were consulted, I don't know if young people were consulted about it at all. I know I wasn't asked my opinion, it was just sprung upon us. ... I think that we have made our voices heard, but I don't think they've taken it on board. I don't think they've listened.
>
> 　　　　Female, sixth-former, 18, white, individual interview

> there's a lack of communication, I think. I know there's television you can watch the debates if you're interested, but I don't think that they make an effort... there's Question Time and there are television programmes, but they aren't necessarily related to issues that students are interested in. I mean I've watched the ones of tuition fees and what-not, but it's not necessarily the debate that young people would have if you had it at university and I think that's probably where the problems lie... It's the nature of politics though isn't it?
>
> 　　　　Female, 21, university student, white, individual interview

The lack of resources for young people within their local communities was also a source of concern for many, especially, but not exclusively, for young men. Many commented on the lack of youth centres or their inability to access local community centres. For some, this was an issue that affected young people in terms of their likelihood to become involved in, or victims of, crime:

> I think it is just to keep them off the streets, I think they should be kept off the streets. They go round nicking cars, you know, burgling houses. They need like a sense of where they can just like go and chill and hang out, and just relax there. I think a young politician would benefit that, they could help with that.
>
> 　　　　Male, 18, sixth-former, white, individual interview

Another respondent discussed the lack of access to community centres in her area and linked it to problems of gang violence and a sense that the community was not being heard:

> it's bad, it's all around really, it's all different crews, it's like an area thing – they're fighting each other. Bang! That's it – nice to see ya. They say it's a black, but... did you hear about the... well it's all the Indians and blacks now, actually there's a lot of fighting going on down Aston... It's just the crews [gangs] all the time, it's really bad... I think [the government] got enough letters, but they're not gonna listen to us, it's bad. I don't think they're listening to us. I bet they've got loads of letters saying things about the crews, like, but they don't work... they don't do nothing for me with the crime and that. They do nothing.
>
> Female, 17, New Dealer, black, individual interview

For others, there was a sense that the lack of local resources and community facilities for young people discouraged their inclusion within local affairs; commonly this was associated with their exclusion from local spaces and having a say about how resources could be used to benefit their age-groups:

> I think [the reason why there aren't enough facilities for young people is] mainly because of the politicians, there's no real young ones, in our area anyway. I think the woman... in our area who was trying to go for it last year, and she was for Labour, I think she won it, and she's 45–50 herself, she's got the experience, but she's too old, she doesn't realise what youth is like today. She just puts herself back to where she was young, you know, but times have changed. Like crimes coming up and everything. They need a centre somewhere, 20 hours a day I'd say, six days a week, cut the crime down.
>
> Male, sixth-former, 18, white, individual interview

4.3.4 Young people as political agents rather than political apprentices

Finally, we argue that there is a need to move away from apprentice-ship models of political participation, and from seeing young people as future citizens, to viewing them as political agents. There is a marked tendency to view young people's participation in governance networks or political institutions as forms of political apprenticeship, rather than as a means of articulating their interests or concerns. For instance, this is captured in the Young People's Parliament model. This is a young people's deliberative assembly, which has been established nationally and in numerous towns and cities across Britain, and these are often (although not always) based on a didactic model of participation; the decisions taken within these assemblies tend not to have any binding effect on politicians or decision-makers. The debates within these assemblies are, rather, generally intended to educate young people, and participation in them is posited as a means of increasing young people's self-confidence and political literacy, rather than as a means of articulating and mobilising around young people's political interests. Whilst some local authorities seek to establish youth consultation panels, there is rather limited impetus for governance structures to directly engage young people in decision-making processes as deliberators or experts. So, Matthews and Limb note that, although the Children Act 1989 requires local authorities to take into account the views of children in respect to certain court hearings and local authority decisions, generally there is no legal requirement on education authorities, schools, health and local authorities, parents or governments to give consideration to the 'ascertainable wishes and feelings of children' (2003, p. 174).

This tendency to see young people's participation as a form of political apprenticeship has meant that young people's voices have been much neglected in the literature and in political arenas, where there has been a greater focus on introducing stylistic changes to the ways in which politics is communicated in attempts to engage young people (such as using celebrities in election broadcasts, or introducing voting by text messaging) – rather than communicating with young people on the issues that affect them.

Bang notes that contemporary democracies now face particular problems of political exclusion, which he attributes to the uncoupling between lay people and formal spheres of politics due to the increased complexity of governance. In large part, this is exacerbated by the reliance on Expert Citizens in patterns of self-governance and co-governance. So, paradoxically, whilst culture governance tends to hold that the 'most effective forms of connection between social research and policy-making are forged through an extended process of communication between researchers, policy-makers and those affected by whatever issues under consideration', it 'has the consequence of ignoring those everyday narratives and forms of life that do not possess this kind of specialisation' (Bang, 2003, p. 250). According to Bang, under the new culture governance regime, with its emphasis on interaction and expertise, Everyday Makers are more likely to become non-participants.

There are, however, additional problems of political exclusion, which Bang does not identify, in the sense that young Everyday Makers may well find that the expertise-driven mode of politics that pertains under culture governance has limited relevance to their own lives, but even when they do have relevance, young people face additional obstacles to their participation. Thus, young people are rarely acknowledged as Expert Citizens, even in relation to issues which do affect them, and young people tend to be regarded as *future* citizens (Wyness *et al.*, 2004).

Indeed, many of our respondents believed that they are excluded from, or marginalised within, mainstream politics *because they are young*, and this was accompanied by a recurring sense of weak political efficacy. There was a strong theme in many of the group and individual interviews that young people generally felt excluded or marginalised from decision-making processes because of their age. There was an acute sense that young people are poorly represented at national and local levels and, with regard to decision- and policy-making, it was frequently observed that young people are rarely consulted or listened to – even with respect to issues which directly affect them, such as the introduction of AS levels, the types of training courses they could access on New Deal, decisions about local amenities or community events and so on. More worryingly, perhaps, there was a recurring sense that young people would not be taken seriously even if they were to participate in the discussions of decision-making bodies:

> I think, say if like there is 20 people my age and they wanted a meeting with [politicians] and 20 adults wanted a meeting with them to discuss the local area, I think they would definitely go with the adults, and they always say on TV we listen to the kids and stuff and you see the kids [being interviewed] and that, that's only because the camera is in front of them ... Otherwise they wouldn't want to know ... maybe if the whole community got together and kids did gather some ideas then maybe but probably not, I wouldn't have thought so anyway, but ... even if they did call meetings they wouldn't let people our age know anyway.
>
> Male, sixth-former, 18, white, individual interview

It was suggested that such attitudes established a spiral of low expectations:

> I think it's like a cycle for us, 'cos we haven't really been interested in it, 'cos ... we haven't been included in stuff, except writing to your

councillor and stuff and then it would have just been seen as kids messing around.

Male, sixth-former, 17, white, individual interview

the children won't talk to older people because they think – oh they won't listen to a young person, they will talk to them and tell 'em yes we want this done and that cos they will really listen, but I reckon they just write it down and go chu!

Female, homeless hostel, 18, black, focus group

Many respondents felt that stereotyped and negative perceptions of young people were common among adults and these acted as barriers both to young people's entry into political arenas and to their effectiveness within them:

they would kind of have the idea that the young are very sort of hot-headed, and you know, sort of react to things as they happen, and don't think about it as carefully as maybe older people would, so they wouldn't have as much respect from people on the Council as they need to get what they wanted.

Female, sixth-former, 18, white, focus group

A number felt that they were not encouraged to participate in politics, commenting that they were not invited to join groups, they rarely had their opinions solicited, nor were they provided with the information to participate:

I know I have no-one talking to me about politics, I don't know much about it, I have no knowledge of it, I have no-one to instigate it or to, you know, say do you want to come and vote?

Male, homeless hostel, 23, white, individual interview

I just don't think young people are encouraged to show their opinions in terms of associating themselves with a group. Show your opinion, you know so you can sit around in a group with someone from the government and tell them your opinion, but you can't, it's like you're not encouraged to join groups.

Female, sixth-former, 18, white, individual interview

Despite the sense that young people were routinely excluded from power, or marginalised within political arenas, there was a common perception that young people's perspectives and concerns needed to be represented and listened to, because young people had experience of the issues that affected them or because they were able to understand their peer-group better than adults or because they were a source of fresh ideas and solutions. Thus, there was a strong perception that representation by young people of young people was crucial for having their concerns addressed; a perception that applied similarly to representation by, and for, women and ethnic minorities:

> it's actually working with the people, not just assuming what can help, but actually finding out, taking the time to spend with the young people, which is what matters today is the young people, you know, and find answers and improvements, and that's the best way to go about it, work with the young not the old, they're moulding the life for us, and we don't want that, we want to mould it ourselves and all these old people are out there voting for us and they really have no idea where they're going, they really have no idea what they're doing for us. You know, the way they're making the life for us . . . You need to work with younger people more, that's what matters.
>
> Male, homeless hostel, 23, white, individual interview

> I think younger people, kind of, when it comes to issues that involve young people and drugs, you know, that sort of thing, even young people that don't, that aren't involved in that kind of thing, because they are in, they might be in the environment where they know it happens, they're the kind of better people to ask over how you would solve those issues, rather than someone, you know, sat in an office somewhere in London in a suit, you know, that's not there, or remembers maybe what it was like when they were young and how to deal with it from that point of view. You need kind of a more up-to-date thing.
>
> Female, sixth-former, 18, white, focus group

> Just a young person to represent [us], yeah, who thinks with experi-ence, who knows what's going on in the world.
>
> Female, homeless hostel, 18, black, focus group

Typically, our respondents stated they were unlikely to vote in either local, national or European elections, concurring with survey data on

young people's disinclination to vote and their levels of electoral absten-
tion. Nevertheless, several felt that the voting age was set too high:

> we can't vote until we're 18, so a lot of people say well our opinion
> doesn't count then because, you know, we're not supposed to vote
> until we're 18.
>
> Female, sixth-former, 18, white, individual interview

> you should be younger as well, should be younger. What's this 18
> thing? . . . 16's old enough, if 16's old enough for you to move out of
> your yard, and look after a yard and pay rent and work, why are you
> not old enough to vote? That is pathetic, do you know what I mean?
>
> Male, homeless hostel, 23, white, individual interview

The ability to vote at 18, however, did not contribute to any sense
among our respondents that their views had become more meaningful
or respected. The lack of a vote at 16 and 17 was viewed as confirmation of the lack of regard that adults and politicians have for young
people, whilst the ability to vote did not confer any sense of political
empowerment or efficacy.

These sentiments were also frequently expressed in relation to our
respondents' perceptions of what it means to be a citizen. For instance,
one male sixth-former suggested that to be a citizen was to be:

> Probably an adult, I would have said, to be honest. It's 'cause a citizen
> is related to a, it's again like with like meetings, and if they want
> to speak out it's normally an adult that does it. I am a citizen and
> stuff like that, I've got my rights, but other than that I can't see.
> A perception of a citizen anyway is someone, it's not our age anyway,
> definitely.
>
> Male, sixth-former, 17, white, individual interview

The problem of political exclusion that our respondents expressed points
to a need to engage young people in politics in a way that addresses them
as political agents. Yet, Cunningham and Lavalette (2004) highlight the
ambiguities that surround notions of young people's political agency in
the promotion, on the one hand, of active Citizenship within the school
curriculum and, on the other, the panic over the anti-war school student
protests of 2003. They argue that 'Children . . . are seen as problems to
be "managed", "moulded" and "reformed" rather than as active citizens

capable of thinking and making decisions about issues that concern them' (2004, p. 258).

4.4 Conclusion

Overall, our data tend to suggest that young people are far from being politically apathetic and are, in fact, highly articulate about the political issues that affect their lives, as well as about the disconnection between these and mainstream politics. Listening to the young women who would not consider voting in general elections, yet who argued passionately about local housing issues, and who would certainly have cast a vote in the referendum on this issue, it seems clear that political apathy does not adequately account for their resistance to voting more generally. The very strong sense among many of our respondents that they are marginalised or excluded from political decision-making or debates suggests that their non-participation can only perversely be attributed to apathy.

By moving from surveying young people's attitudes towards a limited range of political issues and arenas to conducting in-depth exploration of young people's views and experiences, we can begin to develop a much more nuanced understanding of the relationship between young people's lived experiences and their engagement and interest in politics. For instance, the data from the group interviews with young men reveal their very low levels of political efficacy, connected with their view of politics as a series of authority relationships, in which they saw themselves as having only a passive role. We can also see the ways in which young people, particularly our South Asian and female respondents, viewed politics as a site or mechanism for achieving change, whilst perceiving few opportunities for participation at a national level, due to the under-representation of women and ethnic minorities in national politics.

Henrik Bang's work assists in identifying some of the ways in which the changing political environment itself shapes political participation and our data certainly support much of what he suggests about the emergence of Everyday Maker modes of participation. Our respondents were, by and large, disengaged from mainstream, electoral and party politics and were clearly much more likely to be active and engaged in local community politics and issues. They also often saw politics as a form of self-actualisation and their inability to conceive of themselves participating in the national, mainstream sphere is compounded by the low visibility of politicians who look like the society around them.

Yet, the notion that they are disengaged from the state is not supported by our data; rather we suggest that young people do view the state as shaping their life-chances and experiences, but their unwillingness to engage in state-oriented political action is a demonstration of their very low levels of political efficacy. In this respect, we argue that age to an extent structures young people's political participation, particularly in the ways in which it operates as an obstacle to their participation. Thus, Philo and Smith's warning against collapsing the political into the personal is a useful one that alerts us to the need to address some of the specific processes and factors that give rise to young people's political exclusion, and one could draw similar conclusions in relation to ethnicity, class and gender.

Our understanding of young people's non-participation therefore should take account of both changes in the political environment that give rise to shifts in the ways in which young people politically engage (i.e. generation effects), as well as the life-cycle effects that operate as structural constraints on their political participation. In this respect, models of transition assist us in understanding the specific concerns that may affect young people as they become parents, students or trainees. There was a very clear sense among our respondents that their interests and concerns were not being addressed by politicians and few perceived any mechanisms for involvement to bring about change.

In this chapter, we have concentrated on differences and exclusions that attach to age to explain this limited sense of political citizenship among our respondents. It is clear from the data here there are significant differences between young people, particularly in relation to class, gender and ethnicity. Whilst, we argue that age does have particular implications for how young people experience and relate to politics, young people themselves are not an undifferentiated group, as Chapters 5–7 show.

5
Class as a Lived Experience

Class, historically at least, has been one of the key analytical concepts in Social Science generally, and Sociology particularly. It has also been one of the most contested. In section 5.1 of this chapter, we begin with an examination of some of those contestations, because that literature informs both our conceptualisation of class and, consequently, our analysis of the data. In essence, we treat class as a structured lived experience which helps shape how our respondents understand and relate to politics. In section 5.2 we use our data to examine whether and how our respondents 'live' class and whether and how class affects their understanding of, and attitude towards, politics.

5.1 Contesting class

This is not the place to discuss the contestations surrounding class in any detail (for good reviews, see Crompton, 1998; Savage, 2000), but we do need to make a number of points.

First, although the usual starting place for theoretical discussions about class has been the debate between Marx and Weber, almost all the best empirical analysis of the effect of class on social and political outcomes, whether it be wealth, health, education, voting, other forms of political participation and so on, use a measure of class based on location within employment relations, derived from Weberian analysis. As such, much of the empirical work seems to be interested in prediction about how class correlates with other social and economic outcomes, rather than with explanations of how class affects these outcomes. Consequently, most research shows that class, treated as an independent variable and measured in Weberian terms, is correlated, sometimes highly correlated, with dependent variables such as political participation. Unfortunately, little attention is given to the mechanisms or processes involved in producing those outcomes. As a result, many have been strongly critical of much class analysis.

Secondly, in recent years some have gone further in their criticisms, rejecting class analysis entirely. For example, Pakulski and Waters (1996) suggest that, although class was a key explanatory variable in the past, it no longer has relevance in a much more complex, contemporary, some would say postmodern, society. Instead, their focus has been on consumption, rather than production, as the basis of contemporary social cleavages and the chief source of individual identity.

Finally, following Bourdieu, we take a less fundamentalist approach arguing that class is not a fixed category, but a lived experience. As sociologists or political scientists, we should focus on how people experience or live class, and indeed other aspects of their life, thus there can be no privileging of class; however, this 'lived experience' is not totally open, rather it is structured. Let us examine each of these points in more detail.

5.1.1 The problems of contemporary class analysis

As Savage (2000, p. 3) argues: 'The sociological debate on class and stratification has, since at least the Second World War, been organised around arguments between Marxist and Weberian approaches.' In fact, most of these debates have revolved around questions concerning the relative merits of class schema developed from Marxist and Weberian approaches. However, there is little doubt how this particular debate stands; it is John Goldthorpe's Weberian categorisation of class, which focuses on employment relations, not on ownership (as would a Marxist), that has informed most empirical work.[1] This dominance is likely to continue, and indeed grow, because the new National Statistics Socio-Economic Classification (NS-SEC), which was produced by a team from Essex University and is based on the 'Goldthorpe schema',[2] will become the schema used by most empirical sociologists and the UK Government for the foreseeable future.

Crompton and Scott (2002, p. 4) contend, in common with many others (see, for example, Skeggs, 2000, p. 3; Devine and Savage, 2002, p. 185), that there has been too much emphasis on judging the relative merits of various class schema. As a result, they argue (2002, p. 4) that 'debates have become increasingly focused on methodological questions, rather than on substantive issues of class inequality and class action'. We have considerable sympathy with this argument, but it would be wrong not to acknowledge that Weberian-based empirical work on class has produced a great deal of useful information. As Skeggs

(2000, p. 4) puts it, 'the descriptive school of social class is very important for showing how hierarchies do exist and for monitoring social changes'. The problem is that such research usually only takes us so far.

In our view, the strength and the weakness of this empirical work using the NS-SEC schema are clear if we return to Pattie *et al.*'s (2004) work on political participation. They examine class, actually they call it socio-economic status, as a potentially important variable in one of their structural models, civic voluntarism theory, using the NS-SEC to measure socio-economic status. They also use income, which is related to class, as an independent variable. They show that both socio-economic status and income are related to various aspects of political participation. For example, those who are richer and/or with a higher socio-economic status are more politically knowledgeable (Table 3.7), more interested in politics (Table 3.9), more likely to discuss politics (Table 3.11), more satisfied with British democracy (Table 2.17), more trusting of people (Table 2.4), more personally efficacious (Table 2.18) and more politically active (Table 3.4). In contrast, those who are poorer with lower socio-economic status are more committed to rights than obligations (Table 2.12), and particularly to state-provided rights (Table 6.9).

These are interesting findings. In our view, what Pattie *et al.* (2004) have done is assess the utility of a number of predictive models of various forms of political participation and that is a useful and interesting exercise. However, it tells us that those with a higher economic status are more likely to participate; it does not tell us *why* that is so. For Pattie *et al.* (2004), like most social scientists who focus on this area, class or socio-economic status is treated merely as an independent variable. This problem is a general one. Few studies of the effects of class, and certainly not the work of Pattie *et al.* (2004) or Norris (2003), go beyond the first step in moving from correlation to cause. Certainly, they use sophisticated statistics to control for the influence of intervening variables and remove the possibility of a spurious correlation – a relationship between two variables which, in fact, results from the effect of a third variable on those two variables. However, to establish cause we need an understanding of the mechanisms or processes by, and through, which class, or socio-economic status, affects political participation, or whatever. Whilst one's theory suggests those linkages, the extent to which one thinks those linkages can be empirically, or certainly quantitatively, tested depends on one's epistemological position.

Savage makes the argument succinctly (2000, p. 20): 'the conceptual cupboard of classical class theory looks dusty. [. . .] What both Marxist

and Weberian perspectives on class lack is any clear theoretical explanation of why and how class matters'. In fact we need to make two points
here. First, it is individuals who act, so it is crucial how individuals
understand and experience class and, as Skeggs (2000, p. 3) emphasises,
'a central weakness in any classification [is that it] cannot explore the
meanings people give to objective positioning'. Secondly, as Crompton
et al. (2002, p. 5) point out, the class literature focuses on the outcomes of
processes, yet, if we are to attempt to explain how class affects outcomes,
we need to focus both theoretically and empirically on the processes
involved.

In recent years then class analysis has been under significant attack.
In part this results from critiques of the work of class analysts, but it also
reflects both changes in the intellectual climate, in particular the rise of
anti-foundationalism and the 'cultural turn', and changes in society.

The 'cultural and linguistic turn' in Sociology has led many to reject
the idea that class is a key factor affecting identity, because class as
used by most empirical Sociologists is seen as an essentialist category.
Here, class is often seen as strongly associated with Marxism as a grand
narrative and grand narratives are unsustainable. Not everyone has fully
embraced the cultural and linguistic turn, although few now see culture
as a simple reflection of objective class positions. Rather, many sociologists are dubious about the utility of class analysis because of the changes
in contemporary society. In particular, many have emphasised that the
last 30 years have seen: massive changes in employment relations and
occupational structures; increased feminisation of the workforce; long-
term unemployment; a decline in the proportion of manual workers
in the labour force and the rise of the service sector; increased flex-
ibilisation of labour, involving in particular deskilling and reskilling;
job insecurity; and increased globalisation of both capital and labour
markets (see, for example, Cannadine, 1996, p. 4).

Overall then, many have identified an impasse in class analysis to
which there are three possible responses. Some, for example Goldthorpe,
Marshall and Wright, have defended class analysis, and especially either
a Weberian- or Marxist-based class schema with few concessions. As
such, they have paid scant attention to their critics, to social changes
or to the role of other social divisions. Others, for example Pakulski and
Waters (1996), who we focus on in the next section, have pronounced
the death of class. Finally, in response to various critiques of class
analysis, some authors, for example Savage (2000), Crompton (1998),
Crompton *et al.* (2002), have attempted 'to reposition class analysis
within sociology by undertaking a critical review both of class analysis

and the preoccupations of contemporary sociology' (Savage, 2000, p. 8). We identify ourselves with this third strategy and outline the position we adopt in section 5.3.

5.1.2   Rejecting the validity of class analysis

Pakulski and Waters (1996, p. 4) argue strongly for the death of class: 'classes are dissolving and . . . the most advanced societies are no longer class societies'.[3] So, they contend, as we said earlier, that class societies are historically specific societies. More specifically, they develop a periodisation of the development of advanced industrial societies over the last two centuries (1996, pp. 24–25; see also pp. 88–89, 112). They argue that nineteenth-century society was structured by classes based on economic relations, while in the first three quarters of the twentieth century, society was dominated by the state sphere. However, in the contemporary period, social stratification reflects lifestyle differences and is value based. As such, the stratification system is a shifting mosaic, not a set structure. The state is weakened because of globalisation, increasing demands from citizens and much reduced mass support for its legitimacy. The economy is weakened because of the vastly increased importance of symbolic values. The central site for social reproduction is now the mobile, biographically self-composing individual. Indeed, to Pakulski and Waters the future outcome of these changes will be an end to gender, to add to the existing death of class (1996, p. 112).

In Pakulski and Waters' (1996, p. 10) view, class theory is based on four propositions – economism, groupness, behavioural and cultural linkage and transformational capacity – and they reject each of these propositions in turn; thus in their view establishing that 'class is dead'. However, it seems to us that Pakulski and Waters construct a very economistic, Marxist conception of class to which few, if any, modern sociologists, even modern Marxists, would adhere. Pakulski and Waters could claim, probably would claim, that, unless a class theorist adheres to their four characteristics of class analysis, then they are not a class theorist, or presumably a Marxist. Yet, there are many sociologists who do regard class as an important feature of contemporary society (Savage, Crompton, Devine and Scott, to name but a few), but do not hold to those principles. In our view, the test is whether class analysis, as specified by a particular theorist in the light of contemporary debates, helps us explain and understand certain social actions; in our case young people's understanding of, and relation to, politics.

In Pakulski and Waters' view, society is not characterised by structured inequality, rooted, to a significant extent, in access to economic, and related social and cultural, resources. Rather, it is complex, contested and constantly changing experience. In contemporary society, class and indeed society are social constructions, existing only in terms of our understandings of them.[4] While we acknowledge the importance of moving beyond an approach that merely treats class as an independent variable, seeing it also as a lived experience, we do not share Pakulski and Waters's view that 'lifestyle' has become the chief basis of social divisions. Society is more complex than it was (see Chapter 2) and cultural values and patterns of cultural consumption do not simply reflect economic relations or access to economic resources. However, the claim that most, if not all, have access to sufficient scarce resources to make lifestyle choices[5] does not stand up to any empirical analysis. Indeed, in almost all advanced capitalist societies inequalities of wealth and income have increased over the last two decades (see Gottschalk and Smeeding, 1997, 2000; Brandolini and Smeeding, 2006).

In our view, the UK is characterised by structured inequality: inequalities of access to scarce resources, based on age, class, gender, ethnicity and so on, which persist over time and constrain and facilitate the life chances, and indeed the access to certain lifestyles and modes of cultural consumption, of individual agents.[6] Here, we agree with Crompton and Scott (2002, p. 6) who argue that it is essential for 'class analysis to take on board the extensive changes that have been taking place in the spheres of production and consumption in class societies and to recognise the interdependence of class, gender, ethnicity and age'. However, our concern here is not to defend this position at any length, rather to make it clear where we stand and for this reason we next outline our approach, in particular briefly considering the work of Pierre Bourdieu which best articulates the key elements of our view.

5.1.3 Class as a structured lived experience

Our starting point is evoked by Cannadine's (1996, pp. 19–20) position, when he argues:

> where Marx was onto something was in his insistence that the material circumstances of people existence – physical, financial, environmental – do matter in influencing their life chances, their sense of identity, and the historical part which they and their contemporaries may (or may not) play. Whatever the devotees of the linguistic turn may claim, class is not just about language. There is reality as well as representation. Go to Toxteth, go to Wandsworth, go to Tyne side, go to Balsall Heath, and tell people who live in the slums

and the council estates and the high rise ghettoes that their sense of social structure and social identity is no more than a subjective rhetorical construction. It seems unlikely they would agree. [...] Class, like sex, may indeed take place in the head: but it has never existed solely in the head or the eyes or the words of the beholder. Social reality always keeps breaking in.

Secondly, like Savage (2000, p. 51), we contend that the UK is marked by very unequal access to economic resources:

> Broad patterns of wealth-owning and income in Britain point quite unambiguously to the existence of a very small class who earn their wealth from property and a much larger class who predominately rely on income from their labour, in the form of wages and salary. [...] Recent trends have seen a clear polarization, which has favoured the wealthy. Forms of rentier income deriving ultimately from property ownership are more unequally distributed than is income from the labour market, and the expansion of shareholding and investment income in the last 20 years has therefore accentuated, rather than reduced economic inequality.

However, we recognise that access to economic resources does not determine actions, and thus outcomes, in any simple way. Agents, not structures, act and, as Savage (2000, p. 95) argues, 'class processes work through the individual'. As such, and here we follow Savage (2000, p. 67) again:

> Class impacts on economic inequality not just cross-sectionally, as a kind of macro structure which affects the income people can command, but also as something which individuals perform, by accumulating different potentials to unlock income sources which operate later in life.

Here, the relationship between structure and agency is seen as dialectical, that is, interactive and iterative. Structures constrain and facilitate agents, but agents interpret structure and, in acting, can change them. In addition, a series of factors mediate between class structure and the individual: educational qualifications, individual ability and work-life mobility (again see Savage, 2000, p. 88, for a fuller discussion). At the same time, the material, that is access to economic resources, does not determine the ideational, that is, culture. Rather, the relationship is again dialectical, so we need to consider how economic resources constrain and facilitate access to, and the role of, culture, while culture can change both the broad economic structure and the individuals' access to economic resources.[7]

All this means that we choose to view class as a structured lived experience. As such, we reject most empiricist approaches to class, without accepting that class is an obsolete concept, by arguing that class is not a fixed category – defined in most of the approaches we have considered to date largely in terms of occupation – rather it is something we live. Given this approach, we focus on how people experience or live class. Here, the double hermeneutic is taken as axiomatic and the focus is on understanding, not explanation. Given this view, our aim is to understand others' understandings of the world. In this approach class is a lived experience, part of the individuals' understandings of the world, which we as observers do our best to understand. It is not simply an 'objective' independent variable to be plugged into a regression analysis.

We discussed various approaches to the idea of lived experience in Chapter 1. Here, we need to refresh our memories about the interpretivist view, which would see experience as a process, not something we gain or possess. Individuals or subjects have experiences; indeed, they are constituted through experience. So, experience is neither 'self-evident', nor uncontested. Rather, our experience involves our interpretation of their interpretation of their experience. Class here is part of what constitutes individuals and their identity, so the concept is not totally rejected, as it is by Pakulski and Waters, but equally it is not an objective, structural category that shapes attitudes and behaviour. Instead, it is something individuals live.

We do treat class as a lived experience, but as a lived experience that is structured. In that way we not only reject Pakulski and Waters' view that class is dead, but also argue that an individuals' experience of class is shaped by their access to economic, social and cultural resources. For this reason we are very interested in Bourdieu's analysis of class and in particular in the concepts of economic, cultural and social capital and the relationship between them. In our view these ideas help us make sense of our respondents' experience of class and of their understanding of politics, as we shall see when we consider the data below.

Some critics may feel that it is not possible to fuse Bourdieu's views on class with an approach that stresses that class is a lived experience. However, we, like Bourdieu, hold to a middle ground on the structure/agency problem; in our view how our respondents experience the world is through a habitus which reflects structured inequalities in the UK. Their experiences are structured by a habitus that reflects 'real world' processes.

Pierre Bourdieu moves beyond the idea that capital is solely based upon material exchanges, identifying two main 'non-economic' forms of capital: cultural and social capital.[8] In Bourdieu's view, these different types of capital are acquired and exchanged and converted into other forms. Given that the structure and distribution of capital also represent the inherent structure of the social world (here we can see Bourdieu's realist credentials), Bourdieu argues that analysis of the multiple forms of capital will provide an understanding and explanation of the structure and functioning of the social world.

The term 'cultural capital' represents the collection of non-economic forces such as family background, social class, varying investments in and commitments to education, different resources, and so on that influence academic success.[9] Throughout his discussion of cultural capital, Bourdieu suggests that cultural capital is not inherited in a genetic sense, rather it is learnt and grown initially in the family. He argues that the ability and talent of an individual is primarily determined by the time and cultural capital invested in her/him by her/his parents. Similarly, Bourdieu (1984, p. 244) argues that 'the scholastic yield from educational action depends on the cultural capital previously invested by the family' (and) 'the initial accumulation of cultural capital, the precondition for the fast, easy accumulation of every kind of useful cultural capital, starts at the outset, without delay, without wasted time, only for the offspring of families endowed with strong cultural capital' (1984, p. 246). Based upon these claims, it appears that cultural capital regulates and reproduces itself in a similar fashion to habitus. According to this model, families with a given cultural capital would invariably produce children with a similar amount; this might seem a very structuralist position. However, Bourdieu is not a determinist; he rather suggests that structures privilege by facilitating those in a privileged position and constraining those who are disadvantaged.

Bourdieu defines social capital as 'the aggregate of the actual or potential resources which are linked to possession of a durable network of more or less institutionalized relationships of mutual acquaintance and recognition' (1984, p. 248). As such, an individual's social capital is determined by the extent of her/his social network. Two things are crucial here: first, the sum of the resources, both cultural and economic, held by the members of the network and, secondly, how effectively an individual can use, or activate, that network, so calling on its resources.

According to Bourdieu, social networks must be continuously maintained and fostered over time in order for them to be called upon quickly in the future.

The possibility of conversions between different types of capital and the rate, in the sense of both the extent and the costs of exchange, of conversion, is crucial. Bourdieu, in fact, argues that all types of capital can be derived from economic capital through varying processes of transformation. In Bourdieu's view, cultural and social capital are fundamentally rooted in economic capital,[10] but they can never be completely reduced to an economic form. Rather, agents always have space to grow their social and cultural capital, particularly through education. Again, economic capital may facilitate or constrain individual attempts to grow social and cultural capital, but it doesn't determine it. At the same time, social and cultural capital, to an extent, remain effective because they conceal their relationship to economic capital.

In effect, Bourdieu is examining how class actually affects people's actions. He argues that there is a close link between economic, cultural and social capital. Those with more economic capital have privileged access to cultural capital – books, quality newspapers, galleries, theatres, museums and, above all else, education. As such, they develop particular values and interests associated with 'high culture' and high culture is celebrated, while 'low culture' or 'popular culture' – TV, magazines, the tabloid press, soccer – is looked down on. This cultural capital, especially when linked to high cultural capital, gives greater access to more powerful social networks. However, both cultural and social capital make you better placed to acquire more economic capital, for example, through access to better jobs. To Bourdieu then, this is a virtuous circle; it can be broken, but it is powerful.

Even this brief exposition of Bourdieu's position shows it is not unproblematic. It can seem economistic,[11] although, as we emphasised, he is insistent that economic capital does not determine other forms; it merely acts as a facilitator for those who possess it and a constraint for those who do not. Similarly, it is difficult not to look somewhat sceptically about Bourdieu's argument about popular culture in an area where 'celebrity culture' seems to grip almost everyone and such celebrities earn millions.[12] Nevertheless, we are interested in Bourdieu's position because it goes beyond correlations and predictive models to offer an explanation of how class might affect young peoples' attitudes to life and politics. At the same time, it recognises the continued resonance of class and offers an understanding of how it affects contemporary society.

As such, we treat class as a lived experience, in the sense that we are concerned to examine how our respondents view, live and experience class. Our method allows us to approach their understanding and experience of class indirectly, as we made clear in Chapter 3, because we did not ask our respondents about class; rather we examined the extent to which they narrated the images we presented to them in class terms. By this we do not mean we were interested in whether they talked about class, because, as we shall see, the term was rarely mentioned. Rather, we were concerned to establish whether their world was one in which the extent of their access to economic, cultural and social capital, in Bourdieu's terms, affected their life generally, and their understanding of politics particularly, and to what extent they recognised this fact of life.

5.2   The analysis

As we emphasised above, we are treating class as a structured lived experience which has resonance for how people act. As such, we need to address a series of questions which stem from our review of the literature on class. First, do our respondents think in class terms or are Pakulski and Waters right in their assertion that lifestyle choices shape behaviour? Secondly, even if our respondents rarely use a concept of class, does Bourdieu's formulation of the relationship between economic, social and cultural capital help us understand their lived experience? Thirdly, for our respondents, is there a relationship between their class position and their understanding, and view, of politics and does this reflect their lived experience?

5.2.1   Thinking in class terms?

Our respondents rarely mentioned class; it was not a concept they used frequently, or easily. Rather, they used it in only in limited contexts, as we shall see below. This might seem to confirm Pakulski and Waters' analysis. However, our argument here, and throughout this book, is that, although our respondents do not generally talk about class, or indeed gender, this does not mean they do not live or experience it. In our view, this position is supported by our data.

Interestingly, most of our respondents did talk about class in relation to the two images of the political candidates (*Man Candidate* and *Woman Candidate*) and they saw both, although the male candidate more than the female candidate, as middle class. In addition, they were also widely perceived as being out of touch. A few responses convey the tone which was not particular to any site(s), but rather were voiced by respondents from more and less privileged backgrounds. So, one of the focus groups at the FE college site discussed the male candidate in the following terms:

> *Respondent 1*: I think he looks snobby and stuck up . . .
> *Respondent 2*: He looks like he's from a good background. Highly educated.
> *Respondent 3*: In a good environment.
> *Respondent 2*: Oxford I'd say [affecting an upper-class accent].
>
> Females, FE college students, 18 and 20,
> South Asian, focus group

One white male in the New Deal group was even more scathing:

> To be honest I thought he was a toff and a wanker and that he's a Tory bastard. Look at me, I've got a nice rosette . . .
>
> Male, New Dealer, 23, white, focus group

Even the University group took a similar view, with one white female respondent saying of the male candidate: 'a middle class boy, everything you don't want your politician to be'. She commented similarly on the female candidate that 'she looks pretty middle class'. Consequently, our respondents also saw the candidates as not representative in demographic terms either of their constituency or more broadly, because of their class background as well as their age. So, one woman in the University group commented about the female candidate: 'she doesn't look like she kind of fits in there, that particular area, or like she'd normally be there'. Similarly, two female members of the homeless hostel group argued:

> *Respondent 1*: They should have people like us, you know people like you or us . . .
> *Respondent 2*: Yeah, it's unrepresentative.
> *Interviewer*: You don't think they represent us?
> *Respondent 1*: Na, they're just people that have come up and have got money. We need someone who's gone through what we've gone through . . .
>
> Females, homeless hostel, 18, black and white, focus group

At the same time, some respondents felt candidates faced a dilemma in terms of how they presented themselves in class terms:

But, people are automatically cynical about politicians. So, if she turned up in a suit, people are going to go: 'look at her, she's visiting the poor areas. What a snob, what a stunt'. If she turns up in anything else, 'she's trying to be a woman of the people, what a stunt'. Politicians can't win, that's the whole point, because people are inherently suspicious of them, because they want something from you.

Male, university student, 21, white, focus group

As we emphasised, our respondents rarely talked in class terms and they were certainly more likely to discuss lifestyle issues; another finding that might seem to confirm Pakulski and Waters' (1996) claims. This was particularly clear in their discussion of two images: *Mom and Baby* and *Empty Houses*. Indeed, more than half of the groups discussed the first of these images in terms of lifestyle 'choices'. One of the hostel groups made the point about the single mother image:

Respondent 1: well, their mum's wearing a Nike top, so it looks like they got some money.
Respondent 2: You see them people in the street, they've got Nike.
Respondent 3: Yeah, look *we've* got Nike on; we're living here man.
Respondent 2: And we're in a hostel.

Male and Females, homeless hostel, 23 and ages unknown,
white, black and unknown ethnicity, focus group

So, lifestyle choices are important aspects of our respondent's lives. The key question here is, are these choices as open as Pakulski and Waters suggest? In the University group the discussion of the single mother image revolved directly around the issue of choice:

Female respondent: ... she's not too badly off.
Male respondent: Yeah, but if you extend [female respondent's] view, what you see is that, I always get the impression that a lot of people who, you know, have low incomes, their spending priorities are wrong ...
Female respondent: (interrupting) That's not what I am saying ...
Male respondent: (continuing) if you go to council estates, they're the first people to get the ...
Female respondent: (interrupting again) ... but everyone else is saying that ...

Male respondent: (continuing again)...style trainers, the new computer games systems and stuff, yet they don't actually have a decent house and they're not providing for their children.

Female respondent: yeah, but it's a lot easier to buy Sky TV than it is to buy a house.

Male respondent: Yeah, but the point of the matter is, it's personal preference...

> Female and male, university students, 22 and 21,
>
> white, focus group

Most others, particularly those from the less privileged sites, were much less willing to see choice as open. One group almost immediately assumed that the designer t-shirt worn by the women in *Woman and Children* was a fake. The logic was, 'she is working class, she cannot afford a designer t-shirt, so it must be a fake':

Respondent 1: She looks underprivileged because of her children; they're badly dressed.

Respondent 2: She looks like she's struggling to cope with family life.

Respondent 3: Looks like she's wearing a fake t-shirt as well, need I say more.

Respondent 2: Yeah, a fake t-shirt.

Respondent 4: Breadline.

Respondent 1: Working class.

Respondent 4: She's missing a button as well.

Respondent 1: Yeah, she's got a button missing on her cardigan.

> Males, sixth-formers, 17–18, white, focus group

The same theme was taken up by the university focus group:

Respondent 1: Even if she's poor, she's got the Nike t-shirt.

Respondent 2: That's not a proper Nike t-shirt, is it? That's a fake one; it looks like it's a knock-off, so it's, kind of even sadder.

Respondent 3: She's got them down the market.

Respondent 1: Although the label's still important.

> Male and female, university students, 21–22,
>
> white, focus group

So, the label is important, but those without economic resources can only buy a 'fake' or go without other things to afford the 'real' label.

A similar questioning of the reality of open choice was developed by a white male from the New Deal group:

> Yeah. At my little brother's junior school now, he can't wear designer clothes, because it puts the unfortunate kids down, and the other parents have to respect that, because my little brother he's spoilt, he's got Lacoste shoes, Armani jeans, Moschino jeans, Ben Sherman shirts, and he's only 10. There's kids who just can't afford that. But luckily my mom's got a good job and my step-dad's got like, well he's disabled now, but he had a good job.
>
> Male, New Dealer, 23, white, individual interview

This clear relationship between economic capital and lifestyle choice was reaffirmed by a sixth-former in his individual interview when asked about the woman in the *Empty Houses* picture:

> And I don't think she probably has got enough money, probably being a single parent and such, to move out into another area, that's a better class. OK she does have a new pram and the thing is, if you're living in a place you can't neglect everything, like if you've got kids, you can't really say 'OK we haven't got money you're going to go without food for the next couple of days or you're going to go without kind of necessities'. Everyone needs a bit of pleasure or enjoyment, but if you can't really move out into a bigger house and a nicer place, get a car and whatever else, yeah, then, what money you do have, you might as well enjoy what you can. 'Cos I don't think if she puts the pounds aside, she ain't going to, not over a couple of weeks or over a year, I don't think she's going to get into a nice, bigger, house.
>
> Male, sixth-former, 18, South Asian-white, individual interview

He went on to comment:

> I don't really think it's the fault of the individual themselves. OK maybe so . . . someone might say, like you know, [someone like her] should put a bit more effort in, you know, like looking for a job and they were like being dependent on the person, whereas everyone should have like a little independence just in case things do go wrong.
>
> Male, sixth-former, 18, South Asian-white, individual interview

While our respondents did not talk directly about class, except in relation to the candidates, they recognised it around them. Here, we start with one, particularly strong, and extended, example from an individual interview with a male respondent from the hostel group who narrated his personal experience:

Respondent: That would be the whole system, but then again that's when you come back to us, because we are the system, you know. We're all people, every single one of us and we all have different jobs and different roles that make the system the way it is, and maybe it was for the best when the system was set the way it has been set, but, you know, it has got us a lot down in a way, because it's such a particular pattern, you know, that it's getting boring. You know, the whole Job Centre thing, you know, living on benefits and you know, and if you're not working what do you do? You sign on. You know that if you get a property, you've got to pay rent. It's like, when you're working, it's like, in a hostel you're there trying to work on your life, trying to get your life on track and you can't because it's so expensive to live here, you know? You try and, you know, do education, but eventually it gets boring. It's not the proper education that you really need, you know, and then you want to get a job, you try and get a job. By the time you've got a job and you've paid what, say you've got a £100 and you've paid £50 rent, your shopping, your electric, your bus fare to and from work, your money's gone and you're working for nothing. So, you might as well have stayed on your income support, it works out better, you know, than working. So, a lot of people in these hostels, they're influenced more to not work, do you know what I mean, to rely on the system and not go out and get a job because of the situation. You're not supported enough. You know, having to pay, 40 something pound rent out of £100, that is half of your wages and you're left with 50 something, and when you take your living expenses out of it, you know I was paying £9 bus fare a week and then a fiver electric and then the rest on food and munchies, you know, so I was just really working myself senseless just to get by. You know, I wasn't getting no luxuries out of it, you know, I couldn't smoke or anything. You know, not because I couldn't afford it, but I did I quit smoking, it's not like I was spending £40 on that, you know, and even then I never had money.

Interviewer: So you were actually working were you?

Respondent: mm, I was working full-time, sweating my brains out yeah.

Interviewer: Was that part of a scheme or was it a job?

Respondent: It was like a job, like for [names company], and it was so hard and you're taking home a 100 pound a week and I thought that it would have been good, you know, a 100 pound a week, that's better than 42 pound, but by the time you've worked it out, things you've got to do, and the rent, the appalling rent that you have to pay, you know, there's just no point. I was going to go to a work the other week, but by the time I worked out the wages I would be earning it would not be worth it, I'd be tiring myself out, right, to provide food, for my flat, electric, you know, and everything that eventually I was going to tire myself out again. I mean last time I ended up in hospital, you know, I was really, really unwell. And that's what work had done to me, it had really tired me out, not being able to go out when I did get a day off. I was just having to stay in or go and do the shopping or clean my yard on my day off, you know. And it was like, if I didn't have to pay 40 something pound rent, you know, maybe that 40 something pound could have took me out for the day, you know, and I could have rested or gone out for dinner, you know, lunch and looked after myself a bit more, feel like I'm treating myself, but of course I was getting down and the wear and tear, and I was getting tired, withdrawn, and you know, eventually I was getting ill and I was in hospital, and then I lost my job and that's how it goes. You know, and this place. And it's hard to pick yourself back up after that, because it was like, I give it my all, you know, I stopped smoking, I was living better, you know, I got my flat, everything was nice, you know, all my clean clothes, and my flat, everything's clean, nice central heating and that, it was really nice, and then you know, your job's working out, your train is getting there, and then you fall ill, and then you've got no money because you get the sack and you're in arrears with housing benefit, I was in all that, normally had no food, everything just crashed down, it was like harder, I'd give it my all, I did my best and this is how it has ended up. It's the instability that I'm left with and the manager of this place would have kicked me out straight away because there was a problem with the rent, not offering me a chance to try and sort it out, OK you have a problem, I'm very aware of this, which she was aware of, you know, and sort it out, she didn't want to. You know what I mean, I had to go to her with a proposition, I will pay extra rent out of my money that I get every week, when I get my book, I will give you so much money to try and pay off this debt, if you let me stay here. She didn't offer me that, I had to go and beg, you know, and that support should be offered straight away.

Male, homeless hostel, 23, white, individual interview

Another strong argument came from the individual interview of a woman from the hostel group:

People do tend to have everything made for them, y'know? They've got themselves in a good job, they living comfortably, y'know, they're eating meals everyday they don't know what it's all about to be homeless, to not know where your next meal is coming from. Certain people they don't seem to really care, they see someone walking down the street looking scruffy, they tend to cross the road, clutch onto their handbag or whatever the case may be. Y'know, maybe if they was to stop and take a look into homeless people's life, then they would understand It's not all about stealing a handbag, or you don't smell because you want to smell bad, it's 'cos you've got nowhere to wash. You ain't got no clothes to change into, you can't wash your clothes, so maybe, if them kind of people were to stop and take a look and put themselves in that predicament for just one day, then maybe society would change.

Female, homeless hostel, 18, black, individual interview

Equally stark, if much briefer, was the comment of a woman from the hostel in response to the picture of the single mum:

Respondent: Do you know what this reminds me of? Me standing outside Ainsley House [name changed].
Interviewer: What's Ainsley House?
Respondent: Children's Home.

Female, homeless hostel, 16, mixed ethnicity, focus group

Reading these narratives, it is hard to see class as dead and focus on lifestyle choices. Perhaps the most evocative response of all came from a male hostel respondent when he was asked where he expected to be in five years:

To be honest, I can't see myself what I'm going to be in five years, I don't know where I'm gonna be. I don't even know where I'm gonna be tomorrow. That's the chance you take when you move out at a young age and into hostels, you know, you really don't know where you're going to end up, or know what you're going to get out of it, or, you really don't know. You just have to take each day as it comes and just try and use whatever's there. You can plan, but it's very difficult to plan when you're in such an awkward position, because you're really not in control of where your life is going in a place like this. It's very easy to lose control.

Male, homeless hostel, 23, white, individual interview

However, it was not only the less privileged respondents who identified a spiral of poverty. So, a South Asian male from the sixth form argued in his individual interview:

if you're a single parent she would have, she would probably have, lots of difficulty in getting any sort of child care for her child at a low cost. If she isn't, yeah, if she isn't able to do that, she isn't able to get a job and get, build a way out of there. So, because of the fact there's no good child care, she'll probably stay in that situation for a while . . . 'cos it's society's fault in that, in that respect it is. But, if she can't, if she can't get the childcare at a reasonable cost, so she can get a job, or if the workplace don't provide her with a crèche or other such facilities, she isn't able to get herself out of the situation, although she may be willing to. So, to a certain extent it is your own personal fault, some people aren't genuine genuinely, aren't willing to try and try and get out of the situation, but, on the other hand, it could just as easily be society's fault for effectively not providing what she needs . . .

Male, sixth-former, 17, South Asian, individual interview

None of this should suggest that we are arguing that class is the only factor affecting our respondent's lives, but just that access to economic, social and cultural capital, which is discussed in more depth in the next section, crucially affect their life chances and lifestyle choices.

Indeed, it was clear from our respondents that class was not the only, or necessarily the most important, lived experience in our respondent's lives. Obviously, ethnicity and gender played key roles and they are dealt with at more length in the next two chapters. However, family and community were also key elements in many of our respondent's lives. To an extent, but not entirely, this was a reflection of ethnicity and religion. So, there was no doubt that our South Asian respondents talked much more of family and community than did our white respondents. One Muslim male respondent from one of the FE college groups offers clear and fairly typical evidence of these ties in his individual interview:

Interviewer: So do you think you are very involved in a community?

Respondent: Oh, the community is like my family, because where we come from, the whole community is mostly Asian, because it's all based around the mosque. I mean you go to mosque, it's 'ah, it's his son', and you have to behave like his son. They don't know my name, they know my face and it's – 'ah, it's his son, how's your father?' This, that. They don't ask about me, it's not like 'oh, had a good day son?' It's like 'how's your father?' 'You're his son aren't you? Yeah OK'. 'You have to behave yourself like your father expects you to behave', like they think you should behave, which is, I wouldn't say it's a lie, but it's not me. And it's all confusing after that. Like because, as soon as you leave that area, you're back with your mates again, you're sitting in the pub, and they see you in a pub, and it's 'alcoholic! tell his father, he's drinking, damnation, throw him out of the mosque, don't let him in the mosque again, he's going to eternal hell.' It's like that. I've seen it like that, I've seen kids who do drink, and guys who don't drink, who are just messing around with their mates and it's like 'you're going to go to hell for that, and your father's going to disown you', and you actually brick it, you're so scared like. But I'm only having a laugh. That's all I see myself doing is having a laugh, but no, you're . . . 'it's blasphemy', 'it's . . .' something very, very bad. It's like 'oh shit. You've done this and that's it'. And I've seen people get kicked out of the house for months on end and living on the street, who live outside their front doors and sleep in the gardens, because they're scared and they've no family to go to, because once your father disowns you, your whole family says no. So they have to sleep in the front garden, and every morning the father goes to work and there they are begging him 'let me in, I'm sorry, I won't do it again, I won't do it again.' And it's like, the mother's there, and the mother can't look at the kid, because once the father disowns the child, the mother actually can't do anything about it. She can beg her husband but that would be it, and the guy I was talking about now, he begged his father for about three or four months, and his father didn't let him back in again. But his father made him, because when Asian people eat, they all eat out of the same bowl, it's like there's a massive serving of food and then we all just like eat together, and his father made him sit on the floor and eat separately from his brothers and sisters and everyone, and he had to sit in the kitchen on the floor, and everyone else would be sitting together and eating. You know 'if you want to live in this house you are going to have to work your way up again, you will have to earn my respect, because you know, right now you are not my son.' And now, he's fine but, first few months of being at home, he said 'I prefer to live on the streets again, and I can get my 10 pence off someone, and then I'd go eat crisps and I'd be happy, but I'd miss my family and I had to go back to my front garden and beg.' Which was . . . Because we all went to his father's house, and we all begged him, and he goes 'it's all your fault anyway, because you boys, your behaviour has done this to him, you've lost me my son'. And he said it like that, and he was almost crying, but he was angry, so he wouldn't cry 'you've lost my son.'

Male, FE college student, 19, South Asian,
individual interview

There were examples of the importance of family among our white respondents, but they were fewer. However, one white, male, respondent from the New Deal sample provides ample evidence that close family ties are not synonymous with South Asian communities, but among other ethnic groups also:

Respondent: Yeah, she is an Irish auntie, you know. She's always been like – out there. She's a space-cadet. But, yeah, I think everyone looks to her now, because she's got the biggest family, she's got the most respect. You know, I think she's had 13 kids, and she's got god knows how many grand-kids. Because I think my great-grandmother had 50-something grandchildren and then so many great-grandchildren, and I think, when she died, she had 14 great-great-grandchildren, you know, where like they've all grown-up and that.

Interviewer: Wow.

Respondent: And yeah, so you know, we're a very close-knit family.

Interviewer: Yeah and it's quite a big extended family as well.

Respondent: Yeah, and that's just like the English side, and then you've got the Irish side, which my great-grandmother, she's still alive actually, she's 96, and she still runs up and down to the church everyday, saying she's going to help the old folk, so she's the head of the family in Ireland. It's like the mafia, the Irish mafia really (laughs).

Interviewer: Yeah. I've got Irish family as well (laughs).

Respondent: And the way they stick together is nice, I don't think many families do that, you know. The Asians definitely do it, but just the pure English-blood people, they don't do it. You know, it's like, I prefer going out for a drink with my grand-dad than I do my mates.

Male, New Dealer, 23, white, individual interview

5.2.2 Bourdieu as a way forward?

Here, we want to examine whether Bourdieu's argument on cultural and social capital and their link to economic capital has resonance in our data. Certainly, our respondents, particularly our less privileged respondents, were clear that economic capital, education and life opportunities were linked. One male, white, New Dealer commented, when asked about the life chances of people like him, in his individual interview:

Yeah, nah, because say like in the fourth year they should do it [identify potential], so then they can determine what groups they go into in the fifth year. So, like they're intelligent and they don't take their exams, they can end up in the dunce group. You know, when they don't deserve to be there, and they're just labelled a dunce all through their school. And they have to work harder to try and improve themselves. But, once they go to senior school they do need facilities, you know books. I don't know what the government's playing at. They should provide uniforms, because there's single parents, you know. My mom's a single parent, and there was three of us, imagine forking out for three uniforms every year?

Male, New Dealer, 23, white, individual interview

This respondent here was talking directly to the point about cultural capital, its relationship to education and to economic capital – here his references were to his own experience of lack of economic capital. The reference to clothes is particularly important as clothes are an indicator of both economic and cultural capital. He recognised the importance of a 'good' education in deciding opportunity and access to future economic capital. Perhaps most interestingly, he saw this as a political problem, indeed a problem the government should address.

The response of two young people from the hostel site, in their focus group, to the images of the two candidates bear on the same issues:

Male respondent: To me they look like they've achieved something, I don't know what they've achieved, and they look smartly dressed, y'know which is good, presuming they've come from/
Female respondent: /College probably/

Male respondent: /good homes, like good upbringing.
Female respondent: Good school

> Male and female, homeless hostel, 23 and 18,
> white and mixed ethnicity, focus group

Here again, clothes are seen as a marker of home background and education and these key elements in Bourdieu's understanding of cultural capital are viewed as affecting life chances. Throughout this exchange the respondents were identifying the men in these images as from a different background than themselves; though, interestingly, the term 'class' was not used.

It was very common, particularly among our less privileged respondents, to see education, a crucial element of Bourdieu's conceptualisation of cultural capital, as linked both to economic capital, so those with economic capital had better access to education, and to greater life chances and more future economic capital. So, members of the all-male, white focus group at the school argued in response to the image of the male candidate:

Respondent 1: Good qualifications and that.
Respondent 2: Probably got a bit of money and that.
Respondent 1: He looks a stereotypical Tory.
Respondent 2: Probably been to university and you know what I mean?
Respondent 3: His family were involved in politics before. Public school . . .

> Males, sixth-formers, 18, white, focus group

A much more personal take on the value of education was provided in the individual interview of a male member of the hostel group:

Respondent: I'd have got more out of school yeah if I had been disciplined a bit more. But, because I was left to my own device, I did what I wanted, you know, I was left running riot basically. All through school I never done one page of work and I don't know how they let me stay in the school for so many years and not get one drip done, not one drip of sense, you know, it just amazes me. I think the only thing I learnt how to do was to get in with the crowd and do whatever the crowd do, and smoke.
Interviewer: Do you think that's changed now, or do you look at education differently?
Respondent: What do you mean, if I went back to education?

Interviewer: Or, yeah, do you look at education differently now compared to when you were at school?

Respondent: Yeah, it's really important, you know, it's the crucial stage of your life, that's when you most need your information, you know, that's when you need to get all your brain-work, you know, that's when you need to use your brain, and get smarter, and just keep learning and learning. But, you don't realise how much you're gonna need it until you're actually needing it, you know?

Male, homeless hostel, 23, white, individual interview

The individual interview with a white male on the New Deal Programme again reflects our respondent's sense of socio-economic disadvantage, and it also addresses two key themes throughout our work, the remoteness of politicians and their lack of concern about people like the respondent:

Respondent: Let them live in our shoes for a bit and see what its like and our ways. Do you know what he [Tony Blair] gets paid at all?

Interviewer: I know his wife gets paid more than him.

Respondent: Yeah but she's a judge innit or a lawyer . . . But it's like he's been brought up with a silver spoon, you'd want him to come over the other side for a week see what it's like on that side like.

Interviewer: Do you think a week would be long enough?

Respondent: I think it would kill him.

Interviewer: I think he could live on benefits for a week. It's when you've got to live on it for a year or two years of your life.

Respondent: Know the feeling. I'm 25 now and I ain't even had a full time job.

Male, New Dealer, 22, white, individual interview

However, many of our less privileged respondents saw the lack of identification of politicians with them as inevitable, indeed something they would have done in the politician's place. This is well reflected in the comments of a male from the New Deal group in his individual interview:

You're not gonna live in the area that you represent. If I was a member of the council and was going to represent this place, I'd be earning a decent wage, I ain't gonna live in one of these places y'know. What I mean is I'm gonna live in Sutton [Coldfield] and drive a BMW or something, you don't live around here.

Male, New Dealer, 23, white, individual interview

5.3   Class and politics

With regard to the relationship between class and politics, our data tend to confirm the quantitative findings of researchers like Pattie *et al.* (2004). We asked our respondents in the individual interviews whether they had voted at national, local or European elections (if they were over 18) or if they would vote when they were eligible. We found no one in any of our groups who was a member of a political party or actively involved in an interest group. However, the respondents from our more privileged sites and with higher levels of education were more likely to have voted, or to say they would vote in future. Unsurprisingly, they were also more likely to feel efficacious, to have greater political knowledge and to think they would become more involved in politics as they grew older. At the same time, while almost all of our respondents were cynical about politics generally, and politicians particularly, a few respondents from our more privileged groups were more understanding of the difficulties facing politicians.

More interestingly, there were clear examples of what Bang terms Everyday Makers, that is, individuals who became involved in 'political' issues which affected them, but were not political activists in a broader sense. Probably, the best example of this involved a current local issue at the time we were conducting our research. The Council had held a referendum in which tenants were asked to approve the transfer of the council's housing stock to a housing association and had organised a strong and well-resourced campaign to support that change. However, there was also a well-organised campaign against the changes, and in the estate on which our school site was located there were scores of posters urging tenants to oppose the transfer.[13] Interestingly, in that site almost all of the respondents said they would not vote in an election, but would have voted (all No) in the referendum. This issue which directly affected many of their families because they were council tenants had politicised them in a way that Bang would have expected.

A key point here is that such Everyday Maker activity is not 'classed', at least not in any simple sense. So, we came across two other examples of Everyday Maker activity, one reported by a male South Asian in the FE college site in his individual interview:

Respondent: [I would sign] Petitions yes, because our local park has got done up, our local park, the kiddy area, has got done up because of petitions. Because there was a derelict caretaker's house there, where all the junkies stayed. We didn't want that, so the community actually knocked it down. There was no hard hats, no bull-dozers, and no metal fences, whatever, we just went down and started knocking it down. The police came and kicked us off. And then, well actually I wasn't there at the time, it was the older generation they started with their little hammers and chisels and knocking the walls down.

Interviewer: The older generation got it all together, was it mixed generations there?

Respondent: It was mixed, there was even a councillor there, our local councillor, he just sat there watching, saying – you shouldn't be doing this, but he stayed there, and he goes 'I agree with it', because he has got a young daughter and all our kids play together, and now the parks got all these lovely little flowers and patterns on the floors and multi-coloured toys and all that, and it's good. There is no house in there, because before half of it used to be filled up with junkies, and you'd go there and you'd see syringes lying on the floor.

Male, FE college student, 19, South Asian,
individual interview

Similarly, a white male from the New Deal group reported in his individual interview about his involvement in a sit-down protest in his local area on a dangerous stretch of road in order to lobby the Council to install traffic-calming measures after a child had been killed there (for further details, see Chapter 4, pp. 166–167).

Perhaps, most interesting were the results of the sorts conducted at the end of the group interviews from which a clear pattern emerged. The focus groups conducted in the more privileged sites generally included fewer of the images in the 'political' pile. More specifically, they tended to operate with a narrower definition of politics, which, in fact, fairly closely reflected the idea of politics in the mainstream political participation literature. So, both the University and the selective sixth-form focus groups established three piles: a political pile, a social with political aspects pile and a non-political pile. More specifically, the University focus group put the images of *Man Candidate, Woman Candidate, Refugees, Oldham, Hostel, Polls Apart* and *Police* in the political pile, with the *Mom and Baby, Women and Children, Empty Houses* and *School* in the social with political aspects pile and the rest in the non-political pile. The selective sixth-form group put *Refugees, Man Candidate, Woman Candidate* and *Polls Apart* in the politics pile, *Police, Hospital, No Skating, School* and *Protestor* in the social with political aspects pile and *Oldham,*

Hostel, St. George, Cricket Fans, Trafalgar Square, Empty Houses and *Mom and Baby* in the non-political file. The reasoning of these two groups was reflected in the individual interview with a South Asian, white male from the selective sixth-form site:

> political is, erm, things that I think involve the government, straight in kind of thing like, you know, you've got your candidates running for, you know, Parliament and whatever else and you get asylum seekers which is at the main forefront kind of issues that the government's always kind of discussing. You get the MPs and they discuss kind of asylum so that, then you've got your schools, your NHS, which are run kind of organisations which the government has (to) look into, which they kind of look over ... And then you get things like football, cricket and other sort of things which are more on the social kind of side where, you know, you're like social, sports and whatever else.
>
> Male, sixth-former, 18, South Asian-white, individual interview

However, in the other least privileged sites, the New Deal site and the homeless hostel site, the groups put all the images in the political pile. Even in the sites which were more mixed in socio-economic terms, the groups put many more images into the political pile. So, in the three focus groups conducted at the comprehensive sixth form, two only left out *Trafalgar Square* and *No Skating* from the political pile, while the third group added the two sporting images to the non-political pile. Similarly, at the FE college site, one group put only the sporting images and *No Skating* into the non-political group, while the second group added *Trafalgar Square* to that pile.

We do not want to make too much of these sorts, not least because a number of respondents emphasised the difficulty of deciding what was political. It was interesting, nonetheless, that the discussions of what was 'political' that occurred during the sorts were often fairly sophisticated, given that many of the respondents involved would be regarded as apathetic in most mainstream political participation studies. Indeed, this is reflected in an exchange within one of the FE college site focus groups:

> *Respondent 1*: You know this one, this one should be with it as well and the single parent one and that one as well. The trouble is there's quite a few.
> *Respondent 2*: In their own way, in different circumstances.
>
> Females, FE college students, 18 and 20,
> South Asian, focus group

However, it does seem to us that those from the less privileged groups who had much more contact with the state, particularly in relation to social security and welfare-to-work policy, experienced many more things as political. This interpretation seems confirmed by the comments of a white male from the homeless hostel group:

> Yeah, all of them did. I mean we had to put them into categories – which were and which were not, and I still think all of them, you know, government and politics it applies to everything nowadays. If you look at everything, and it's all government and they are involved. So, I think every picture really has its political side.
>
> Male, homeless hostel, 23, white, individual interview

5.4 Conclusion

As always, we have only been able to give an overview of our rich data, but a number of things seem clear. In the first place, it is hard to read the transcripts of our focus groups and interviews and conclude that class does not exist or matter. Our respondents rarely talked of class, but they lived it. The groups we talked to with limited access to economic capital knew they had little and that many people had much more. They also appreciated how that affected their life chances; their experience was that origins strongly shaped destinations, as expressed by a male respondent from the New Deal group:

> Well, there is a whole system isn't there, that you kind of go into, like the whole way of life, you know, if you come into this world, there's a map set out for you already. If you're not doing this, you're going to be doing this, and if you're not doing this, you're going to be doing that. You know, you don't really get to do what you want, what you really, really want to in life.
>
> Male, New Dealer, 23, white, individual interview

Secondly, it seems to us that Bourdieu's work has a great deal to offer. Our work convinces us that, while class is a lived experience, it is an experience rooted in, but not determined by, structured inequalities. Furthermore, it seems clear to us, and our respondents often agreed, although without using Bourdieusian terminology, that there is an evident link between economic, cultural and social capital.

Thirdly, class does relate to politics in the sort of ways mainstream authors emphasise. The more privileged in terms of economic and cultural capital are more knowledgeable, feel more efficacious and more likely to vote. However, insofar as we identified examples of Bang's Everyday Makers, they were not drawn exclusively, or even mainly, from those who were privileged in economic and educational terms. However, we did find that the less privileged had a broader conceptualisation of politics, in our view because they lived in a world in which they constantly needed to negotiate their relationship to the state.

Finally, our respondents did not experience class independent of other aspects of their lives; so the experience of class is gendered and raced and the next two chapters deal with these issues.

6
Gender and Participation

Feminism has changed the way social scientists think about gender. At the same time, gender, like class and ethnicity, continues to be a contested topic. Here, we begin by briefly tracing the development of ideas about gender and the relationship between the different positions on gender and ideas about citizenship and political participation. The major section of this chapter presents our data on how our respondents experience gender, and how that affects their ideas about, and participation in, politics.

6.1 Feminism, gender and citizenship

There are many approaches to categorising the development of feminism, but a common classification distinguishes between first-wave, second-wave and third-wave feminism, although we recognise that the last in particular is very diverse. In this section, we address the relationship between these different feminist approaches and how these inform perspectives on citizenship and participation. In particular, this involves considering the putative distinction between the public and the private which has been a core concern in the development of feminist ideas.

First-wave or liberal feminism is most obviously associated with the women's suffrage movement. Here, the argument was that women's subordinate position in society resulted in large part from their absence from positions of political power, symptomatic of which was women's exclusion from political offices and the suffrage. Central to the justification of such exclusions was the normative separation between the public and the private, which, historically at least, was crucial in liberal thought. Squires (2000, p. 25) emphasises this point in her discussion of Shklar's (1991) work:

> Liberalism has only one overriding aim: to secure the political condi-
> tion necessary for the exercise of personal freedom. These conditions
> are held to require the clear demarcation of the spheres of the
> personal and the public... Given this, the line between the public
> and the private has to be drawn, and must under no circumstances
> be ignored or forgotten.

Early liberal theorists thought that, once full suffrage was obtained, women would have a more equal say in the public realm. Increased public political participation would lead to a more represent- ative government; representing women in demographic terms and, consequently, responsive to their interests – paving the way for gender equality and a more meritocratic system of achievement.

However, even when women in the UK achieved suffrage on the same basis as men in 1928, political, as well as social and economic, inequalities persisted. Few women became MPs and many fewer Minis- ters. Indeed, a recent report entitled *Sex and Power: Who Runs Britain?* from the Equal Opportunities Commission suggests that, at present rate of progress, it will take 200 years for women to achieve equal represent- ation in Parliament. Furthermore, women achieving the vote did not make governments noticeably more responsive to women's concerns.

Second wave feminism developed as a critical response to the liberal ideas of first-wave feminism and has been characterised as materialist feminism or radical feminism. Second-wave feminism particularly prob- lematised the liberal distinction between the public and the private arguing that the distinction was a key ideological aspect of the repro- duction of patriarchy. As such, they criticised four related elements of the liberal view.

First, and most broadly, for the liberal, 'the political' was equated with the public sphere and civil society with the private sphere. In this view, the state should confine its activities to the public sphere while in civil society the individual should be free to pursue personal goals with minimal constraint from the state. Yet, to a second-wave feminist full citizen rights can only be exercised if individuals have sufficient resources – in Bourdieusian terms, economic, social and cultural capital (see Chapter 5) – to become active citizens. Individuals may have both the right to engage, and even the responsibility for engaging, within the public realm as an active citizen, but the ways in which these rights and duties are experienced or lived are classed and gendered. In essence, to operate as a citizen in this model means being able to maintain oneself as an 'economically active' member of society. Yet, even those women who do engage in waged labour, particularly historically poorer women, continue to retain primary responsibility for the undertaking of (unwaged) domestic labour, especially in relation to childcare (Lister, 2003). This leaves little space for being an active citizen. Indeed, as we shall see in this chapter, many, if not most, of the poorer young women in our sample were constantly faced with balancing the need to gain an education and the skills to be able to work, with domestic responsibilities. This was a key political context of their lives. So, to the second-wave feminist, one of the key problems with the liberal view of citizenship is that it erroneously presupposes a level playing field for men and women.

Secondly, radical feminists argued that this distinction had clear policy consequences. So, Lister (2003) contends that, because women are traditionally either missing or invisible within the public realm, their rights and interests are subsumed beneath the rights and interests of men and regarded as essentially private matters. As an example, second-wave feminists argued that issues such as domestic violence were ignored by the police and the courts because they were seen as belonging to the private sphere.

Third, the second-wave feminists saw the clear demarcation between the public and the private spheres as most often accompanied by a view that, while the public sphere was male, the private sphere was female. Again, they suggested that, for women, this resulted in an imbalance between rights and responsibilities. Indeed, Miraftab (2004, p. 3) argues:

> The binary constructs of public/private spheres feed the construction and the legitimisation of needs associated with the public sphere, versus the delegitimisation of 'wants' the category associated with the private sphere. Such discourse thus de-politicises what occurs in the private sphere associated with women's activities.

Fourth, Cornwall (2002) emphasises that liberals' conventional focus on formal forms of political participation legitimises participation only within a framework defined by external agents, notably the state. This conceptualisation of the political arena ignores the agency of women in grass roots, neighbourhood and community-based arenas, which are arenas that are more available to both women and young people (Desai, 2002; Lister, 2003). A similar point is made by Miraftab (2004, p. 4), drawing on Cornwall's concept of invited and invented spaces.

She criticises the focus in the International Development literature on collective action sanctioned by neo-liberal policies:

> Its narrow focus on collective action that highlights the coping mechanisms used by the poor, legitimises their actions selectively as civil society's celebrated social capital... Limiting the recognition of participation in citizenship only to actions within officially sanctioned channels (invited spaces) constitutes yet another state-centered perspective. Just as liberal views assigned the citizenship-granting agency to the state, this perspective assigns to the neo-liberal state the agency to grant status as civil society, and defines the space where citizenship can be practiced.

Second-wave feminism saw gender differences as structural; increasingly defined in terms of patriarchy. There were significant differences between those socialist feminists who saw patriarchy as, in large part, a reflection of class differences, and those radical feminists who saw gender divisions, and thus patriarchy, as the dominant social division. However, for all second-wave feminists, gendered structural inequality, particularly in the labour market, was the problem and had to be resisted and overcome. Political equality meant little, if women remained economically subordinate to men. Indeed, if women were to achieve genuine political equality, then they had to fight for women's liberation from economic, and resultant social and political, oppression. Given this view, citizenship involves much more than formal citizenship rights, like the vote, or participation in formal political processes, like membership of political parties. Rather, full citizenship involves social and economic, as well as political, rights and is impossible in societies where there is persistent social and economic inequality.

Given their critique of the liberal position, radical feminists recognised and rejected the idea that citizenship is granted by the state, and experienced by the population, in a gender-blind way. In addition, they argue that citizenship is dependent on a set of practices that are gendered. As Durish (2002) argues, the formal inclusion of women will not change the structure of citizenship which relies on such gendered hierarchies. This critique has influenced policy developments in some countries. So, for example, the Netherlands has developed a programme (Van Drenth, 1998) that aims to increase young women's awareness of available life choices in order to enable them to make 'non-traditional' choices, to ensure future active social and economic citizenship. Whilst, first-wave feminists, with the notable exception of Sylvia Pankhurst, thought that increased formal participation in politics by women would lead to much greater gender equality, as we shall see below, our young women did not share that rosy view.

Second-wave feminism was influential, although there are interesting debates about how influential it was. However, from the late 1980s it came under increasing criticism from a variety of directions. One key criticism came initially from black feminists in the US, but was also taken up by working-class feminists. The critique attacked what was seen as the white, middle-class bias of much of Western feminism (Carby, 1982; Amos and Parmar, 1984; Knowles and Mercer, 1992). From this position, because second-wave feminism was dominated by white middle-class women it had little to offer black or working-class women.

This was a crucial criticism which caused deep splits in the feminist movement. However, the most fundamental criticism of second-wave feminism came from anti-foundationalists, sometimes termed 'post-structuralists' or 'post-modernists'. We have dealt with elements of this argument in the last chapter. In this view, gender is a social construct, not a structural social division. As such, patriarchy is not a reflection, and a cause, of structured inequality; rather it is a discourse, although in almost all societies a dominant discourse, about the differences between, and the relations between, men and women. Consequently, the achievement of full citizenship is only possible if difference is recognised, perhaps even celebrated. The dominant discourse of patriarchy has to be opposed with a discourse of difference, if women, or indeed ethnic minorities or the disabled, are to enjoy full citizenship. Just as gaining the vote will not lead to such a politics of difference, neither will the achievement of equal pay (which, given the dominance of the discourse of patriarchy, is very unlikely anyway). It is through a discursive struggle to recognise diversity that difference can be acknowledged and become the basis of our society and polity. The position is outlined by Bashevkin, discussing the work of Voet (2002, p. 8):

[In] the view of post-structuralist feminists, political representation occurs through the crucial vehicle of language or discourse, and not simply in the formal institutions of public office and public admin-istration. By analysing linguistic representations, post-structuralist analysts reveal the power of multiple interests spoken as well as written text or, conversely, their lack of influence. In Voet's words, this third variant endorses the opening of public discourse toward 'an inclusive politics that listens to the voices of groups for whom policy-making is intended'.

From this perspective, listening to the voices of women is a key step in understanding (and transforming) the political, and here methodologically our research is very much in sympathy with this perspective. Where we differ from post-structuralism is in insisting that lived experience is structured, in terms of this research by age, class, gender and ethnicity. Consequently, we are operating from a second-wave position. While not prioritising gender, or for that matter age, class or ethnicity, we argue that age, class, gender and ethnicity are crucial lenses through which our respondent's experiences are interpreted. At the same time, they are lenses that interact.

6.2   Gender and politics

Walby (1997) asks, 'is participation gendered'? In our view, we also need to consider how does gender affect both ideas of politics and political participation? Pattie *et al.*'s findings suggest some gender differences in the ways in which men and women relate to politics and participation (2004, p. 86, Table 3.4). They found that all forms of participation – that is, individualistic, collective and small scale – whilst related to age, education and socio-economic status, were not related to gender. However, they also found that women were less knowledgeable about (Table 3.7), interested in (Table 3.11) and likely to talk about (Table 3.11) politics than men. At the same time, women were more liberal (Table 2.21) and men more libertarian (Table 2.16). Finally, women were more likely to trust the police (Table 2.15) and respect the law (Table 2.19), but less likely to feel personally or politically efficacious (Table 2.18). While these results are interesting they tell us nothing about either how women, and men, experience gender or how they understand and experience politics. It is these two areas that we examine here.

As Lister (2003, p. 37) argues: 'Citizenship as participation can be understood as an expression of human agency in the political arena, broadly defined; citizenship as rights enables people to exercise their agency as citizens.' However, agency is gendered, that is, it is structured. For example, as we shall see, the experiences of politics of some of the single mothers in our study are constrained by their lack of economic and educational resources, which result, in some cases from their being single mothers. In addition, they are also constrained by the patriarchal nature of the dominant distinction between the public, as male, and the private, as female.

Our data show that our respondents live gender in different ways and this is related to politics broadly conceived. For that reason our data on gender addresses a number of issues in the feminist literature as well as allowing us to reflect back on the literature on political participation and citizenship. As such, in the next section, we consider how our respondents experience gender. Following this, we then look at how gender affects ideas of politics.

6.2.1 Living gender

As we saw in Chapter 5, Pakulski and Waters (1996) argue that class is dead and gender is dying as a social division, to be replaced by social divisions based on lifestyle and consumption choices. We took issue with that argument in the chapter on class. Here, we turn to the question of whether gender has ceased to be a crucial factor in the experience and discourses of our respondents.

Women, and indeed men, can experience gender, and gender inequalities, without necessarily articulating them. Griffiths (1995) makes this point very strongly when she argues that girls who live in a society where the term 'slag' exists cannot just ignore the label; the mere non-recognition of a term does not make it go away and certainly has little, if any, effect on the impact this label can have on a young woman's life if it is attached to her. Similarly, for the young working-class women in our study the fact that they avoided speaking of class does not necessarily mean that class does not impact on their lives (Walsh, 1997); the link between class and life chances and educational achievement does not go away because we choose not to speak of it. In our transcripts, an absence of class discourses is mirrored by a relative absence of direct references to gender. What seems apparent, though, is that our respondents, both women and men, use a discourse which might be termed an 'equal opportunities discourse'; yet it is a 'knowing' discourse. Many women particularly talk of equal opportunities, but contend, as one of our respondents asserted, that women are equal, but 'have to work harder for it'.

Whilst our male respondents tended to talk about gender even less than our female respondents, they still lived gender. To put it another way, they may live their masculinity, but they did not talk about it. When men did talk about gender and relationships, it was generally in relation to pregnancy and, especially in the case of some, rather older less privileged respondents, about the difficulties they experienced in 'providing' for their partners. However, in relation to pregnancy and parenthood, the voice of men is relatively absent.

In the rest of this section, we focus upon three (related) themes which emerged in relation to our respondent's experiences of gender: first, the relationship between poverty/class and gender; second, the issue of sexuality, but more particularly 'reputation' and pregnancy and the constraints of being a single parent; and thirdly the role of education as a route out of gendered inequality.

6.2.1.1   Poverty/class and gender

As we saw in the previous chapter, a recognition of poverty and how it crucially constrained opportunities available to them was a constant theme within the discourses of the young people from our disadvantaged sites. These young people talked of economic poverty as an experience, either direct or through friends, which often involved real dependency on the state. In their view, this poverty was both reflected in, and reflected, their limited access to citizenship, so they knew that people rarely listened to them, and, at the same time, it meant that they were less able to/likely to participate. However, at the same time, respondents from the disadvantaged groups, particularly, knew that poverty had a particular affect on women especially because of its link to unwanted pregnancy.

This recognition of poverty was particularly evident in responses to the picture of the woman with two children (*Women and Children*). So, a white male from the New Deal site argued:

> *Respondent*: That's poverty, innit. You know she's pissed off with the government, she hasn't been provided for... and the kids they aren't wearing good clothes probably bought from a charity shop or something. Yeah, she's depressed; she wants the government to do something about it, she just looks miserable. [Poverty] is a political issue; it shouldn't be ignored by the politicians.
> *Interviewer*: And do you think that it is, it is ignored?
> *Respondent*: Yeah, it is ignored. There are loads of people in poverty, and that, or in run-down council estates. You know, but at the end of the day, it's probably not like her fault.
>
> Male, New Dealer, 23, white, individual interview

Here, the respondent assigns responsibility for the children's poor clothing, which are seen as indicators of poverty, mainly to the government. He recognises the interaction between the woman and the state, but says it is probably not her fault, thus both recognising the constraint on the woman and suggesting that the state is ignoring people in poverty.

As we emphasised in Chapter 3, the responses to all the images were complex. In particular, many respondents constructed quite sophisticated narratives around the images, offering a great deal of 'imagined' detail about the lives of those in the pictures. The crucial point here, however, is that indicators of poverty were invariably evident in the construction of these narratives. One focus group's response to the image of someone who they perceived as a single mother (*Mom and Baby*) shows how the respondents constructed a story of poverty for the young woman:

> *Respondent 1*: No, I think this picture right, it's like she's young and she probably/
> *Respondent 2*: /And she's not wearing any make-up.
> *Respondent 1*: Na, it's not that. She's probably in a baby unit or something, y'know [showing her] how to look after a child, 'cos she really does look young, 16, 15, 'cos you hear of young pregnancies.
> *Respondent 3*: Yeah.
> *Respondent 1*: Yeah, pregnancies, yeah.
> *Respondent 2*: Looks like my brother's girlfriend.
> *Interviewer*: Why do you say that?
> *Respondent 2*: 'Cos it looks like her . . . Her name's not [X] or [X} is it by any chance?
> *Interviewer*: I don't know what her name is.
> Females and male, homeless hostel, 18, 23 and age unknown, mixed ethnicity white, focus group

Here, respondent 2 is drawing on his own experience. He can directly relate to the image of a young woman with a child, because his brother's girlfriend is in a similar position. As the researchers, we had no idea if the child was the child of the young woman in the image, or whether she was a single parent, but the respondents 'read' this message so that it dominates their narratives. For example, in a focus group of FE college students, there was the following exchange:

> *Respondent 1*: They're a single parent family living on an estate.
> *Interviewer*: Why do you think they are a single parent family?
> *Respondent 1*: Because there is no father in the picture, unless he is taking the picture.
> *Respondent 2*: You can tell from the houses as well.

Respondent 1: Plus their expressions as well.

Respondent 3: From the face, yeah, especially from the face.

Respondent1: And from the faces you can tell they're not happy.

Respondent 2: And may be she's got like a crap sort of job as well, where she's not earning enough income to support her family.

Respondent 1: They might be in debt also and have problems.

Interviewer: You talked about the house; what else made you think they are poor?

Respondent 2: From their faces.

Respondent 1: Their clothes.

Male and females, FE college students, 19–20,
South Asian, focus group

6.2.1.2   *Pregnancy, being a single mother and 'reputations'*

In our disadvantaged groups, poverty, pregnancy and single parenthood were often narrated together, particularly by the women. So, in response to the image *Mom and Baby*, one woman drew on the direct experience of living with, and having friends with, babies, while, subsequently, a young man offered his interpretation of why the woman in the image is a single parent:

Respondent 1: Na, she's going through a hard time. You can see the look in her face, 'cos she ain't had no sleep, 'cos the baby's up crying with colic.

Respondent 2: Or her man's a drug dealer and he's locked away, yeah.

Female and male, New Dealers, 19 and 23,
black and white, focus group

Many of our respondents emphasised the difficulties of being a single parent. Here, an excerpt from a comprehensive sixth-form focus group is typical:

Respondent 1: She looks tired and just like completely withdrawn.

Respondent 2: Probably because the father's pissed off.

Respondent 3: Yeah, but the baby looks healthy and it looks alright and it's just that the mother, the mother just looks . . .

Respondent 1: Yeah, looks like she's having to sacrifice her childhood and that for the sake of the baby.

Females, sixth-formers, 16 and 17, white, focus group

Such talk about how being a young single parent involves the 'sacrifice' of youth defines explicitly the threat of unplanned pregnancy to some of the young people in our research. Overall, the volume of material that this image generated shows the very real fear, particularly at the less privileged sites, of the effect of unplanned pregnancy on young women in particular. In this vein, the respondent below talked about gender in relation to his experience of teenage pregnancy; he has a young daughter, but does not live with her mother:

> the responsibilities are different for a man and a woman. You know, because at the end of the day if the woman gets pregnant, and the man does a runner, she's got the responsibility... They might be proud to have the baby, and love it to bits, but if they're still in school, they've buggered it up... Basically a lad can just walk off. I mean, he'll get in trouble with the CSA [Child Support Agency], but, do you know what I mean, it's nothing. If you don't want nothing to do with it, you don't have to have nothing to do with it. All the CSA can say is 'yeah, pay this bit of money'.
>
> Male, New Dealer, 23, white, individual interview

This person's experience of, and insight into, pregnancy recognises that early pregnancy often means that young women have to leave school with no qualifications. In this way, becoming a mother hinders life choices; choice is not as open as Pakulski and Waters (1996) suggest. Early pregnancy also increases young women's contact with the state, with benefit agencies and, in some cases, social services. Such contact is far from unproblematic. The young New Dealer continued:

> *Respondent*: pay the money and don't do nothing else. But even then, when you're paying the money to the CSA, because I'm not with my daughter's mother, and they take the money off me, and it don't go to them, it goes to the government. And then, she's like, 'well I don't get it', and they [the CSA] go 'well you're on Family Allowance'.
>
> *Interviewer*: So they penalise her because she's on benefits?
>
> *Respondent*: I did say once, ignore the CSA and I'll give you the money each week or each month when I get paid and that. We was gonna do that, but the CSA just moaned.
>
> Male, New Dealer, 23, white, individual interview

Both this respondent and the mother of his daughter are constrained by their relationship to the state. He wants to fulfil what he sees as his role, take responsibility for the upkeep of his daughter, to become a full citizen, but her unemployment means that she is dependent on state benefits and unable to accept money from him without losing benefit. This situation is known to many of the disadvantaged young people in the study; teenage pregnancy leads to teenage poverty, with little or no opportunity to gain employment or education. The gendered nature of this poverty is clear as the poorer young women are unable to access affordable childcare in order to work or resume education. In this way, as second-wave feminists argue, the interaction between the individual and the state is highly gendered. Young women with children are maintained in a situation of poverty, unable to access citizenship through being economically active; this is a direct, and very political, experience.

Our main point here is that the disadvantaged young women's lives are more precarious specifically because the threat of pregnancy can, would and does spoil escape plans, particularly those based around education, an issue we discuss at more length below. At the same time, if they become single mothers this also brings them into direct and continuing contact with the state. It is interesting that in all focus groups, and regardless of class or ethnicity, both young women and young men when responding to the image of the young woman and the baby (*Mom and Baby*) presumed that the baby was hers, not a sibling or a cousin, but her child. Subsequently, the respondents from disadvantaged backgrounds went on to construct emotive stories about deceit and betrayal: she has been abandoned by the baby's father; her parents do not want to know. No one narrated a positive story. A focus group at the homeless hostel presents a typical example:

Respondent 1: Basically, if the baby's dad was there he would be in the picture.
Several people: Yeah, that's right.
Respondent 1: There's no excuse for him not being in the picture.
Respondent 2: She's young, ain't she, and he's probably run off or whatever.
Respondent 1: Or, if she's listened to 'I still love you, I do love you, I want you to have my kid.' And yeah right, soon as she gets pregnant and he sees how fat she's getting, he runs off with the next skinny girl he can see.

Females, homeless hostel, 18–22, black, focus group

One does not need to be a Foucauldian to acknowledge that, in our interviewees' responses, there is clear evidence of social control or discipline in relation to women's bodies, particularly perhaps working-class women's and black women's bodies. As Finch (1993) argues, the sexualisation of working-class women and black women leads to a perception, often a self-perception even, of sluttishness; of pollution and decadence. It seems clear from our interviews that the clash between the public and the private, the cultural and the natural, is much more vivid for working-class and black women. This was a clear theme in the way two young South Asian women, interviewed together, discussed the reasoning behind their choice of FE college:

> *Interviewer*: Why did you go to [names the college they attend] rather than [names their local college]?
> *Respondent 1*: I dunno, it's reputations innit?
> *Respondent 2*: They've got reputations.
> *Respondent 1*: . . . they've got a bit of a bad reputation, they've been given the reputation; [names local college] girls.
> *Interviewer*: Really I haven't heard this one. I've heard other things about [names local college] but not [names local college] girls.
> *Respondent 1*: Oh yeah, it's like, if a lad asks where you're from and she turns round and says I'm from [names area]
> *Respondent 2*: Especially if you're Asian.
> Females, FE college students, 18 and 20,
South Asian, focus group

The threat of a bad reputation and its effect on the lives of young people cannot be underestimated. For the respondents above, being labelled a 'slut' is a real threat to their standing within their local community and it has major implications for their social capital and, therefore, their life choices. This may be exacerbated by the fact that we are working with young people from a large urban conurbation and this shapes their experiences. It is certainly well established that young people's spatial awareness and their perception of themselves within the physical environment are gendered. As we indicated earlier, young women experience social control of their sexuality, of their sexual selves, in the streets and areas in which they live.

As Tolman argues (1994, p. 326), on the basis of her research on young urban women's sexual identities:

> The fact that girls who live in the urban area experience the visibility of and the discourse about violence, danger and the consequences of

unprotected sex, and that the suburban girls live in a community that offers a veneer of safety and stability, informs their experience of sexuality. Awareness of these features of the social contexts in which these girls are developing is essential for listening to and understanding their narratives about sexual experiences.

Discourses of vulnerability arising from 'inappropriate pregnancy', as well as social vulnerability in the form of getting a 'bad reputation', were reflected in the accounts of the people we interviewed.

Conversely, a 'reputation' can be a 'positive' thing for a young man, as one male respondent argued when talking about young women's perceptions of young men, and some young men's attitudes towards themselves, in his area:

> They think it's better to have a reputation for going into prison than it is to be a nice person and that. Y'know, it's just because, I don't know, it's hard to explain. Y'know people, well girls around my area find it more attractive if they can go out with a lad and turn around and say: 'yeah, he's been in the nick'. Y'know, and I don't know why they're like that. I'd never do anything to put myself in prison. Yeah, but, it's an attraction, y'know, violence.
>
> Male, New Dealer, 23, white, individual interview

As such, reputation, as a form of social capital in Bourdieusian terms, can work in different ways for these young people. For the young women, a bad reputation is threat to their social capital, but a bad reputation for some young men can give them sexual status with some young women. Breaking societal norms, and consequent exclusion from societal acceptance, may be seen as less valuable than being attractive to young women.

6.2.1.3   Education as an escape route

Given the experiences of our disadvantaged respondents, it is interesting that education is perceived as an escape route out of their present situation, although much more for young women than young men. As one woman argues:

> Some, I don't know, some of them do find it easy 'cos they've always got their family, or they've got the child's father around. Most of them, the child's father, is nowhere to be seen or he's had to be deported 'cos he's not from here or some of them are psychopaths.

They're mad, some of the things that go on, you think, how can you have a child with such a person? They say: 'oh but I do like him'. I think liking someone and having a child are two different things. I know it's madness some of the time. It's like one of my friends she does drink, she drinks mad stuff like Crest and Super Tennants, and stuff like that, and her little baby, sometimes he's walking around drinking from her can. I'm thinking he's only one years old, what are you doing? You need to wake up man and see what he's carrying on with and she's got no control.

She goes on to say:

Most of my friends, before they even left school, they were pregnant and most of them have got kids . . . but they're not getting an education out of it. My friend says, oh after she's had her baby she's going back to college and she still hasn't done that and her baby is nearly a year old now. It's not as if her mom wouldn't help out. I'm sure her mom would do anything to help her look after her son or get him into a nursery, 'cos most nurseries, they're expensive as well.

Female, New Dealer, 19, black, individual interview

This woman's irritation with the fact that her friends with children do not complete education reflects a general attitude among many of our respondents, of both sexes, to what can be viewed as inappropriate pregnancies. They do not just blame the state for failing to provide cheap childcare, they also recognise that the woman, and the man, had some choice. Nevertheless, the key point is that, in the experience of many of our respondents, the problem of childcare constrains young women from being educated to become economically active. It is also interesting that, while the woman respondent above offers a logical solution, getting mother/grandmother to look after the child, she does not acknowledge that this only moves the problem from one woman to another, by reducing the opportunity for the grandmother to be economically active. In fact, her 'solution' does not match her own family experience, as her own mother has actively pursued education as well as working:

[Mom's] always been at college from when I can remember. She's always been studying something. Even now she's just completed her level three NVQ for Health Care Assistant 'cos she's thinking about going into nursing or something. But she's always been studying and I'm thinking if my mom can do it, so can I.

Female, New Dealer, 19, black, individual interview

Her positive attitude to education is obviously informed by her mother's experiences and she certainly sees education as a means of engaging with the public realm and improving her life chances. However, the rest of her response indicates how vulnerable young women like her can be:

but then I've got the family aspects of everybody watching me, expecting me to follow my mom and become pregnant at seventeen. [...] Now I've actually passed that age, it's like: 'oh well done [name] you're really getting on with college and everything.' So, everyone's interested and I'm thinking well, you weren't interested before, so why are you interested now? I dunno it's just mad.

Female, New Dealer, 19, black, individual interview

Here, it is clear that she knows the danger of early pregnancy and becoming a single mother; she was/is frightened of mirroring her mother and recognises her friends' experience of exclusion and having to work harder to maintain their citizenship identity.

For the men, particularly the disadvantaged men, among our respondents, the desire to earn enough to 'settle down' is evident in the transcripts. Those young men, who are already living independently, talk of the difficulties they have experienced in trying to remain independent. For those who are trying to make the leap into independent living, the difficulties are even more apparent:

Interviewer: So what do you see for the future, where do you see yourself in five years time?
Respondent: The same really, nothing changes.
Interviewer: What is it you want?
Respondent: To get a job, me and me girlfriend to get our own place, y'know, our own baby, but you can't bring one up on the dole. It's not fair, y'know, not having anything.

Male, New Dealer, 22, white, individual interview

Similarly another male respondent talks of people he knows who have never worked:

Interviewer: Who are those people?

Respondent: Just knobs really. I've got friends who are doing it. They haven't worked, y'know, they're 21, haven't worked since the day they left school, y'know. Left school, claimed Hardship Allowance, then claimed the dole and stuff like that. It just isn't right.

Interviewer: So, you think you should get a job or try and find a job and provide for yourself?

Respondent: Yeah, because at the end of the day, know what I mean, if you want to get married, you want to have kids and stuff like that, you can't bring up your kids on the dole, you know, you've got to provide for them.

> Male, New Dealer, 23, white, individual interview

The impact of socio-economic changes on the experiences of the interviewees should not be ignored, especially in the light of the way these changes are gendered. As discussed in Chapter 3, youth transitions to adulthood have become more complicated with the traditional routes that many of our respondents would have taken into 'adulthood' having disappeared. Indeed, respondents from our disadvantaged sites had no expectation that they would leave school and enter full-time employment, let alone secure employment. Indeed, such expectations were probably not even held, and certainly not fulfilled, by their parents. As we have already indicated, education and skills are perceived as the key to employment, regardless of gender. Yet, many of our disadvantaged respondents had fairly negative experiences of education and training programmes designed to 'shape the pathway' to employment.

As we saw in Chapter 5, many respondents felt constrained or left out by the education and training route and this is particularly clear in the quote from one respondent, a disadvantaged white male, which we discussed in Chapter 5(see pp.139–140). His unsuccessful attempt to gain independence from the state and to establish his own home and independence shows just how constraining a lack of resources – again in Bourdieusian terms, economic, social and cultural capital – can be.

Education is the key by which some of our disadvantaged respondents might escape from the 'cycle of deprivation'; it gives them some chance of exercising more control over their own lives. Indeed, many of our disadvantaged young women were undertaking or planning more education, much more so than were their male counterparts. However, they knew that this path was one that was very difficult.

6.3   Gender, the political and political participation

Here, we focus on the extent to which conceptions of the political and, to a more limited extent, forms of political participation were gendered for our respondents.

The responses to the images of two political candidates, one female (*Woman Candidate*) and one male (*Man Candidate*), were interesting. It was noticeable that the narratives about the image of the female candidate only focused on whether she was from the area, that is, a local person; there was no engagement, either positive or negative, about her gender. In contrast, the male candidate, who is pictured standing in a quiet country lane with cottages in the background, was seen by most of our respondents, regardless of site, as coming from a privileged background:

> *Respondent*: I don't like that guy whatsoever. He's a knob. Trust me, he is, he is just the smarmy politician that I expect politicians to be, y'know?
> *Interviewer*: So do you think he's typical?
> *Respondent*: Yeah, typical, just got into politics, trying to prove a point . . . Closet homosexual, weekend drug user.
> Male, New Dealer, 23, white, individual interview

Here, the main point is probably that politicians are seen as removed from these young people's experience, as being privileged, but it is also interesting that there were no references to the woman's political candidacy.

At the same time, the picture of the *Woman Candidate* raised, for some of the respondents, issues of equality and particularly of the unrepresentativeness of Parliament in gender terms. The following two examples make the point, but there were others. In a focus group of young women from a comprehensive sixth form, there was the following exchange:

> *Respondent 1*: I don't know how many years ago it was, when women weren't allowed to be in power, they weren't allowed to appear in Parliament, so therefore, if there's all men, women are just starting to catch up. Obviously there's gonna be a load that comes in all at once.
> *Respondent 2*: Yeah, I think maybe at the moment, it's still going through that period where women are still catching, there has been a lot of progress, but there's still, there's gonna be more progress,

where there's gonna be more women, and being more confident, because it, it is very male-dominated and that might be intimidating for women as well, I think. You know, you've got to be a kind of, you'd have to be very dominant, you'd have to be someone who was constantly seeking power all the time. You'd probably have to have more confidence than a man.

Respondent 1: You'd have to be very strong, because no doubt there might be quite a few men in Parliament who would look down on you because you are a woman, because it was mainly a male thing.

Interviewer: Do you think it matters whether or not there are more women in Parliament?

Respondent 1: I'd like to see more women.

Respondent 2: Yeah, I'd like to see more women now. I think, generally, there needs to be more women in there because it's like they seem to be in a minority and women aren't a minority. So, there needs to be more.

Females, sixth-formers, 18, white, focus group

When asked about why there was such under-representation of women, one woman respondent from the same group again emphasised the male culture in Parliament in her follow-up individual interview:

Respondent: . . . if I wanted to go into politics, you know, I wouldn't be frightened to do it, or frightened to try. But, I do think, on the whole, because it's, because there are more men involved than there are women, I think generally, one, women are put off by that. And then, secondly, the nature of the whole, of the whole government, that things happen behind closed doors, everything happens after hours, and you know late nights, and the whole sort of gentlemen's sort of idea of government. It is difficult for women if they have, it is a real generalisation, but if they have a family, because on the whole women aren't going to want, not that men want to be away from the family, but it's more difficult for them to be away from their family than it is for, well, you know it's just, I think that women find it difficult to be away from their family for a whole, that amount of time. Especially with children and things, it's a lot more difficult. I don't think it would put me off, but I think that, I think a lot of people would find it difficult or stressful to be an MP as well as balancing that with a family, as well because of the roles that women are given in the home I think.

Interviewer: So you think it's practical things that make a kind of male culture?

Respondent: Yeah, there is definitely a male culture, like you know, like I said this whole idea of a gentlemen thing, it's really, it's a really difficult thing for people, for women to think about getting involved in. And I also think that the amount of, I think it's a very stressful sort of environment for anyone to be in.

Female, sixth-former, 18, white, individual interview

Despite this, it seems to us that it is when we look at the contact individuals have with the state that we see the gendered nature of politics more clearly. This was particularly evident in the focus group with a number of young women with children, who are unemployed and living in a hostel. In response to the image of the couple in the park (*No Skating*) the women began talking about the pressure put on them by staff members to take their (i.e. the young women's) children to the local park to play and to get some fresh air:

Interviewer: Does it look like parks round here?

Respondent 1: No

Respondent 2: . . . not that park over there. That park is full of rats man. I think the rats go to the park to go on the swings and that.

Respondent 1: Na, this park doesn't look like a park round here. This park looks like a park in London.

Respondent 2: Na na, not round here. There's a park like this where all the birds go and it's a really nice park. I forgot what it called now and it's a little, a little park, innit right, and it's got all these different things, innit right . . . I can't remember the place [Another group member names a well known Birmingham park]

Respondent 2: Yeah, and it's really nice there. So we have got a nice park, but not round this area, because that park over there, right, it's horrible. You go there and there's big massive rats and they're horrible. Ooh, I see, I see Asian people playing football and I think they're mad. I couldn't watch them playing there, they, they ooh they're horrible and at night time you go to make a phone call, we went to the phone call I swear there was like three or four . . .

Respondent 1: About six of them.

Respondent 2: And I swear the council aren't doing anything about it man. That is disgusting, that is, aw have you seen them at night time?

Interviewer: Why aren't they doing anything about it then?

Respondent 2: I don't know, probably scared of them.

Respondent 1: I mean you get told to bring your kids to the park.

Respondent 2: I don't know what her name is. Yeah, yeah you get people saying, 'cos they don't know, 'cos they don't live here and they don't go to the park over there. They go 'take your children to that nice little park', 'cos they think it's a nice park, it's horrible.

Respondent 1: It's a rat trap.

Respondent 2: I mean people have sex over there and they chuck their condoms on the floor. I think it's disgusting and everything else and people have got raped over there and sometimes you see their knickers and bras. I mean, come on, don't ya, come on, seriously it's disgusting, it's just horrible.

> Females, homeless hostel, 18–22,
> black and white, focus group

There is pressure here to be seen to comply with the model of a 'good mother'. Yet, the definition of the good mother is 'classed' as the idea of taking your child to play and getting some fresh air is in direct conflict with these women's experience of the park as a place of potential danger for them and their children. If they resist the pressure to go to the park, they run the risk of being seen as inattentive or bad mothers and the need to be, and to be seen to be, a good mother is particularly pertinent for these young, poor, single women. The monitoring of their activities outweighs the opportunities they have to make decisions in their lives. Their response in the circumstances shows strength; they all refused to go to the park, but also made it known that the area is unsuitable for them and their children. Their analysis of, and response to, the use and suitability of this space is political. There is no voting, no membership of political parties or interest groups and no signing of petitions; rather there is a stand-off against staff members.

This returns us to a key theme of this book; access to the mainstream arenas of participation may be gendered and limited by age. As such, it is important to recognise the role of participation in local/personal arenas, no matter how unusual these may appear to those who focus on formal political arenas. To put it another way, these women are behaving much more like Bang's Everyday Makers than Pattie *et al.*'s political participants.

We saw earlier that the threat of pregnancy features in the lives of many of our less privileged female respondents. Here, it is important to emphasis that, for these young women, pregnancy and single parenthood in a sense establishes a partially institutionalised boundary between the public and the private. Pregnancy tends to confine young women to the private, in this sense domestic, sphere, and effectively to exclude them from the public arena. Indeed, many young women will find it physically difficult to move far from home. In this vein, one respondent, a single mother from the hostel site, reflects on the photograph of the man with a pushchair (*Empty Houses*) in the light of her own experience of having to use public transport with a pushchair:

> London wasn't built for mothers, [. . . it's] no pushchairs (on) public transport. Whereas Birmingham, that's one thing I'm glad, Birmingham has seen that there is mothers who do have to catch the bus, 'cos we can't all afford taxis and cars. Yeah, we need to get on a bus with our buggies and our heavy shopping.
>
> Female, homeless hostel, 18, black, individual interview

For many women in this position, engagement with state agencies is something imposed on them, much more than men, especially if they become single parents and this experience is key to their understanding of political institutions.

It was noticeable that there was limited identification with, or discussion of, feminism among our female, let alone our male, respondents. This was evident in the responses to the female candidate discussed earlier; she was narrated almost as if she was 'gender neutral'. In fact, feminism was seen as part of a bygone age, so in her individual interview, a woman university student saw feminism as having little or nothing to do with young women's identity:

> *Interviewer*: So would you say that there's been a change since your parents' generation in interest in politics? Or is it just that young people are apathetic. I mean do you think there's been a shift at all?
> *Respondent*: I think there probably has been a shift, because you have to, um I don't know, you remember, like the swinging sixties, burning your bra and all that kind of stuff [laughs]; they were interested. Students were known for being politically interested, so it must have changed a bit.
>
> Female, university student, 18, white, individual interview

At the same time, many of our young female respondents were keen to assert themselves as independent and active agents, and that, in some ways at least, is probably a legacy of feminism, although the extent of this self-assertion was not unproblematic. In this way, one young woman from the New Deal programme discussed negotiating roles with male colleagues working in a hotel kitchen. She begins by talking of the perception that she could not lift heavy bags of sugar and then continues:

> And, I'm like, I'm not that feeble, but it's like, I dunno, if you go on in a certain way as a female, they'll just, I dunno, give you stick, but if you kinda give it back as good as ya get, they kinda think: 'she's a nice person, she's more laid back, she's more relaxed, she very likely like one of the lads'.
>
> Female, New Dealer, 19, black, individual interview

So, she is defending her corner, but suggesting that, to stand up for herself, she has to behave like 'one of the lads'. Later, in the same section of her interview, she was asked whether she thought that there are equal opportunities for women:

> There are, but you have to work harder for them. [...] Society is mostly male orientated, most big companies – you don't really see women managers, they're mostly men. (Even) if they think that, y'know, you could be 10 times better than a man at the job, but he will still probably get a job because oh, he's a man, he should be at the top, women can't handle this, and all the rest of it.
>
> Female, New Dealer, 19, black, individual interview

Many of the men thought that there was more equality. In this vein, one young white male from the New Deal programme argued:

> *Interviewer*: Do you think that responsibilities and opportunities for men and women are different?
> *Respondent*: Yeah.
> *Interviewer*: What about things like equality, and ...
> *Respondent*: Now that will sort itself out, equality, that's already come.
> *Interviewer*: How?
> *Respondent*: Women are getting paid just as much as men nowadays. I mean you've women football teams and that, ain't you?
> *Interviewer*: Yeah.
> *Respondent*: *** League,
> *Interviewer*: Oh right.

Respondent: And they've got a World-Cup for women as well. So, yeah, equality . . . So, they're righting themselves. Yeah, well, two-thirds of them I reckon. Only need about another say, yeah, about 10 years. It should be there.

Male, New Dealer, 23, white, individual interview

For some women, the idea of feminism and equality caused difficulties because they felt unsure what feminism, and being a feminist, involved. One woman sixth-former's response when asked for her views about feminism and whether she thought she was a feminist was fairly typical:

I wouldn't really no, because I think that there are some people that take this word feminism, they think it's quite a radical thing, whereas some people that like call themselves a feminist seem to want female dominance, and I don't think that's right. I think equality is right, but you have to bear in mind there are differences between men and women.

Later she continued:

I don't know whether I would associate myself with the word feminism, but I do think at the moment we haven't, in some areas we have equality, but in others, we're severely lacking in it.

Female, sixth-former, 18, white, individual interview

The response of some of our male respondents to the image of Muslim police women (*Police*) was interesting:

Respondent 1: I think it's the uniform as well, when women wear a uniform they become more powerful; you get because (she's) a police officer.
Respondent 2: Yeah that's it.
Respondent 1: They're more like, you know, it makes them look more powerful. So, when they take it off and go outside' they need to say, 'yeah I'm a police officer', when they've not got the uniform on.
Interviewer: You think it goes to their heads?
Respondent 3: When they're wearing the uniform; behind the uniform is the power.

Respondent 1: 'Cos, that's when they're more stuck up, and it's more of a man's job.

Respondent 2: Big power.

Males, FE college students, 17–20, South Asian
and black, focus group

Here, the women are not seen as powerful, or having authority in their own right, only because they have a uniform which symbolises, a largely male, authority system.

6.4 Conclusion

We agree with Lister (2003, p. 199) when she argues that:

> Through an inclusive definition of political citizenship (and particip-
> ation), women's 'accidental activism' in the interstices of the public
> and private spheres [. . .] come to be acknowledged and valued as acts
> of citizenship. At the same time, by linking agency and structure as
> mediated by culture (we keep) in view the ways in which the political
> stage is structured both materially and symbolically to disadvantage
> women. (our addition in first brackets)

Liberal theories see education as a leveller, arguing that equal access to education will enable women to enter the job market on equal footing to men. These liberal theories do, to an extent, inform the way some of our young people think; certainly, there was a discourse of equal oppor-tunities in our more privileged sites. However, our less privileged female respondents, as Lister would expect, were well aware of the constraints on their social mobility through education. Indeed, overall, probably the strongest theme to emerge from our interviews concerns the rela-tionship between class and gender. Among our respondents, class does not wash out gender divisions, anything but, rather it reinforces them. As such, our data would seem to support a second-wave, materialist feminist, position. To put it another way, and as we saw in the last chapter, in our view this analysis shows how economic, cultural and social capital are related and how the experiences of our disadvantaged, working-class women are shaped by their lack of these capitals.

7
Young People and the Politics of 'Race', Ethnicity and Identity

7.1 Lived experience, identity and political engagement

Throughout this book, we have argued that, in order to understand young people's political engagement, it is necessary to understand politics as 'lived experience'. As we saw in Chapter 2, this approach has some parallels with Beck's (1994b) concept of 'sub politics' or Giddens' (1994) view of 'life politics'. It also resonates with Bang's (2003; 2005) argument that, under the conditions of culture governance, politics is increasingly seen in terms of individual projects of self-actualisation, where the 'political is increasingly personal and self-reflexive' (2005, p. 163). These approaches share a view of political engagement as involving everyday choices and actions aimed at contesting or establishing rules, practices, norms, forms of decision-making, outcomes and so on, particularly where these rules, practices, norms and so on are no longer necessarily governed by tradition. This perspective owes a great deal to both feminist and social movement politics, which have re-politicised the micro and personal spheres that were defined out of the realm of politics by liberal political discourses. As a consequence, this approach views the range of arenas in which political action may be theoretically analysed as including those in which everyday experiences and actions occur.

Fundamental to such perspectives on politics are the ways in which questions of identity are bound up with everyday 'life politics'. Thus, Giddens (1994, p. 91) defines life politics as a 'politics of identity as well as of choice', where identity is seen as something with which individuals reflexively engage. This understanding of identity and lived experience formed a key aspect of the ways in which our respondents expressed their political engagement, and they tended to view questions of identity as *political* questions that they confronted and articulated in their everyday lives.

We have also argued that politics should be viewed as *structured* lived experience – in other words, that expressions of identity politics should take account of the factors that shape or constrain the ways in which such politics is expressed and experienced. As Giddens remarks, 'Life politics is not, or not only, a politics of the personal' (1994, p. 91), it is rather a reflexive engagement with the world, which in turn structures individuals' lived experiences. Our data illuminate the ways in which state policies and social practices relating to 'race', ethnicity and multiculturalism shape young people's life politics.

Bearing these issues in mind, the following sections will focus on the particular ways in which our respondents expressed their political engagement and the connections between everyday actions and their views of macro-political institutions. In section 7.1.1, we begin by examining how identity shapes young people's engagement with politics and, particularly, how 'race' and ethnicity had an impact on our respondents' conception of politics. Our data show that for many of our respondents, experiences of racism and racialisation have politicised their lived experiences, although, as we argue, much of the literature on political participation pays insufficient attention to these experiences. In section 7.1.2, we explore how living in a multicultural city shaped many of our respondents' life politics – particularly in relation to how they related to identity, space, community, citizenship and some of the tensions surrounding, as well as their visions of, living in a multicultural society. In each of these sections, we will highlight the intersections between young people's lived experiences and their engagement with more formal, macro-political institutions.

7.1.1 Young people, 'race' and the politics of lived experience

In this section, we explore how 'race' and identity shaped young people's conceptions of the political and how they related to political institutions. In particular, our data show that racism and racialisation (Murji and Solomos, 2005) had a profound impact on black and minority ethnic respondents' conceptions of, and engagement with, the political. Our black and minority ethnic respondents, particularly but not exclusively, identified 'race' as inherently political due to racial inequalities in employment, education and other public and political institutions, or racism and racial violence.

The literature on youth political engagement rarely deals with issues of 'race', ethnicity and identity, however. In the first place, quantitative studies of political behaviour and attitudes among young people rarely disaggregate by ethnicity, whilst studies of black and minority ethnic groups' political participation rarely disaggregate by age. We, therefore, have little by way of analysed data or reports on black and minority ethnic young people's political participation and attitudes. Given that the crisis of electoral engagement that is so often identified among the young is also a cause for concern among many black and minority ethnic groups (Saggar, 1998), this gap in the literature is particularly problematic.

In the 2001 General Election, for instance, MORI estimated that the turnout among black and minority ethnic voters was 47 per cent, that is, 12 percentage points lower than the overall turnout (Richards and Marshall, 2003), and it suggested that this turnout remained static in the 2005 General Election (MORI, 2005b). In addition, there are studies suggesting that levels of electoral registration are very low among some black and minority ethnic groups (Purdam *et al.*, 2002; The Electoral Commission, 2005b). It is important to note that there are significant differences between black and minority ethnic groups in terms of electoral participation. For example, a 2004 report commissioned by the Electoral Commission and ICM found that the adjusted estimated turnout[1] in the 2004 European Elections among Asian voters was 50 per cent, compared with 42 per cent among white voters and 38 per cent among Black and Black British voters (Curtice/ICM, 2004). Although these findings clearly suggest differential patterns of voting across ethnic groups, and highlight that some black and minority ethnic groups' electoral engagement are *higher* than overall levels (OBV, 1998), they also potentially obscure some key variations. Previous studies of electoral engagement point to significant differences among 'Asian' voters, suggesting in particular that voters of Indian origin are more likely than whites to vote, whilst Pakistani and Bangladeshi voters are much less likely (Anwar, 2001; Purdam *et al.*, 2002). These differences between groups of black and minority ethnic voters tend not to be particularly rigorously analysed in many election studies, often due to low sample sizes, which make the generation of reliable results difficult. Indeed, this problem is identified as one that limits the analysis of black and minority ethnic political and electoral turnout generally (Fahmy, 2004). Thus, Purdam *et al.* in their 2002 report for the Electoral Commission, comment on the, 'lack of reliable and compelling survey evidence regarding BME turnout' (2002, pp. 50–51).

Pattie *et al.*'s (2004) analysis of ethnicity in their study of civic and political participation found that ethnicity was not particularly significant in relation to propensity to engage in political action (Table 3.4) or in terms of civic beliefs and citizenship values (Table 3.18), although interpersonal trust was higher among white respondents (Table 2.14), whilst trust in the police was much lower among the merged categories of non-white groups. However, they also report that non-white categories of respondents were more satisfied with the state of British democracy (Table 2.17) and more likely to be involved in micro-political actions concerned with public services such as education or health than white respondents (Table 4.9).

Their analysis of the data by ethnicity used ethnic identification categories of 'Asian', 'East Asian', 'Black' and 'Other' which were merged into one category in the reporting of their data. However, as noted above, a number of studies suggest that there are significant variations between black and minority ethnic groups in terms of electoral registration and voter turnout, thus the merged category of 'Black/Asian/Caribbean/Other' has somewhat limited value in terms of what it tells us about electoral engagement and participation more generally. Their data, furthermore, do not explain the lower levels of electoral participation among black and minority ethnic groups that are revealed in other surveys and, we argue, their data reveal even less about *why* this might be the case.

Problems in disaggregating data on electoral participation by age *and* ethnicity are generally a problem within the survey literature, although Purdam *et al.*'s (2002) report indicates that minority ethnic young people are even less likely to be engaged in electoral politics than white youth and black and minority ethnic groups overall, although they present little direct data on this group (2002, p. 50). This view is supported, however, by MORI's (2005b) report, which suggested that levels of claimed turnout in the 2005 General Election among black and minority ethnic 18–24-year-olds and 25–34-year-olds were much lower than the overall claimed turnout (48 per cent against 72 per cent overall claimed turnout). Similarly, Operation Black Vote's (1997) report, *Into the Millennium*, argued that 'Young Blacks are consciously opting out of a system they believe has no place for them and nothing to offer them.' Nevertheless, we have little by way of survey data to confirm the extent of this longitudinally or between minority ethnic groups, nor do we have much by way of qualitative data to explore *why* particular groups might be relatively more disengaged from electoral politics.

Whilst, there are several very good and interesting studies of black and minority ethnic young people's everyday or life politics, particularly in relation to experiences in the labour market (Solomos, 1988;

Brah, 1996), identity formation (Alexander, 1996; Brah, 1996) and style (Back, 1996; Hebdige, 1987), the relationship between these political lived experiences and young people's views of political institutions and processes have been less well explored. Aside from Kum-Kum Bhavnani's (1991) psychological study of black and minority ethnic young people's perspectives on politics, which illuminated the ways in which these were shaped by policies and practices relating to 'race' in the period of the late 1980s, there have been relatively few studies that directly explore such connections.

Instead, as Bhattacharyya and Gabriel (2000) point out, policy debates and studies on black and minority ethnic young people have tended to be much more concerned with crises in relation to these young people's identities or social integration. In the same vein, Back (2002) argues that debates on black and minority ethnic youth have tended to focus on 'lawless masculinities', yob culture or the pathologies of the inner city. Similarly, but earlier, Hall *et al.* (1978) drew attention to the succession of moral panics in the 1970s around black young people, notably in relation to black masculinity and crime in the construction of 'mugging' as a black phenomenon. In many ways, according to Alexander (2000), such themes around black masculinity and criminality have been reconfigured in contemporary debates and transposed onto Asian masculinity.

Back and others also identify 'concern about the aftershock of immigration', conceived as the destabilisation of 'settled identities', as a recurring motif in discussions of black and minority ethnic youth (2002, p. 439). This is manifested in the frequent characterisation of young people as 'caught between cultures', in conflict with their parent's generation, whilst not fully integrated into British society. Back's (1996, 2002) work on youth identities suggests a more complex picture, in which young people's identities are not reducible to a simple conflict between their parents' and British culture. Rather, black and minority ethnic young people express what might be seen as a hybrid British identity, which may also be appropriated and shared by white young people.

This theme of identity conflict has been reinvigorated in recent narratives of Muslim youth, as a consequence of the 2001 disturbances in Bradford, Burnley and Oldham and the London bombings of 7th July, 2005. Public debate around both issues has been preoccupied with the lack of community cohesion in Muslim communities, disaffected youth and the failure of 'community leadership' (Ouseley, 2001). Frequently, then, when black and minority ethnic young people appear in public debates, it is in association with crises (of masculinity, family relations,

social connectedness, educational attainment, etc.), rather than in relation to their opinions and views about political institutions, policies
and processes. As such, we agree with Les Back when he argues (2002,
p. 441), 'any credible discussion, both politically and sociologically, of
issues of youth crime or racism or multiculturalism needs to begin by
appreciating that young people can speak for themselves, and it might
be worth us taking the time to listen'. Below, we set out our data on
young people's conceptions of the political and political institutions and
how these interacted with issues of 'race', racism and the recognition of
difference.

7.1.1.1 'Race', identity and defining the political

In our interviews, the relationship between experiences of racism and
racialisation and views about the British political system and processes
were frequently expressed by our respondents, particularly our black
and minority ethnic respondents. 'Race' had an impact on their lived
experiences in a number of ways and these were significant in shaping
their views on political institutions and processes.

For instance, one focus group of FE college students of South Asian
(Indian, Pakistani and Afghan) origin interpreted virtually all the images
that we distributed in the focus group (for details of these, see Chapter 3)
as relating to issues of racial equality or racism. Furthermore, during
the sorting exercise (when we asked the respondents to sort the images
into those they considered political and those they did not) they sorted
and defined the images as political on this basis. Thus, in the sorting
exercise, these respondents, in common with several other black and
minority ethnic respondents, identified one particular image (*Hospital*)
of two black men dressed in white coats standing next to a hospital bed
occupied by an elderly white man as political because of its associations
in their view with issues of racial inequality:

> This one [is political] because there's two black men and there's a
> white person there, and obviously he's looking at these two men and
> because they're both the same colour, it could have been either one
> black, one white, because there's two black men and there's not many
> black people doing it [working as doctors] . . .
>
> Female, FE college student, 18, South Asian,
> individual interview

Similarly, in relation to the same image, a respondent in another FE
college focus group asserted:

I would say it is [political] 'cos not a lot of black people are high up in that kind of profession.

> Male, FE college student, 18, black, focus group

One respondent from the group of South Asian FE college students, in talking about her perspective on politics, explicitly defined politics as the expression of racism and racial intolerance:

I never talk about politics. This is probably the second time I've actually spoke about politics . . . but I find it interesting talking about politics. But I dunno I think it would be better if there was like no political thing happening as in racial attacks, all these things that happen. All the bad things that happen: it would be better if all that kinda died down because like it is the 21st century now, so like give up! Basically you're working with different people, your whole life is based on working or doing things with different people – not just one colour. 'Cos like we've got over that, it's just like passed our heads now, it's like doing other things now. But some people are just stuck in the 1960s, 50s, 70s and all those, and thinking 'no this is what happened to us this is so-and-so we should stand our ground' . . .

> Female, FE college student, 18, South Asian, individual interview

For this group, their views of politics were intimately connected with issues of racism and racial violence, a view echoed by a sixth-former (of Pakistani/English origin):

it can be made political because, well, it's a black issue, a black man was killed, so that is definitely political from day one . . .

> Male, sixth-former, 18, South Asian/white,
> individual interview

7.1.1.2   *Far-right politics and the politicisation of young people*

This perception that issues relating to race equality were political was also expressed in relation to respondents' awareness of far-right racist activity. In particular, awareness of, and reports on, the activities of the British National Party (BNP) and the National Front (NF) were highly politicising for many black and minority ethnic respondents and had a significant impact on how they viewed political institutions and processes, and this was particularly heightened among our South Asian respondents. For instance, in one particular interview, which took place shortly after disturbances in the northern English towns of Bradford,

Burnley and Oldham, and when there was speculation that the BNP would march in Birmingham that weekend, the respondent, a young FE college student who self-identified as British Asian, reported feeling that a highly racialised political discourse had increasingly come to the fore. He felt this was due to, among other things, the aggressive and predatory campaigns by far-right parties and groups such as the BNP and the NF:

Politics before for me was either about Conservative or Labour, nothing else. But over the past few years, [that's changed] . . . now, it's like, there is a story, ages ago, I actually found it really funny, that my dad was told that all the immigrants are coming here now, but soon the government's gonna fling 'em all back out again. Which I found funny, and he goes . . . when the Asian and black people start getting rich and they all become successful, the poor white people are going to feel threatened and they are going to evict us, as it were. And, everyone was just laughing, and even my dad was laughing . . . But, he actually thought that, that we'd get kicked out, which I found funny. But right now, it's not funny. Now it's like, it could happen, with all this racism going on, maybe people will stop voting for conservatism, will stop voting for the Labour party and vote for the BNP, vote for them and National Front will become more up-front, and they'll get in politics, and then all hell will break loose. And then it gets all confusing, and you say – ah, my dad was right.

Male, FE college student, 19, South Asian, Individual interview

Many other black and minority ethnic respondents were similarly concerned with far-right racist activity and this had a significant impact on how they experienced and defined politics:

It's all politics. It's racism, racism and the fight and the NFs.

Female, FE college student, 17, South Asian, focus group

I think that it [race] is a matter of politics, because they're in the news recently all this BNP party, and, you know what I mean, and it's politics isn't it? . . . this BNP parties and parties like that, the racial tension that is going on at the moment. That's all politics . . .

Male, FE college student, 18, South Asian, individual interview

This assessment of, and concern with, far-right activity also formed a key aspect of many respondents' analyses of the causes of the disturbances in Bradford, Burnley and Oldham in 2001:

> They [the BNP] brought all the racist issue to the top again, even when it had died down, it just came, then they became 'Britain for the British', 'we don't want this', 'we don't want that', and it all came to the surface . . .
>
> Male, FE college student, 19, South Asian,
individual interview

For those who saw far-right activity as highly determining of political discourses, there was some dissatisfaction with the responses of local authorities and the national government to this issue. Such views were expressed on several occasions when respondents raised the prospect of far-right organisations being permitted to stage a march in Birmingham:

> *Respondent*: . . . the NF march I think they allowed that to happen because they were protesting, freedom of speech, but they knew that there was gonna be a riot but . . .
> *Interviewer*: Which NF one is this?
> *Respondent*: In Bradford OK? By knowing that was gonna happen, oh OK they probably didn't know it was gonna happen or not but by it happening now there's gonna be another march in Alum Rock and it's allowed.
>
> Female, FE college student, 18, South Asian,
individual interview

7.1.1.3   *Voices or noises? The interpretation of the disturbances of 2001*

The disturbances in Bradford, Oldham and Burnley over the summer of 2001 were identified particularly by black and minority ethnic respondents as a political issue and this was connected with their analysis of racism in British society. Coverage of the disturbances of 2001, however, has tended to focus on disaffected youth, rather than issues of far-right activity (Bagguley and Hussain, 2003). Thus, the responses of politicians and social commentators to the disturbances tended to express concerns that ethnic minority, and especially Muslim, youth were politically disaffected. The Home Office's follow-up report to the Cantle Report noted that the 'disengagement of young people from local democratic processes is clear to see . . . ' (2002, p. 23).

There are parallels in the ways in which the 2001 disturbances were reported and analysed with the disturbances of the early 1980s in Brixton, Toxteth and Handsworth (Solomos, 2003). In both periods, there were divergences between those reports that viewed the disturbances as 'riots' and explicable by reference to the attitudes and cultural outlook of black and minority ethnic communities (the pathologising arguments); those that focused on socio-economic deprivation and saw the 'riots' as disorganised expressions of frustration and resentment; and those that saw the 'riots' as confrontations and inherently political (Benyon, 1986; Solomos, 2003). Dikeç (2004), in his study of social unrest in the French banlieues in the 1990s, argues that a key issue at stake in the analysis of such events is the ideological struggle over the definition of such events as 'noises' or 'voices'. Such differences in the assessment of the disturbances were expressed among our respondents. In particular, the analysis of 'riots' differed across ethnic groups. Generally, our South Asian and black respondents were much more likely than white respondents to see rioting as a way for communities to have their voices heard or as a means of challenging racism – or indeed for their problems to be made visible:

> when it comes to that you have to make a statement and let people know that yeah you are there and you're not just gonna be pushed about. The community itself – they're not being heard, or whatever the case may be, so therefore they have to make themselves be seen. A lot of people think it is when that they're not being heard, the only way to be heard is to create a scene. That way you will definitely get some attention y'know, because society itself don't hold with violence, but a lot of people do turn to violence for the only resource.
>
> Female, homeless hostel, 18, black, individual interview

> *Respondent 1*: I think it's built up so much in their head because no-one's done something about it. I mean some things tend to build up and build up.
> *Respondent 2*: Obviously it started out with racism.
> *Respondent 1*: But in their heart it will explode and it will explode out of a person when it tends to build up in their head. Well I think that's what's happened. I think that's why: 'we've done all that to get some attention or get something across', that: 'hello! Are you

gonna do something about it? Well we can do something about it' –
so I think they've just taken control and power yeah.

Females, FE college students, 18 and 20,
South Asian, focus group

Oh is it Oldham? Yeah like that there must have been some racist
thing that was happening and they're just putting their point across,
so they're participating 'cos it's happened to them.

Female, FE college student, 18, South Asian,
individual interview

Some people have ways of showing their emotions in different ways,
some resort to violence, some resort to other methods of releasing
anger, d'y'know what I mean? And they're now, they're just gonna
think, I'm petrol bombing this, petrol bombing that, causing destruc-
tion: y'know what I mean? But people look up to 'em though 'cos,
y'know what I mean, for what they're doing and that and that's how
they get their boosts to do what they do.

Male, FE college student, 20, black, focus group

I think they're doing that, 'cos they're trying to put across a
point ... the Bradford riots were a minority of people, but the fuel
was there.

Male, FE college student, 21, South Asian, focus group

Some expressed a general discomfort about justifying violence, whilst
arguing at the same time that the disturbances had happened for a
reason, as the anxieties expressed by these respondents of Pakistani and
Pakistani/English origin suggest:

it's their anger, because maybe they're trying to show their point, but
they're maybe not being listened to, or they're trying to get attention,
in a bad way. Whereas to them, they, they're maybe people doing
it for a laugh or whatever, or there may be certain people who are
doing it to put a point across, they'd rather be heard, and they think
that it's an important issue, because like that, it looks like a riot or
something, and maybe that could have been stopped, if you know
what I mean, if they were being heard.

Male, FE college student, 18, South Asian,
individual interview

I don't think big scale, big scale violence, I don't think is justified at all. But local, small scale can be justified in a way that people can understand . . .

Male, sixth-former, 18, South Asian, white,
individual interview

Most black and South Asian respondents tended to identify causes of the disturbances and were frequently critical of institutional responses to them, as the comments by two young women FE college students show:

Respondent 1: I think the police turned a blind eye to that [the disturbances in Bradford, Burnley and Oldham] as well, cos y'know you hear them saying, the Asians saying 'oh well', y'know, 'we've been telling the police and they haven't done anything about it' and y'know, to them it might sound like minor things that just gonna blow over but look what it turned into now and what are they gonna do now?

Respondent 2: They should have done something before but they never, they just turned their backs on them.

Females, FE college students, 18 and 20,
South Asian, focus group

Where they were not supportive of such action, some South Asian respondents denounced them because of the negative impact they would have for minority groups:

Respondent: So they're making trouble in their own area, but innocent people maybe really be discriminated against because of the trouble, do you understand, because of the tension between whites and Asian, whites or blacks, or whatever.

Interviewer: Do you think it brings to a head then, or makes it worse, or?

Respondent: I think it makes it worse, yeah. Because at the moment, their behaviour caused a riot. Or take an example, Bradford, where there is quite a lot of racism in Bradford, and most of the businesses there, restaurants and that, they're all with English people and you know, white people, who eat all the food and that, but now that the riots have happened, and I've been there just there after the riots, and it's all completely dead. It's like a no-go area now . . .

Interviewer: for?

Respondent: Well, for like, I'm not just saying whites, there are whites walking around, but people may because of the tension there, because of the divide, people are fearing to go there. And at the end of the day, if you look logically at the aspect, it's their own people who suffer: the businesses and that. I mean the businesses are things people will want, do you understand? So, in a way they lose out, and in a way they . . . so I mean, it's not, I don't think it's a good thing.

Male, FE college student, 18, South Asian, individual interview

These responses resonate with Bhavnani's (1991) study of black young people's assessments of the implications of the disturbances of the 1980s. She found that some respondents were uncomfortable with rioting as a form of action, fearing that it would serve to reinforce stereotypes about black people.

Our white respondents, on the other hand, tended to focus on the violent aspects of the disturbances and saw them as unjustifiable in principle:

I don't think it's justified at all . . . I think violence is always wrong even if somebody starts with violence, then it's difficult to react effectively without using violence again, but the violence should never have been started in the first place.

Male, university student, 21, white, individual interview

I think I understand the issues involved which would incite this sort of behaviour, but at the same time I absolutely hate violence of any kind and I think it doesn't deal, . . . I mean there it's a racial issue and they're not helping their issue by becoming violent. I think you know in, you know, however many years that Britain and the IRA have been dealing with each other and the northern Ireland problem has been going on, in all those years violence has achieved nothing and it does not make people back down and I think that violence between these sides isn't going to improve each other's opinion of each other with their respective opinions and I think it's really just so destructive. I don't think it's a good idea at all.

Female, university student, 21, white, individual interview

I remember the talk about violence and yeah it kind of shocked me really. I don't think that there's ever a need for this kind of violence. I think it's more damaging than it is anything else. And yeah, OK, it makes people listen but it makes people prejudge the issue before because if someone burnt the building down then they're not necessarily going to sympathise.

> Female, university student, 21, white, individual interview

Maybe I'm not in their circumstances, but I just think that it just, well, the bad thing is that whatever message they're trying to get across by using the violence, it makes people kind of turn away from it and what they're trying to say and it detracts from that and they think, you know, they come across as more kind of thugs and stuff.

> Female, university student, 21, white, individual interview

Rioting's not really right in any sense of the word but the reasons that were behind this were stupid – religion or stuff.

> Male, sixth-former, 18, white, focus group

7.1.1.4 Community voices and the failures of representative institutions

The analysis of street disturbances as an expression of frustration or a stand against being ignored was closely linked for many with their perceptions of the lack of representation and accountability of mainstream political institutions. As one (Pakistani-origin) sixth-former argued,

> I think having a good representation . . . with respect to there of the rioting: had an Asian person from that area been in the House of Commons or someone Asian high standing within the House of Commons, perhaps they felt he could have associated with them better than someone else could have, because he's been through similar histories as they may have done . . . so it is important to get a good spread of people, so that more and more people can associate with them and become more personal with politics . . .
>
> Male, sixth-former, 17, South Asian, individual interview

There was a strong perception across all our groups that political and public institutions failed to represent Britain's ethnic and cultural diversity. Generally, the expectation that political institutions should reflect the diversity of the society that young people inhabited was coupled with a perception that they failed to do so.[2] The perceptions among our respondents that Parliament and politicians failed adequately to represent ethnic diversity had a negative impact on many respondents' assessment of their ability to address issues relating to ethnic inequalities and racism.

If the politicians started mixing with different races, they might understand about what people actually need and maybe they could make a difference.

Male, FE college student, 19, South Asian,
individual interview

And like you don't really hear MPs and whatever making state-ments saying like something needs to be done, or maybe I'm just not watching the news enough, but I haven't heard them mention anything about racism, about how to stop it and I haven't seen them try. I haven't seen them going out of their way to do something, organise something, an organisation or something. I haven't seen them do that. And I haven't seen them go deep into it, y'know, find out what's causing it, what they can do to prevent it.

Female, FE college student, 20, South Asian,
individual interview

Respondent 1: I don't really think MPs, the Prime Minister, MPs are gonna listen. Not until something really happens.
Respondent 2: Bet they all just think it's just another letter, y'know, about racism, and it happens, it comes and it goes, it'll be there for a few days and it will blow over.

Females, FE college students, 18 and 20,
South Asian, focus group

There are a number of studies which argue that the under-representation of black and minority ethnic groups in Parliament is a key factor in the lower levels of electoral engagement among these groups (Purdam *et al.*, 2002). Yet, many respondents, across ethnic groups, commented on the narrow social base of Parliament and, for many, this created a perception of Parliament as being unlike the society that they themselves were familiar with and therefore contributed to their sense that Parliament is 'full of people, people like me can't relate to'. The failure of Parliament to reflect back to our respondents the diversity of their own society created a perception among them that it was out of touch with people's lives and concerns. In other words, poor representation of black and minority ethnic groups was not only an issue that undermined black and minority ethnic young people's assessment of political institutions, but created scepticism about these institutions' accountability and responsiveness across all ethnic groups. As one white hostel resident commented, most of them are just snobby white people to me, and I wouldn't give them the time of the day, I wouldn't, and I'm white myself . . . because they're always sitting in a room full of the same sort of people, not going out there talking to the people in the streets.

Male, homeless hostel, 23, white, individual interview

In many respects then, our data reflect Bang's (2003) argument that young people frequently share in common with Everyday Makers the expectation that politics should involve the recognition of difference. This expectation is linked with his argument that the political is increasingly seen as a form of self-actualisation, which is linked with an expectation that their own and other people's identities should achieve expression and recognition through politics. In other words, the recognition and inclusion of ethnic and cultural difference (as well as gender, age and class difference) lie at the core of how young people expect politics to be expressed, and this sentiment was echoed across interviews with white university students:

really important to have a cross section of opinion and very important . . . full of too many men (laughs) to be honest! Middle-aged men, particularly, like the House of Lords and yeah it would be good to get a lot more women involved and then like people from different cultures to have their opinions and stuff as well. I think they're getting better, but for them it's very much the minority of people they're getting from different cultures and ages and genders and stuff so . . .

Female, university student, 21, white, individual interview

7.1.1.5 Community activism as racism/politics-free

This negative assessment of how mainstream politics expressed issues relating to 'race' and racism was contrasted by one FE college student with his experience of political action at a local community level. In this particular case, even though politics was conflictual, it was viewed positively because it was viewed as connected to, and representative of, local communities:

There was no, we were all against one person, we were against the Council, we were forcing the Council to do the park up, and that would be it, and the Council there's no, we don't see the Council as being racist at all, because it's the Council . . . and the Council doesn't get racist – not like politics at all.

Male, FE college student, 19, South Asian,
individual interview

In common with many of our black and minority ethnic respondents, he viewed politics inherently as an expression of racialised divisions – as evidenced by his assessment of community action as free of racism and 'not like politics at all'. His view of community activism as racism-free, and hence non-political, is extremely interesting in terms of what it reveals about his views of political institutions. It also suggests why he was much more likely to engage in local community actions rather than with mainstream politics.

7.1.1.6   Accountability and public institutions

These expectations about diversity of representation, equality and accountability applied also to other public institutions such as schools, the NHS and the police. Solomos (1988) and Benyon (1986) argue that experiences of discriminatory policing practices, combined with the tendency for young black men especially to be objects of police attention, serve to politicise both policing practices and the young people involved. Among black and minority ethnic respondents particularly, perceptions of unequal treatment in relation to policing were frequently highlighted by men and women as problematic and prevalent:

> so behind closed doors it's all, it's all different. It might look sweet when the officers are out and about in the street and thinking, oh they're looking after us. But you don't know what's going on inside of them . . . I don't think I've got faith in police officers at all . . . I think they don't, I'm not saying that they don't do their job, right, I think it's their attitude towards society, you know what I mean?

Female, FE college student, 17, South Asian,
individual interview

> *Respondent 1*: Being black on a Friday night (laughs) or swearing, yeah they've done that to me before, took me saying I was swearing when I never and I was cautioned for it as well. It was just stupid.
>
> *Respondent 2*: There is always a minority, they will never stamp out racism even some times when you walk around, you see some officers and it's there.

Respondent 3: That's happened to me a few times – seriously.
Respondent 2: And why at the end of the day? Because they're racists.

Male, FE college students, 17–19, black and
South Asian, focus group

Another young South Asian respondent reported that he thought his peer group's perceptions of, and trust in, the police had deteriorated in recent years.

Interviewer: Do you think it's getting worse now, or was it always like that?
Respondent: I doubt it was always like that. If it was, it was less evident to us. We wouldn't have saw it like that. We probably would have just had a laugh. But now racism has come into it, nobody is having a laugh at all. Now it's, there's a copper over there, it doesn't matter. A few years ago, we would have had a laugh, we'd probably walk up to them and take the mickey, and that would be it. They'd take the mickey back: 'ah you're bald', 'you're this' and: 'you're a copper, you sit in a car all day', that's it. But now, no-one goes up to a copper anymore. It's like: 'it's a copper, let's walk away'.
Interviewer: So what's happened, that you're worried about now approaching them.
Respondent: /just what would happen if we approached to them. Would there be a racial clash, would they beat the crap out of us? That would be it. Tactics of just being afraid. Everyone's afraid.

Male, FE college student, 19, South Asian,
individual interview

In one focus group of black, mixed ethnicity and South Asian male FE college students, respondents linked these issues of discriminatory practices, which they saw as being a feature of police conduct, to wider issues of accountability:

Interviewer: So you think that it [policing practices] can't be changed?
Respondent: I think it can if police put more public points of views, y'know that the police have got their badge number there? Say that police officer is going on disrespectful, they should have advertisements on the telly saying that if a police officer is being disrespectful in any way you can make a complaint or even the one's that are good positive attitude you can have a certain hot line that you can phone up give the badge number and d'y'know what I mean?

Male, FE college student, 19, black, focus group

The perception of a lack of accountability and diversity in such institutions had a highly negative impact on respondents' assessments of these institutions. As in the case of political institutions, there was a widespread view that institutions such as the police should be representative of diversity in order to be properly accountable and effective in addressing issues relating to identity and difference:

> I think it's absolutely essential for [the police force] to represent all the different groups . . . because you know Britain, the face of Britain has changed now . . . And you know there's issues to be understood with different races and different groups and I think, you know, to have people involved in the police force who know and like have personal experience of these different groups is going to do nothing but benefit the police force.
>
> Female, university student, 21, white, individual interview

In addition, principles of both gender and ethnic representation were frequently invoked, as this sixth-former (of Pakistani-origin) maintained when describing his encounter with police in making his daily journey across Birmingham to attend school:

> it has been in the papers quite a lot just a while ago it would suggest that there is racism in the police prejudice in the police force, it is true . . . you see very few coloured people in the police force whether you're inside or outside the police station. For example, I go by train every morning and there are police officers at the New Street train station, different ones every few days and they're mostly white, or white males. You'd think that if they were trying to promote a fair image, if they had a fair image and they're trying to promote it, they'd have more Asian people and females visible so people would perhaps think that these reports by the press and media are unfounded but by the fact there isn't and all we see is white males generally we can only assume that what the what the papers say is true and there is institutionalised racism . . .
>
> Male, sixth-former, 17, South Asian, individual interview

7.1.2   Ethnicised geographies and political engagement

In this section, we argue that lived experience is bound up in the ways in which young people experience a multicultural society in their everyday lives. In particular, our data drew attention to the ways in which young people experienced diversity simultaneously with highly ethnicised urban geographies, and this was manifested in their views about mobility, equality, personal safety, community and a sense of belonging.

Pilkington and Johnson (2003) suggest that, within youth studies, there has been a move towards seeing youth identities within the framework of reflexive modernity (see Chapter 2 for a discussion of reflexive modernity), where lifestyle and consumer choices form the basis of young people's identities – rather than more stable collective identities based on class, ethnicity and so on. Citing Miles, they suggest that youth studies increasingly see young people's identities as constructed through 'deterritorialized lifestyles that are as flexible as the world around them' (2003, p. 265). In this view then, paradoxically, 'modern' ethnic identity constructions are used by young people to stabilise their everyday lives, in a post-modern environment where such categories are increasingly destabilised. However, Pilkington and Johnson are critical of the lack of empirical content to such theorising, as well as its lack of awareness of the *local* contexts in which global, post-modern cultural forms are enacted. It is in these contexts, they suggest, that 'modern' identity markers, such as gender, 'race'/ethnicity and class, may in fact retain their resonances (2003, p. 266). In this respect, we agree with Pilkington and Johnson's contention that the reflexivity of young people's identity needs to be refracted through an understanding of the structures that shape them. In particular, we found that local spaces are stable reference points in young people's accounts of their identity and materially determine young people's experiences and expectations – particularly in relation to the ways in which they view racial divisions within the city. As Caroline Knowles points out, 'Race is generated in the social texture of space, and so the analysis of space reveals its racial grammar, as forms of social practice to which race gives rise' (cited in Back, 2005, p. 31).

Additionally, many writers have emphasised the significance of *urban* local contexts to black and minority ethnic identity and politics. Keith (2005), for instance, argues that issues of racial divisions and intercultural dialogue must be understood in relation to the urban context in which they take place, whilst Gilroy (1987, p. 228) points out that 'Britain's "race" politics are quite inconceivable away from the context of the inner city.' Similarly, Goldberg (1993) observes the racialisation of urban space in the body politic of the city and argues that racialised space conditions access to resources, education, employment and so on. Such issues are certainly vividly expressed in Birmingham, and issues relating to ethnic diversity, multiculturalism, segregation, race equality and changing identities were clearly reflected in our respondents' views of politics, their own identities and their local spaces.

In this respect then, the fact that the research was conducted in Birmingham was highly significant for the analysis of these particular issues. As noted in Chapter 3, Birmingham has a large and diverse black and minority ethnic population (of 29.6 per cent according to the 2001 Census). Birmingham City Council actively promotes an image of Birmingham as a global and multicultural city, positing the city's ethnic diversity as an integral part of its heritage and key to its future success (Bhattacharya, 1998) and this ethnic diversity is reflected in the local geographies and cultural life of the city. Nevertheless, Birmingham's ethnic minorities are clustered in nine of Birmingham's 40 wards,[3] and seven of these wards[4] are estimated to have 'at least 75 per cent of their population falling within the 10 per cent most deprived Super Output Areas[5] in England', according to Birmingham City Council, indicating that they are among the most deprived areas in the country. Indeed, a report commissioned by Birmingham City Council, following the release of the Report of the Stephen Lawrence Inquiry in 1999, found evidence of a highly segregated city, where ethnic minorities are socially excluded and geographically segregated. The Commission's report, *Challenges for the Future – Race Equality in Birmingham* (2001), described the city as a 'doughnut' of deprived inner-city ethnic minority areas surrounded by white middle-class suburbs. It also highlighted the persistent under-representation of black and minority ethnic groups in the public life of Birmingham. At Birmingham's first Race Summit, held in January 2003, Council Leader Albert Bore acknowledged, 'it is clear that some parts of our communities, particularly our young people, continue to experience high levels of unemployment, low educational achievement etcetera, and they feel therefore that they have little stake in this City' (2003). These patterns of deprivation and spatial concentration among Birmingham's black and minority ethnic groups were factors invoked in explanations of the disturbances that occurred in the Lozells area in Birmingham in 2005.

7.1.2.1   'Race' and space

Our data show that there was a very strong awareness of the ways in which the city expressed ethnicised geographies and racialised divisions. For instance, many respondents from different sites and ethnic groups identified particular areas of the city with high levels of racism:

> It was a good school, I went to Cardinal Wiseman, but that was racist, a lot of NF, not the school, the school was a good school alright, but the area . . .
>
> Female, New Dealer, 17, black, individual interview

My area is very racist . . . you see it everywhere. Like Kingstanding [an area of Birmingham] NF, Kingstanding APL, you know what I mean, Anti Paki League, or whatever. And er, KKKK, which is Kingstanding Ku Klux Klan. And you know, I just look at it and I think, well why? You know, there's no point to it. My best friend, she's black, you know, I have to watch my back when I walk down the street with her, and you know people, they don't just see the person they see the colour. Around my area, and it shouldn't be like that man, I've had a hiding because of it. I took her out for a meal, to treat her, and I got beat up in the restaurant, all eating, and you know there is a very lot of racism. It's just not as exposed as up north you know, televised and that. Yeah, there is a lot of racism.

> Male, New Dealer, 23, white, individual interview

back where I used to live in Chelmsley Wood, most of the people I mixed with, black and white, was so small minded. They did not understand at all Slavs, Muslims or Afghanistanis or Pakistanis or anything at all they just did not understand it and because they did not understand it, all they could do was criticise, d'y'know what I mean? And a few lads I know used to go around all the time looking for Asians, particularly males, and beat them y'know and these were just innocent Asian lads . . .

> Male, homeless hostel, 23, white, focus group

A strong theme of the responses of the young people in Birmingham was their experiences of segregated everyday lives and their perceptions of certain city spaces as highly ethnicised:

at sixth form college I met mixed races, but even in high school I still had respect for say Asian people and black people even though I didn't meet any until I went to sixth form. So for me, I didn't really think that there was a race problem but coming to Birmingham . . . I've noticed it more and I think you can notice it in the town centre, there's a divide I think between black and white people.

> Female, university student, 21, white, individual interview

7.1.2.2 Traversing ethnicised geographies

There were a variety of accounts of the impact of such geographies on people's mobility within the city. For this sixth-former, of Indian origin, the city's ethnicised geographies were experienced in terms of restricted mobility:

> For me, I've, I have actually got a lot of hassle and all that off my cousins and, look, like my parents support me all the way, but my cousins and my friends are thinking well 'why you want to do that?' 'You're going into a white area, you're not, how can you adjust to them? You're going to be surrounded from morning to night, 24/7 a day by white people, how can you adjust? You can adjust as much as you want, you'll end up just being white.' But I've said 'no I won't, because I'll change them as well, I'll change, yes, but so will they'. That's why they've said 'if you go in there you'll lose who you are' but I said 'no, I won't'...
>
> Male, sixth-former, 16, South Asian, individual interview

In contrast, for others, boundaries between certain areas were not traversable and the city was seen as segregated:

> Basically... there's whites versus Asian. I've been told that 'keep away from here', 'don't go here', 'don't go Solihull anymore because... you're an Asian person'... 'and you're gonna be on your own'... and it's like why? 'Ah because we heard this is going to happen', 'this is going to happen'. And everyone's walking around looking scared and watching their backs. And you see with white people, you see them and they actually step aside when there's, this is a fact now, I was at the cinema last week I think it was, and there was five or six of us, a couple of black people, the rest of us was all Asian, and we were walking through town and we got looks.
>
> Male, FE College Student, 19, South Asian, individual interview

> I mean, if I brought a black person down to see some of the people I knew in a certain area where it was majority white, you know, they'd just stare, you know, they wouldn't, they'd be like 'nah man'. I mean I lived there, and I didn't see a black person until I was about eight years old and I was, you know, I was a bit thrown back when I saw it, I was like what's that? You know, I'd never seen it before, you know, and now it's just like a normal thing, black, white, Asian, whatever, you know, whatever you are, they treat you the same. You know, if you treat me fair, I'll treat you fair, you know.
>
> Male, New Dealer, 23, white, individual interview

For many, such ethnic segregation was viewed as highly problematic as was suggested in one group interview with two young South Asian women attending FE college:

> *Respondent 1:* . . . and Alum Rock is like full of Asians, packed out, and I don't know how they done it.
> *Respondent 2:* And in Alum Rock they've written on the walls like 'no white people after a certain hour' . . . It's not very nice. It's horrible innit? And then like, you know, a white person's gonna see that and go 'alright then', go back into his area, no blacks, no Asians, in certain areas. Y'know, it encourages them when they see things like that.
> *Respondent 1:* That's horrible. It's like an eye for an eye.
>
> Females, FE college students, 18 and 20,
> South Asian, focus group

7.1.2.3 *Ethnicised geographies and 'safe spaces'*

For some respondents, however, living in majority black or South Asian areas as a young black or South Asian person provided a sense of community and security. In other words, for some, being a member of the majority ethnic group within an area or in certain spheres provided a positive experience of an 'alternative black public space' (Dudrah, 2002). One respondent (of Indian origin) felt there were positive aspects to his own experience of living in an area where there were few white people:

> I mean myself, I live, I actually live in an area which actually doesn't have many white people: there's a lot of Asians and a lot of black people around my area, but I do live with other white people. And there's, it might sound stupid, but the white people are actually a minority for once and they'd actually learned they had to adjust to the world around them and they have, that's why everybody can get along. But even if there's equal parts I think you should still be able to get along 'cos you can adjust to whoever who's who.
>
> Male, sixth-former, 16, South Asian, individual interview

Similarly, one young woman, who described herself as British and Asian, living in an area of Birmingham where whites constituted a minority, observed,

> I've never really experienced any racism from around here, that's a lot, there's a few white people, there's a lot of blacks, there's a lot,

there's a lot of Asians. I've got on with them but I've always kept myself to myself, y'know? And yeah and I've never really experienced any sort of racism here.

> Female, FE college student, 20, South Asian, individual interview

Back (1996, p. 106) warns against loading into such responses a perception of such areas as an 'inner-city Eden', however. Given that inequalities between areas are highly significant in Birmingham, this warning is pertinent.

7.1.2.4 'Mixing in': Young people's vision for the future

Across most respondents (with some notable exceptions, as we shall see below) a recurring theme was the importance of different ethnic groups 'mixing in' and it was striking that the motif and language of 'mixing' was used and referred to across our range of groups. Many sociologists are unhappy, however, about the term 'mixing' particularly when it is applied to 'race' (see, for example, the British Sociological Association's Equality and Diversity guidelines, 2005), because of its connotations of the existence of prior 'pure' 'races', or a belief in objective categories of 'race' (Hutnyk, 2005). Whilst our respondents may have meant many different things by the term 'mixing in', it seemed to us that this term was generally expressed within a discourse of difference, rather than necessarily or only informed by biological ideas about 'race' (although beliefs about the biological basis of 'race' were frequently expressed). In other words, this term seemed to us to be used by respondents to invoke claims about the desirability of living with and encountering difference at the level of everyday experience.

For example, the perception that mixing-in was crucial to resolving problems of racism was shared by many of our respondents from across different groups. One sixth-former felt that segregation was wrong in principle:

> I think you should have mixed areas I should, I don't think you should have a white area over here, a brown area over here, a black area over here.
>
> Male, sixth-former, 16, South Asian, individual interview

Several respondents from different ethnic backgrounds, including those who had grown up in majority South Asian schools, or majority white areas (which they described as racist), expressed their concerns about the lack of 'mixing in' that they had experienced themselves, and believed that mixed schooling was crucial for overcoming prejudice. As one young South Asian female student, commenting on the existence of mainly white, or mainly South Asian schools, argued,

> I think they should by putting people into schools they should do it fifty-fifty so everyone mixes in, and . . . by doing that all the racist remarks will stop because at a young age they're learning how to mix in with different colours.
>
> Female, FE college student, 19, South Asian,
> individual interview

Schools, in particular, were cited as key sites for mixing-in as a counter-measure to racialised boundaries. One British-Asian Muslim respondent argued that the mixing-in of young people was the key to the future resolution of ethnic conflicts. As such, mixing-in would equip young people to resist the bigotry of older generations. In this respect, he opposed the principle of faith-based, including Muslim, schools:

> it's all about how much people mix when they're kids, how much kids mix with different races and that's what makes the difference when you're older. You get told that black is white, or white is white, and then it's all confusing and you just stick with that, but when you're younger, you can make your own mind up. As you grow older, you grow in that mixture of people, like when there are black people who you've grown up with and you think that's not all that bad. He's alright. White people aren't all that bad, because he's not bad, and I know him, and I know his parents, I stayed over at his house one night, and no-one said anything to me, and his brothers and sisters, they're alright, they can't be all that bad a person as well . . . I think there are the ones that say – oh no, it all has to come back to religion. You may be Pakistani but you may be also Muslim, just because you live in this country, it doesn't mean that you stop being a Muslim. It all comes back to the Islamic schools and all that, which drum into people that we should be separate, so that you can't get corrupted. And, I don't know about that.
>
> Male, FE college student, 19, South Asian, individual interview

Those who had experienced mixed schooling felt that it had contributed to the easing of tensions over racism.

> Yeah, it probably starts from when they get to school – if they're not mixed, you know, they ain't gonna know other people's cultures, or

other people, they're just gonna know pure white people, or pure black people, and that's no good. At the end of the day, it's like, my school was well mixed, you know, there was all sorts man, I've got loads of black friends, and Asian friends, and I've even got gay and lesbian friends you know. And luckily I've been brought up to think like that.

Male, New Dealer, 23, white, individual interview

I wouldn't say [colour] was an issue now like it was years ago. You'll still get some people – oh you black this, oh you white that; it's their ignorance basically, it's how you're brought up. If you're brought up in that atmosphere you will carry on with it, but if you're not it isn't, 'cos schools nowadays, they're totally mixed. There's a lot of wide-ranging people. You've got people from all over the world even and you get children interact with different kinds of people so from that age group they grow up knowing different things.

Female, New Dealer, 19, black, individual interview

This perception that mixing-in was crucial to resolving problems of racism was shared by many of our respondents from across different groups. One white respondent from the New Deal group argued,

The only thing you can do is give 'em an insight. So I wouldn't have like just like round here [in a mainly white area of Birmingham], or new just Asian schools, just black schools, just white schools. I'd just throw them all together, you know, and then let them learn other people's countries, let them become mates with black people and gradually over a period of time, through the school, hopefully it will die out. . . . if they're not mixed, you know, they ain't gonna know other people's cultures, or other people, they're just gonna know pure white people, or pure black people, and that's no good.

Male, New Dealer, 23, white, individual interview

Other respondents talked of communities and community centres as key sites for 'mixing-in':

I think just visiting communities, different communities, and seeing how y'know, how it's done, how kids mix in with other races and y'know you go out and interviewing kids and what their point is sitting them down and making them think but putting good things in their mind not saying you should hang around with your colour and it's wrong putting good things in their head kids from a young age y'know they know it's good that we're all one that we should mix altogether.

Female, FE college student, 18, South Asian,
individual interview

Despite the perception that ethnicised barriers to mobility operated within the city, and that there were high levels of segregation, there was among most of our respondents a frequently and keenly expressed desire for what might be termed 'cosmopolitanism'.

I'd like to go somewhere where it's mixed, properly, loads of whites, loads of blacks, loads of Asians. I know it's not, racism it's gonna take a lot to stop it . . . It is, and, you know, to go into an erm a one-coloured area, your chances are high in, y'know, experiencing racism. I do believe that. So I'd like to go somewhere where it's properly mixed, where people haven't got a problem with colour . . .

Female, FE college student, 20, South Asian,
individual interview

7.1.2.5 White identity and 'local patriotism'

As suggested above, this vision of Birmingham expressed by an array of our respondents stood in contrast to that expressed by one partic- ular group of young white men, whose views on Birmingham's diversity and multiculturalism were much more defensive. These young men, attending sixth form in a predominantly white working-class area of Birmingham, viewed their local area as synonymous with white iden- tity, evoking what Back has described as 'local patriotism' (1996). Many of these young men reacted negatively to the prospect of ethnicised boundaries being crossed. Such sentiments were expressed particularly in relation to rumours that a community centre on a square in their local area which had closed down was due to re-open as a mosque. This was viewed extremely negatively by the group and as opening their area out to those who were not from their own (white) community:

It's not the best area in the world, and there is trouble, and I think bringing, building a place in where like where we live for people like of a different religion to come from out of the area to use it then yeah people are going to have a problem with it no matter who it is it doesn't matter what religion, if you're building something for someone else to come in and use it when it should be for us, then, yeah, people will have a problem with it . . .

> Male, sixth-former, 17, white, individual interview

but the worst problem was is that hardly any of the people like Asian people or Muslims or from a different religion live round here, so there is obviously more people gonna come in . . . [it's a] predominantly white area, yeah, so obviously when they found out it was for Muslims it was obvious that people were gonna come in out from the area and use our space or whatever, that's what it was mainly about, that's what it's all about, it's nothing really to do with the religion it's just cause there's no, it's a white area really, there's like about one family that's probably well Muslims that live round this area, that live by the square so it's obvious that they're gonna come from outside this area.

> Male, sixth-former, 17, white, individual interview

over in [the square], they're building a mosque aren't they, so, you know, I mean that will influence people to come to [this school] if they're gonna live local. I wouldn't be surprised if in the next couple of years, everything's gonna change.

> Male, sixth-former, 18, white, individual interview

There was agreement among members of the group that the citing of the mosque on the square was an attack on community rights and this was interpreted as signifying the neglect of their community on the part of the local Council:

the council's focusing on other people 'cos they like, 'cos [the community centre has] been closed down, it's been closed down for a while and people from our area put in, let's get it as a community centre or whatever, and all of a sudden we found out ah someone's bought it, we've let some other people use it, I mean especially, I mean this is the thing, I mean it was a different religion right to start with, it was a problem for some people . . .

> Male, sixth-former, 17, white, individual interview

Although the respondents shared a consensus that the square was a white area, the topography of the square itself suggests something rather more complex given that several of the enterprises there are run by minority ethnic entrepreneurs. Thus, the square features a balti restaurant and a Chinese takeaway. Parker (1995) and Ram *et al.* (2002) point to the invisibility of minority ethnic groups operating such enterprises. In addition, the disputed centre itself displayed evidence of the contested nature of the interpretation of community rights. On the wall of the centre, some graffiti had been amended so that the message daubed there read 'Racists [daubed over the original word] Out [original word].'

The hostility raised by these respondents to the idea of opening their area out to ethnic diversity indicated the purchase of both racist discourses as well as multiculturalist discourses about community rights. In other words, much of the group's attack on the siting of the mosque was justified by positing whites as a disadvantaged ethnic group in their 'own' country. In common with many contemporary right-wing ideological campaigns for 'rights for whites', targeted particularly at white working-class areas, the respondents posited this in terms of cultural encroachment especially by Muslims into white communities:

> with a different religion, if they like want to celebrate like and do like erm, carnivals in town, no one has a problem with it, but say like, I dunno, say or even a sport like, say all the English went out and there would be like riots, like it would be in the paper the next day saying what a disgrace and whatever, so it's much easier for the other religions than just the English people just to go out and have a good time and everything without like being saying like these are thugs or hooligans these are going to cause trouble.
>
> Male, sixth-former, 17, white, individual interview

> if we went into a predominantly Muslim area, and wanted to build like, use one of their centres, like a white area then it would be exactly the same, probably even worse... It's alright for them 'cos the council backs it up as well, the government. It's alright for them to come into the like, to use our, say if wanted to have planning permission for an area where it was mainly Muslims lived, or other religions, then it would be kicked up and probably kicked out, saying 'no you're not doing that'.
>
> Male, sixth-former, 17, white, individual interview

Although a running feature of such discussions among this group was the use of the term 'religion' to refer to non-white groups, we did have different religions [in our school], like black and Asian people, but everyone was fine, we all got on well. Whether it was different in other years I don't know, I'm not sure. Generally we do have our fallings out and stuff, but it was nothing like over because you are black or whatever, anything like that, it was just y'know someone did your head in or whatever or you didn't agree with what they were saying.

Male, sixth-former, 17, white, individual interview

The group then tended to see multiculturalism as a strategy that ought to confer upon them a defensive space, into which their own, white, community could retreat. The reactions of our respondents to issues relating to 'race' and space confirm Brah's contention that 'both black and white people experience their gender, class and sexuality through "race"'. She notes, furthermore, that 'Racialisation of white subjectivity is often not manifestly apparent to white groups because "white" is a signifier of dominance, but this renders the racialisation process no less significant' (cited by Nayak, 1999, p. 73). Whilst Nayak (1999) points to the history of research on youth subcultures which focus on the intersections between 'racism' and 'class' in the construction of white, working-class identities, he also points out that these can obscure questions as to why such expressions of identity are also gendered, and why it is that not all white, working-class men invest in such identity constructions. Indeed, our own data flag up these very questions – whilst some of the young women we met at the same site shared the young men's formulations of their own community as under attack, these were much more marginal views among the women, and, when such views were expressed, they were always contested. Furthermore, young white, working-class men who we encountered in other sites did *not* subscribe to this particular construction of white identity.

7.2 Conclusion

To conclude then, it is clear from the above that issues relating to identity, ethnicity and 'race' have a clear impact on young people's conceptions of the political and political institutions. Our data show how these conceptions are expressed at the level of lived experience very clearly in relation to urban spaces. These findings demonstrate how racialised political discourses, mono-ethnic political institutions and ethnic segregation shaped young people's perceptions of political and public institutions. Clearly, these processes had very different impacts across our respondents and, particularly, in relation to the way they articulated the political implications of issues relating to racism, 'race' and difference.

Yet, such perspectives counter the notion that young people's disengagement from mainstream political institutions can be read as a simple story of political apathy. For many of our respondents, perceptions of political institutions as unrepresentative, unaccountable and unresponsive to issues of racism and ethnic equality offer a powerful account of their disengagement from these institutions.

Conclusion

As always in research of this sort, there are a large number of conclusions that can be drawn. Here, we begin by briefly summarising our findings about the extent to which young people are apathetic or alienated. Subsequently, we focus on our core concern, how young experience politics; in our terms identifying in what ways politics is a structured lived experience. Following this, we return to the work of Henrik Bang and discuss whether new forms of political participation are developing; in particular to what extent and with what possible consequences a new type of Everyday Maker participant is emerging. The final section of this conclusion turns to the question of the nature of British democracy and what our research suggests about the future of democracy and citizenship in the UK and how it might be invigorated.

Apathy or alienation?

As we argued at the outset, much mainstream literature on political participation and media discourses see young people as politically apathetic. In essence, this is because politics and political participation are too narrowly defined. So, many researchers have tended to focus on participation in terms of voting, joining a political party or interest group, contacting public officials, or going on a demonstration. Consequently, when they find low, and in most cases declining, levels of participation of this sort among young people, they read this as evidence that young people are politically apathetic. Such a view is often shared by the government who view declining voting among young people in particular as a problem, reflecting what might be seen as a democratic deficit. However, if we take a broader view of politics and political participation, then our research suggests that most young people are not politically apathetic. Indeed, the quotations in earlier chapters indicate that many are, in fact, highly articulate about the political issues that affect their lives, as well as about the disconnection between these and mainstream politics. For example, the depth of feeling was expressed among young women in one of our focus groups in relation to local housing issues sat alongside a general antipathy to participation in electoral politics. It seemed clear to us that it is not political apathy that accounts for their resistance to voting.

In our view, we can't merely measure political participation in terms of the respondent's responses to the type of questions in Pattie *et al.*'s (2004) study. That is not to say such data are irrelevant; indeed, it is very useful and Pattie *et al.*'s work represents a major step forward from previous quantitative studies. However, in our view, we need a better understanding of how people understand politics and, as such, to view politics as a lived experience.

As Bang argues, viewed in this way the decline in formal political participation is not a 'free rider' problem, but rather a problem of political exclusion. Although some young people may be politically apathetic, in our view, the more serious problem is that many are alienated from the existing political system. It is evident that many of our respondents felt that they were marginalised or excluded from political decision-making. As such, it is perverse to suggest that their non-participation in formal politics reflects apathy. As Giroux (2003, p. 184) argues in the context of America:

> The growing attack on youth in American [*and, we argue, British*] society may say less about the reputed apathy of the populace than it might about the bankruptcy of old political languages and orthodoxies and the need for new vocabularies and visions for clarifying our intellectual, ethical and political projects, especially as they work to reabsorb questions of agency, ethics, and meaning back into politics and public life. [Our observation in italics.]

Indeed, it is impossible after reading our focus groups and interviews to see our respondents as non-political. It is true we found no one who was active in formal politics, although there were several whom Bang might regard as Everyday Makers. However, most of our respondents lived politics; they were consistently faced with the consequences of politics and often recognised these experiences as 'political'. At the same time, they saw politicians as remote and uninterested in them. While they often recognised politics affected them, they felt they had no chance of influencing it. Formal politics was something 'done unto' them and they, particularly those with less economic, cultural and social capital, had to constantly negotiate the consequences of being the objects of political institutions and processes. The key point here is that, if we treat politics as something outside people's experience, that is, in a sense, as merely something that is 'done unto' them, then we ignore how people view, experience and live politics. Yet, we almost inevitably do that if we start from most social scientists' understanding of politics.

By carrying out an in-depth exploration of young people's conceptions of politics, rather than surveying young people's attitudes towards a limited range of political issues and arenas, we can begin to develop a much more nuanced understanding of the relationship between their lived experiences and their engagement and interest in politics. For instance, as we have seen, data from one focus group of young men revealed their very low levels of political efficacy, which was related to their view of politics as a series of authority relationships, in which they saw themselves as having only a passive role. We can also see the ways in which some young people viewed politics as a site or mechanism for achieving change, whilst perceiving few opportunities for participation at a national level, a perception that was exacerbated by failure of political institutions to properly express the social and ethnic diversity that they saw around them.

Politics as structured lived experience

Our approach has been to view politics as a lived experience, encompassing what Mouffe (1993) and others (see, for example, Rasmussen and Brown, 2000) describe as a struggle over identity. Unlike Mouffe, however, we see politics as a *structured* lived experience. As such, we see questions of class, gender, ethnicity and youth as part of the way in which individuals negotiate their political identity. Our respondents' experiences of age, class, gender and ethnicity were both structured and political, and many saw it as such. In other words, the economic, social and cultural resources that young people had access to shaped their experiences and these in turn shaped their definitions of politics and views of political institutions. We develop this argument through a brief consideration of each of these elements of young peoples' experience.

Youth

As we have argued, age did have an impact on the ways in which our respondents politically engaged. In particular, certain life-cycle effects were evident in shaping the issues that they viewed as politically significant (such as access to education, training, employment, welfare and community resources). As we suggested, there was a very clear view expressed by our respondents that their interests and concerns were not being addressed by politicians. Furthermore, there was a strong sense that their ability to enter into political arenas was significantly hampered by perceptions of them as 'political apprentices' rather than political agents. Hence, very few respondents perceived any mechanisms for substantive involvement through which they could bring about change. Our data suggest that young people perceived their political citizenship to be highly limited and this perception underpinned their disinclination to engage with formal, mainstream politics, although we found evidence for engagement in more local, *ad hoc* and community-orientated action. We are in agreement with Philo and Smith (2003), however, that the valorisation of the arenas and practices that young people *do* engage in should not lead us to disregard the ways in which 'adult political domains' structure young people's lived experiences.

Class

It is hard to read the transcripts of our focus groups and interviews and conclude that class doesn't exist or matter. Our respondents rarely talked of class, but they certainly lived it. The groups we talked to with limited access to economic capital knew they had little, and that many had much more, and appreciated how that affected their life chances. Many viewed these issues as inherently political.

In relation to how we understand the relationship between politics and class, Bourdieu's work, in our view, has a great deal to offer. First, our data convince us that while class is a lived experience, it is an experience rooted in, but not determined by, structured inequalities. Secondly, our respondents often agreed, although without using Bourdieusian terminology, that that there is a link between economic, cultural and social capital.

Indeed, the results of our sorts, discussed in Chapter 5, were particularly interesting. In our two least privileged sites, the focus group members regarded the vast majority of our images as political, while the sort in our most privileged sites indicated a much narrower, arena-based definition of politics and one which closely paralleled Pattie *et al.*'s understanding of politics. In our view, this reflects the fact that politics and the State penetrated much deeper into the life of our less privileged respondents and, consequently, they saw politics as something that affected their day-to-day lives (in often negative or coercive ways). We reiterate a point we have made a number of times, politics is something our respondents, particularly our more disadvantaged respondents, lived.

Gender

Our respondents were more likely to talk about gender than class, although there was an obvious relationship between gender and class among our respondents. So, it was our disadvantaged women who were more likely to talk about gender and gender inequalities. Our middle-class female respondents, and most of our male respondents, tended to use a liberal discourse of equal opportunities; arguing that gendered inequality was reducing and opportunities were increasingly available to women. In particular, they saw education as a way of achieving greater gender equality. In contrast, our less privileged female respondents were well aware of the constraints on their social mobility through education.

As such, our female respondents lived gender, but they did so differently, largely dependent on their access to economic, social and cultural capital. Indeed, in our view, class doesn't wash out gender divisions, anything but, rather it reinforces them. Consequently, our data would seem to support a second-wave, materialist feminist, position. To put it another way, as with class, we think our analysis shows how economic, cultural and social capital are related and how the experiences of our disadvantaged, working-class, women are shaped by their lack of these capitals.

Ethnicity

It is evident from our respondents that issues relating to identity, ethnicity and 'race' shaped their lived experiences. Furthermore, our respondents were much more likely to name issues of 'race' and ethnicity as political than they were to cite gender or, especially, class. In part, this may reflect the city, Birmingham, within which the research was conducted, given it is one of the most multi-ethnic cities in the UK, although writers such as Pakulsi and Waters (1996) and Bang (2003; 2004) might argue that issues of identity and difference are increasingly coming to the fore of individuals' political imaginaries. One might perhaps expect this to be particularly expressed among the young.

The differences between the ways in which our respondents narrated youth, class, gender and ethnicity were interesting. They might suggest that ethnicity is the most important source of our respondents identity and, certainly, this is the way our results would be interpreted by authors such as Pukulski and Waters (1996), given they argue that class certainly, and gender increasingly, are no longer key social divisions which shape social and political attitudes and behaviour. In contrast, we would argue, on the basis of our data, that class and gender are still important social divisions which shape people's lives and experience. To put it another way, choice is not open: those with less access to economic, social and cultural capital have fewer choices. As such, we would argue that class, gender and ethnicity are all crucial lived experiences which have political dimensions. However, they cannot simply be read off in the identities, attitudes and behaviour of young people. They result in 'political' action, with political here used in the sense of the narrower understanding of Pattie *et al.* (2004), only to the extent to which people recognise such structural inequality, and that there are mechanisms through which those individuals can be mobilised politically. Many of our disadvantaged respondents recognised that their unequal access to economic, social and cultural capital constrained their choices, although they never narrated this inequality in terms of class and rarely in terms of gender.

Our data demonstrate nevertheless how racialised political discourses, mono-ethnic political institutions and ethnic segregation shaped young people's perceptions of political and public institutions. These processes had very different impacts across our respondents and, particularly, in relation to the way they articulated the political implications of issues relating to racism, 'race' and difference. Again, such perspectives counter the notion that young people's disengagement from mainstream political institutions can be read as a simple story of political apathy. For many of our respondents, perceptions of political institutions as unrepresentative, unaccountable and unresponsive to issues of racism and ethnic equality offered a powerful account of their disengagement from these institutions.

Bang on?

We argued in the Introduction, Chapter 1 and, especially, Chapter 2 that Bang's work offers an interesting contribution to the current discussions of political participation. In particular, we focussed on Bang's argument that a new type of political participant is emerging, the Everyday Maker. If Bang is right, and particularly if there are a growing number of Everyday Makers (for an attempt to assess this quantitatively, see Li and Marsh, 2006), then people, perhaps especially young people, are redefining politics as part of their 'lived experience'. Everyday Makers would not be seen by most of the mainstream literature as involved in politics; or at least only in so far as they also voted. However, Bang's claim is broader and it is a view shared by Mouffe (1993): identity does not shape politics, rather political action is a crucial way in, and through, which

Everyday Makers construct their identity. In large part, this is an empirical question: how common are Everyday Makers and how important is 'politics as doing' in constructing their identity?

In our view, Expert Citizens are a feature of modern polities, but that is a subject for further study. Here we focus on Everyday Makers, particularly examining three of Bang's contentions: Everyday Makers do not relate to concepts of right and left and are critical of politicians and parties; they participate on the lowest level, in concrete issues and on a short-term basis; and they are disengaged from the state, neither seeking influence within it, nor engaging in opposition to it.

Our respondents were cynical about politics and politicians. There was a dominant perception that politicians were disconnected from the lives of ordinary, and especially young, people; this was exacerbated for most by the inadequate number of black and minority ethnic, female or young politicians. Our respondents' view that politicians ought to be demographically representative tends to confirm Bang's view that Everyday Makers see politics as being about the recognition of difference. The failure of political institutions to adequately recognise difference is thus seen as deeply negative and this has implications for the future of British democracy which we return to below. At the same time, the hostility among our respondents towards seeing politics as an expression of ideological differences also confirms what Bang describes as a preference for community organisation.

As we have already emphasised, very few of our respondents could be characterised as conventional participants. We found no party members and only few members of single-issue groups, and none of our respondents could be described as activists in the conventional sense. Those who had actual experience of political participation tended, overwhelmingly, to have participated in local community actions or campaigns. Consequently, respondents expressed higher levels of political efficacy in relation to local participation, in sharp contrast to their lack of political efficacy in relation to the national level.

However, contra Bang's argument, our respondents' conceptions of the political tended to be intensely state-centred, with many of our disadvantaged respondents believing that their lives were constantly determined by the state. In our view, many young people do view the state as shaping their life-chances and experiences, but their unwillingness to engage in state-oriented political action is a demonstration of their very low levels of political efficacy. In other words, young people and especially disadvantaged young people, did not see the state as irrelevant to their everyday lives. Indeed, they tended to believe that the state had a big impact on their lives and this was connected to their very low levels of political efficacy, because they felt it was unresponsive and did not think that they could have any impact on it.

In this respect, we argue that age, to an important extent, structures young people's political participation, particularly in the ways in which it operates as an obstacle to their participation. Thus, Philo and Smith's (2003) warning against collapsing the political into the personal is a useful one because it alerts us to the need to address some of the specific processes and factors that give rise to young people's political exclusion (and one could draw similar conclusions in relation to ethnicity, class and gender).

It seems to us that Bang's work deserves more attention and empirical investigation (see Li and Marsh, 2006 for an attempt to test Bang's arguments using quantitative data). By broadening the focus of studies of political participation, Bang moves attention away from a concern with the free rider problem to a consideration of the role of government in extending or constraining democracy, a point we focus on in the next section.

The future of British democracy

The most important question raised in discussions of political participation concerns what a decline, or a transformation, in participation tells us about the future of citizenship, or more broadly democracy, in the UK. We would argue that, to a large extent, one's view on the extent of participation, the meaning and consequence of any change in participation and what, if anything, needs to be done to broaden participation depends upon the normative conception of citizenship which one adopts.

As we emphasised in Chapter 2, if one operates with a liberal conceptualisation of citizenship, then the problem is apathy. Some liberals would probably suggest that, to the extent that people don't vote or participate more widely, this indicates that they are satisfied with the way the polity functions. In contrast, other liberals would suggest that, if people don't participate, even when they are unhappy with the polity, that is a matter of individual choice. However, the majority of liberals would probably contend that they need to encourage people to take part in the formal political arena, and to vote at least. This might be done by making voting easier, perhaps by using more postal ballots, voting in shops, voting via the Internet and so on. In contrast, a social liberal conceptualisation would recognise that participation is related to resources and probably suggest that higher levels of welfare expenditure lead to higher levels of participation (see Lister, 2005).

Communitarians or civil republicans would also see the problem as one of apathy, but would focus on the obligations that citizens have to participate. To the communitarians the state needs to encourage, and perhaps even enforce, such obligations; a communitarian might even advocate compulsory voting, although that is a 'remedy' that might be most associated with the neo-conservative's position. On the other hand, the communitarian might favour the 'remedy' which would be advocated by civic republicans, that is, citizenship or civics education in order to inform individuals of both how the polity functions and their duty to participate to ensure a healthy polity.

In contrast, those operating with a more participatory view of citizenship, whether they are what we have termed 'radicals' or 'post-structuralists', have a very different idea of the problem. In this view, the problem is not apathy or 'free-riding'; rather it is alienation and unequal power structures. So, the problem lies in the nature of the political system, the inequalities of access to political resources and the distance of politicians from citizens. Consequently, tinkering with the system, by increasing the use of postal ballots or ICTs, will not address the real problems. More importantly, compulsory voting would mask, and indeed exacerbate, the problem. Recent calls by think tanks and government ministers for compulsory voting suggest that the problem of voter disengagement is one of apathy and the responsibility for that lies with citizens and that the act of voting is a duty rather than simply a right. In our view, the introduction of compulsory voting would allow governments to elide the factors underlying the democratic deficit expressed by falling electoral participation. Our data show that disengagement from electoral processes among young people flags deeper problems of the lack of responsiveness of political representative institutions to citizens and especially to young people, who are rarely directly addressed by politicians even in relation to issues that directly affect them. Instead, there are intense debates *about* young people, which tend to focus on anti-social behaviour, educational deficits, drugs, crime and so on in ways that rarely acknowledge the perspectives of young people themselves. Furthermore, given that a key factor underpinning many of our respondents' disengagement from representative political institutions is their experience of government in terms of coercive interventions in their lives, the introduction of compulsory voting we believe is more likely to compound their lack of efficacy and sense of themselves as agents able to act on political institutions.

Radicals would advocate a much more fundamental 'solution', which would involve both economic and political reforms. In economic terms, the stress here is on a much stronger concern with social justice and sees political alienation as bound up with social and economic inequalities. In political terms, reform at the level of both high and low politics would be necessary for the UK to move to a more participatory political system in which people were listened to and felt that what they had to say mattered. In this vein, participatory democracy theorists in particular would advocate the use of participative decision-making and deliberation across various political arenas in order to undermine elite domination of the political process.

Having briefly outlined different perspectives, we shall turn to exploring our own position in more depth, paying particular attention to the difficulties involved in establishing a thicker, more participatory, form of citizenship in the UK. This involves returning to the question of the nature of the British political tradition, which we raised in Chapter 2.

Democracy in Britain: The British political tradition and the democratic deficit

As we emphasised in Chapter 2, the New Labour Government embraced ideas associated with both liberal and communitarian/civic republican conceptions of citizenship. Liberal notions were particularly evident in the idea of citizen-consumers associated with public sector reform generally and welfare reform particularly. The communitarian and civic republican approach that emphasises duties rather than rights is evident in many of the initiatives around social exclusion and in the introduction of citizenship education. New Labour's putative move towards participatory governance is associated with more generalised trends from government through hierarchy, towards governance through networks.

Our argument, developed in Chapter 2, however, was that hierarchy remains the key mode of governance in the UK, a fact which reflects the emphasis on a limited liberal notion of representation and a conservative notion of responsibility in the British political tradition. As such, in our view, the move towards participative governance can easily be overestimated. Increased citizen involvement in the policy process at the lowest levels has been a feature of New Labour's governance, but, as we saw in Chapter 2, this does not necessarily reflect a move towards a more participatory democracy or an emphasis on an active citizenry with significant input into policy-making.

We want to emphasise three points here. First, in our view, participatory governance cannot occur in areas of 'low politics' unless it occurs also in the area of 'high politics.' Unfortunately, New Labour doesn't have a commitment to participatory democracy at this level. Gamble (2003, p. 101) argues, 'a democratic vision of a reformed British state, less centralised, more responsive, [. . .], is what New Labour requires, but has so far not produced'. However, while this seems to us to be an accurate judgement of what is needed, it fails to recognise that New Labour remains influenced by the British political tradition, an interpretation which, in our view, is supported by the fate of its constitutional reform programme (Marsh, 2005).

Secondly, and unsurprisingly given our first point, the shift towards participative governance is partial at best because only some groups are given an active role on the policy-making process. Of crucial importance to us is that one of the groups most often excluded from a more active role in citizenship is the young. Third, even when groups are consulted, this is often with the aim to enhance government's claims to legitimacy and increase government control, rather than to involve citizen's in the policy-making process. This process is exemplified in the variety of deliberative and participative initiatives that have been introduced at the local and neighbourhood levels, deploying a rhetoric of democratic inclusion and participation. Several critics have questioned the extent to which such strategies create space for *substantive* participation (Dryzek, 2000), suggesting they are often aimed at disciplining, rather than empowering, citizens (Newman, 2005c). For instance, according to Barnes *et al.* (2007), participatory initiatives at these levels have not been invested with real power, whilst highly centralised institutional frameworks have still persisted in shaping the practices of deliberative forums. In addition, they see many state-sponsored initiatives as an extension of governmentality rather than participatory democracy. Although they note that citizens sometimes disrupt such structures by 'refusing to play the game', this point recognises nevertheless that the 'game' is not set up to redistribute power between state and citizens.

Overall, like Bang, we think that the problem is not that young people are apathetic, or that there is an information and communication deficit, which might be solved by more political spin, but rather it is the elitist nature of the British political system. Government needs to listen to what people, and especially young people, are saying: they don't trust politicians and political parties and they have very low levels of political efficacy in relation to national politics, because they feel that politicians and government aren't interested in them or engaging with young people in relation to the issues that affect them. As we argued elsewhere (O'Toole *et al.*, 2003), 'political literacy cuts both ways'.

In our view, what is needed in the area of 'high politics' is a move towards a more participatory system in which citizens enjoy the possibility of an active citizenship within a structure of responsive and accountable governance. This would involve substantial constitutional change, with electoral reform, more effective scrutiny of the executive by the legislature and genuine freedom of information. It would also involve much greater subsidiarity and genuine participatory governance, with political decisions being taken at the most appropriate, that is the lowest, level, rather than in the centralised way they are at present. The first step must be to challenge the dominance of the British political tradition and, in particular, the supposed link between centralised government and effective government. We need to emphasise and proselytise an argument that most of our respondents would have no problem with: government doesn't inevitably know best.

As far as the area of 'low politics' is concerned, in our view we need a genuine move towards participatory democracy in which user-involvement, new localism and so on open up the possibility for citizens to engage in framing and deciding issues that concern them, rather than simply being mobilised by government to provide expertise for, or legitimacy to, its policy agenda.

In relation to young people, there are particular barriers to their inclusion and recognition within participative governance initiatives. In particular, we have argued, they are rarely acknowledged as expert citizens, even in relation to issues which do affect them, and young people tend to be regarded as *future* citizens (Wyness *et al.*, 2004). Despite the wave of initiatives in recent years aimed at increasing youth participation and inclusion, the political domain is still mostly regarded as an adult domain, with many initiatives seen as a means of inducting young people into the world of adult politics, rather than as a means of giving young people a political voice. In our view, participative governance initiatives can open up political spaces for young people to organise around and articulate the issues that concern them (O'Toole and Gale, 2006), but these need to be premised on the recognition of young people as full citizens, rather than as political apprentices.

Notes

Introduction

1. See also the special edition of *Journal of Youth Studies* on Youth and Politics, 2003, vol. 6, no. 3.
2. South Africa constitutes a notable exception to this trend.
3. Such views were expressed by those who saw the disturbances as primarily a confrontation between (Muslim) youth and the police. For a more nuanced analysis of these events, see Bagguley and Hussain (2003) and Hussain and Bagguley (2005).
4. Consequently, the UK Government is particularly interested in boosting turnout and, for that reason, has encouraged experimentation with postal, SMS and Internet voting – despite the misgivings expressed by the UK Electoral Commission about the security of such methods.
5. The Programme was made up of 21 individual projects representing a range of disciplines. It claimed that the 'high levels of citizen participation and strong civic norms that fostered political stability and effective policy-making' which characterised Britain in the 1950s have changed, 'and there is now a widespread perception that the political institutions of the British state are losing their effectiveness and legitimacy and that the policy-making process is not sufficiently democratically accountable'. They note that: 'These views appear to be a key motivating force behind the Government's current reforms' (see http://www.essex.ac.uk/democracy/).
6. ESRC Award: L215252015: *Explaining Non-Participation: Towards a Fuller Understanding of the 'Political'*.
7. It is also worth noting here the tendency to consider developments in the UK as unique. So, in this case political participation in the UK is too often viewed independently of developments elsewhere in similar countries. As such, any explanations of trends fail to use a comparative perspective, yet that is essential.

1 The study of political participation

1. The key features of the research design are outlined in Pattie *et al.* (2004, p. 30).
2. In particular, they report a growing awareness among their respondents that people will have to provide for their own retirement (Table 9.2). Nevertheless, they also report a fairly consistent commitment to higher tax and higher spending and suggest that this only fell during the early Thatcher period, when the government moved towards cutting tax and expenditure and this temporarily received popular support that quickly eroded (see Table 9.3).

Similarly, the demand for government to promote equality has also grown (Table 9.3).

3. They found that socio-economic factors, including, in particular, education, but also wealth, age and voluntary association membership, were the most important determinants of participation. Those with higher levels of socio-economic resources are most likely to participate, conversely the 'almost inactives' had the lowest levels of socio-economic resources.

4. For a discussion of the meaning of politics which, among other issues, deals with the distinction between arena and process definitions, see Leftwich (2004).

5. There is an implicit epistemological argument here which is discussed below.

6. To be fair, Pattie *et al.*, to a limited extent, avoid this problem by extending their definition of 'politics' to include both 'micro-political' action and consumer boycotts. In addition, they are also very careful to distinguish between disaffection and apathy.

7. For a more extended discussion of how political participation might be conceptualised, see O'Toole, Marsh, Lister, Jones and McDonagh (2003).

2 The context and consequence of political participation: citizenship and governance in the UK

1. We would like to thank John Dryzek and Andrew Knops for particularly useful comments on this section.

2. Although these are economic rights, particularly freedom from state intervention, rather than social or citizenship rights.

3. The normal distinction is between arena definitions, where politics occurs within formal political arenas, Whitehall, Westminster and town hall, and process definitions, where politics can, and does, occur in all social relationships and processes (see Hay, 2002, Chapter 2; Leftwich, 2004).

4. The liberal would expect a citizen to be involved to the extent that she/he benefits instrumentally from such participation.

5. In the UK, women only gained the same franchise as men in 1928.

6. Although classically Marxists argued that the private sphere, and particularly the economic and class relations within it, determined the public sphere, modern Marxism questions this view (see Marsh, 2002).

7. To Giddens (1994), a 'high-modern' period preceded reflexive modernism, or, as he prefers, 'institutional reflexivity'.

8. So, in this view, globalisation is both a consequence and a cause of this increased risk. Here, the focus is upon the globalisation of money markets and US economic, cultural, military and political hegemony. These changes accelerate risk.

9. In addition, and more broadly, Beck argues (1994a, p. 178) that increased risk has undermined the legitimacy of institutions such as the 'political parties, labor unions, science, law, national borders, the ethics of individual responsibility, [. . .] the nuclear family'.

10. It is worth emphasising here that these are much the same processes as those identified by Pattie *et al.* (2004) as leading to a renewed interest in discussions of citizenship.

11. These claims are expressed in New Labour's Civil Renewal, Neighbourhood Renewal and Active Communities programmes. According to the Home Office, 'Civil renewal is at the heart of the Home Office's vision of life in our 21st century communities' and this includes 'active citizenship', 'strengthened communities' and 'partnership' between public bodies and local people. See: www.active-citizen.org.uk.
12. Such initiatives are certainly not exclusive to the UK as Johansson and Vinden (2005) emphasise.
13. The distinction between 'high politics' and 'low politics' was invoked by Bulpitt as a key aspect of what he termed the 'dual polity theory' (1983). He argued that in areas of high politics (economic policy, foreign affairs, defence and, we would suggest, constitutional matters) British Governments (Bulpitt thought particularly Conservative Governments) jealously guarded their authority and were reluctant to share powers, whilst in areas of low politics (particular areas concerned with the delivery of services) they were less concerned and more willing to cede powers to local government. In the current situation one might extend the dual polity thesis to suggest that the area of low politics includes not only local government, and devolved government, but also most of the scope of the so-called 'network governance'.
14. Interestingly, Walters (2004, p. 36) argues in a similar vein: 'governance discourse seeks to redefine the political field in terms of a game of assimilation and integration. It displaces talk of politics as struggle or conflict. It resonates with "end of class" and "end of history" narratives in that it imagines a politics of multi-level collective self-management, a politics without enemies.'

3   Methodology

1. We acknowledge that this is sometimes a difficult distinction to make. For a more detailed discussion of the relationship between quantitative and qualitative methods, which broadly reflects our position, see Marsh and Read (2002).
2. Bourdieu and Wacquant (1992) see fields as objective relations of difference that both reflect, and are relected in, differential access to the various forms of capital. As such, the precise structure of the field is determined by the overall volume of capital that agents in the field possess.

4   The politics of youth

1. This type of accommodation is made available to young homeless people on condition that they undertake education or training.
2. In 2001 the Department for Education phased out the standard post-16 qualification, the A (Advanced) level (based on a two-year full-time course), and replaced it with a two-tier qualification, comprising the AS and A2 levels (where the one-year AS course results in a stand-alone qualification, which may lead to entry to a further one-year A2 course to

achieve a full A level). This reform was not piloted and the first generation of completers received their results in 2002 amid controversy over the marking criteria and allegations that thousands of students had been unfairly marked down. Following re-marking of over 90,000 entries, 1945 students were awarded higher grades; see Department for Education and Skills news release: www.dfes.gov.uk/qualifications/news.cfm?page=0&id=89 (accessed 15.10.02).

5   Class as a lived experience

1. Goldthorpe distinguishes between three basic class positions – employers, self-employed workers and employees – but these groups are then subdivided, to produce 11 categories in the fullest categorisation, although those are often reduced to seven, or even five, by authors conducting empirical studies.

2. The aim was to develop a more theoretically grounded and empirically useful classification. The new classification identifies 27,000 occupations that are reduced to 353 occupational groups, which are further combined for most purposes to produce eight social class categories (see www.statistics.gov.uk/methods_quality/ns_sec/). Like the Goldthorpe schema, it aims to differentiate categories according to the labour market position and the work situation of a typical employee in a given occupational category. The assessment of a person's labour market position is based upon the source of income, economic security and prospects of economic advancement in the particular job they hold. The assessment of an individual's work situation is based upon the location of the job in the system of authority in the workplace and the extent of autonomy involved in the job. The key thing to note about the NS-SEC is its intention to ground the class categories in theoretical and conceptual work on class in Sociology; in this respect Goldthorpe's work was crucial, as is clear to anyone who compares the NS-SEC classification with the previous Goldthorpe's classification; as such, the classification is rooted in a neo-Weberian conception of class.

3. In fact, they distinguish (1996, p. 5) between class theory, in which, they argue, class is the sole determinant of outcomes, and class analysis, which sees class as a privileged explanatory variable.

4. Interestingly, Pakulski and Waters don't make clear their ontological position. However, they argue strongly that economic class did structure society in early capitalism – suggesting they do not take an anti-foundationalist position. Yet, their description of contemporary society has a very culturalist, even anti-foundationalist, tinge.

5. For example, Pakulski and Waters argue (1996, p. 79), 'if class is dependent on the distribution of material property then an equalized redistribution of that property is consistent with the decomposition of class'.

6. It is also worth emphasising, as Skeggs (2000, p. 21) does, that: 'Class as the central object of analysis has a different place in the different theoretical spaces in Sociology. Those who work on education and health have never noticed a retreat from class in the same way as those who work on feminism, race and sexuality.'

7. As Devine and Savage (2002, p. 195) put it: 'What establishes the relationship between class and culture (i.e. what establishes the classed nature of cultural dispositions) is not the existence of class consciousness, or the coherence or uniformity of a distinct set of cultural dispositions. Rather, the relationship is to be found in the way in which cultural outlooks are implicated in modes of exclusion and domination.'

8. Bourdieu also identifies a fourth type of capital, symbolic capital, which involves the acknowledgement and legitimation of other forms of capital; it is this legitimation process that converts capital to power. Consequently, cultural capital has to be legitimated before it can have symbolic power.

9. In fact, Bourdieu distinguishes between three forms of cultural capital: embodied, objectified and institutionalised.

10. So, as Skeggs argues (2000, p. 14): 'What ultimately defines cultural capital as capital is the ability to convert it into economic capital.'

11. So Devine and Savage (2002, p. 193) argue, 'there is still a tendency in Bourdieu's work to "reduce" cultural forms to specific material bases and to adopt an instrumentalist orientation to culture. Despite his own intentions, a somewhat crude and simplistic economic determinism still underpins his account of the relationship between class and culture.'

12. Savage offers three criticisms of this aspect of Bourdieu's work, arguing that he: (i) proposes a cultural hierarchy, with middle-class taste seen as superior and the increasing existence of what Peterson and Kern (1996) call 'cultural omnivores', that is, people adopting aspects of 'high' and 'low' culture, ignored; (ii) pays no attention to popular culture; and (iii) fails to recognise both the stigmatisation and the importance of working class culture.

13. There was a turnout of 65.5 per cent in the 2002 referendum among council house tenants to approve a transfer of the city's housing stock to housing associations; a turnout which was more than double that at the local election. There was great political interest in this issue and the Council's policy was rejected by a 2/1 majority.

7 Young people and the politics of 'race', ethnicity and identity

1. The adjusted turnout takes account of over-claiming of turnout that surveys frequently report. The overall claimed turnout in this survey was 51 per cent, whilst the actual turnout in 2004 was 39 per cent. The researchers have therefore adjusted all disaggregated turnouts by 12 per cent to reflect this discrepancy. Their report concedes that it cannot establish whether the discrepancy between claimed and actual turnout is consistent across all ethnic groups.

2. Although the representation of black and minority ethnic groups (BME) in the House of Commons is higher now than it has ever been (Ali and O'Cinneide, 2002), with 15 BME members out of 646, the present level still greatly under-represents black and minority ethnic groups (proportionately this amounts to 2.3 per cent black and minority ethnic representation within the House, compared to 7.9 per cent of the population overall. If representation were to be merely proportionate to the general population, then we would expect to have at least 51 black and minority ethnic members in the House).

3. These nine are Aston, Bordesley Green, Handsworth Wood, Lozells and East Handsworth, Nechells, Soho, Sparkbrook, Springfield, and Washwood Heath. See the Economic and Strategy division of Birmingham City Council at www.birminghameconomy.org.uk/wards.htm

4. These seven are Aston, Bordesley Green, Lozells and East Handsworth, Nechells, Soho, Sparkbrook and Washwood Heath. See Birmingham City Council 2001 Census results at: www.birmingham.gov.uk

5. 'Super Output Areas' are the new system of measurement for deprivation indices used by the Office for National Statistics and other statutory agencies, which replace the old units of measurement based on ward. They are designed to be more stable than ward boundaries and more consistent in terms of population size. For further details, see www.statistics.gov.uk/geography/soa.asp

Bibliography

Alexander, C. *The Art of Being Black: The Creation of Black British Youth Identities* (Oxford: Clarendon Press, 1996).

Alexander, C. '(Dis)Entangling the "Asian Gang": Ethnicity, Identity, Masculinity', in Hesse, B. (ed.), *Un/Settled Multiculturalisms: Diasporas, Entanglements, 'Transitions'* (London: Zed Books, 2000).

Ali, R. and O'Cinneide, C. *Our House? Race and Representation in British Politics* (London: Institute for Public Policy Research, 2002).

Amos, V. and Parmar, P. 'Challenging Imperial Feminism', *Feminist Review*, 17 (1984).

Anwar, M. 'The Participation of Ethnic Minorities in British Politics', *Journal of Ethnic and Migration Studies*, 27, 3 (2001), 533–549.

Back, L. *Who Represents Us? Racialised Politics and Candidate Selection* (London: Dept. of Politics and Sociology, Birkbeck College, University of London, Research Papers, no 3, May 1992).

Back, L. *New Ethnicities and Urban Culture: racisms and multiculture in young lives* (London: UCL Press, 1996).

Back, L. 'The Fact of Hybridity: Youth, Ethnicity, and Racism', in Goldberg, D.T. and Solomos, J. (eds), *A Companion to Racial and Ethnic Studies* (Oxford: Blackwell, 2002).

Back, L. ' "Home from Home": Youth, Belonging and Place', in C. Alexander and C. Knowles (eds), *Making Race Matter: Bodies, Space and Identity* (Basingstoke: Palgrave Macmillan, 2005).

Backett-Milburn, K. and McKie, L. 'A Critical Appraisal of the "Draw and Write" Technique', *Health Education Research*, 14 (1999), 387–398.

Bagguley, P. and Hussain, Y. 'The Bradford "Riot" of 2001: A Preliminary Analysis', paper presented to *Ninth Alternative Futures and Popular Protest Conference* (Manchester: Manchester Metropolitan University, 2003).

Baines, M., Newman, J. and Sullivan, S. Discursive Arenas. Case Studies in Participation (Bristol: Policy Press, 2007).

Bang, H. (ed.) 'A New Ruler Meeting a New Citizen: Culture Governance and Everyday Making', *Governance as Social and Political Communication* (Manchester: Manchester University Press, 2003).

Bang, H. 'Everyday Makers and Expert Citizens: Building Political, not Social, Capital' (Canberra: Mimeo, Politics Programme, Research School of Social Science, Australian National University, 2004).

Bang, H. 'Among Everyday Makers and Expert Citizens', in Newman, J. (ed.), *Remaking Governance: Peoples, Politics and the Public Sphere* (Bristol: The Policy Press, 2005).

Banks, M. *Visual Methods in Social Research* (London: Sage, 2001).

Barber, B. *A Place for Us* (New York: Hill and Wang, 1998).

Barnes, S. and Kaase, M. *Political Action: Mass Participation in Five Western Democracies* (Beverley Hills, CA: Sage, 1979).

Bashevkin, S. 'Training the Spotlight on Urban Citizenship: The Case of Women in London and Toronto', *International Journal of Urban and Regional Research*, 29 (2005), 9–25.

Bauman, Z. *Liquid Modernity* (Cambridge: Cambridge University Press, 2000).

Beck, U. 'Self-Dissolution and Self-Endangerment of Industrial Society: What Does it Mean?', in Beck, U., Giddens, A. and Lash, S. (eds), *Reflexive Modernisation: Politics, Tradition and Aesthetics in Modern Social Order* (Stanford, CA: Stanford University Press, 1994a).

Beck, U. 'The Reinvention of Politics: Towards a Theory of Reflexive Modernisation', in Beck, U., Giddens, A. and Lash, S. (eds), *Reflexive Modernisation: Politics, Tradition and Aesthetics in Modern Social Order* (Stanford, CA: Stanford University Press, 1994b).

Beck, U., Giddens, A. and Lash, S. *Reflexive Modernisation: Politics, Tradition and Aesthethics in Modern Social Order* (Stanford, CA: Stanford University Press, 1994).

Beer, S. *Modern British Politics* (London: Faber and Faber, 1965).

Bennett, W.L. 'The UnCivic Culture: Communication, Identity and the Rise of Lifestyle Politics', *PS: Political Science and Politics*, 31, 4 (1998), 741–761.

Bennett, W.L. 'Communicating Global Activism: Strengths and Vulnerabilities of Networked Politics', *Information, Communication and Society*, 6, 2 (2003), 143–168.

Bennett, W.L. 'Communicating Global Activism: Strengths and Vulnerabilities of Networked Politics', in van de Donk, W., Loader, B.D., Nixon, P.G. and Rucht, D. (eds), *Cyberprotest: New Media, Citizens, and Social Movements* (London: Routledge, 2004).

Benyon, J. 'Spiral of Decline: Race and Policing', in Layton-Henry, Z. and Rich, P.B. (eds), *Race, Government and Politics in Britain* (Basingstoke: Macmillan, 1986).

Bhattacharya, G. 'Riding Multiculturalism', in Bennett, D. (ed.), *Multicultural States* (Basingstoke: Routledge, 1998).

Bhattacharyya, G. and Gabriel, J. 'Racial Formations of Youth in Late Twentieth Century England', in Roche, J. and Tucker, S. (eds), *Youth in Society* (London: Sage, 2000).

Bhavnani, K.-K. *Talking Politics: A Psychological Framing for Views from Youth in Britain* (Cambridge: Cambridge University Press, 1991).

Birch, A. *Representative and Responsible Government* (London: Allen & Unwin, 1964).

Birmingham Race Action Partnership, *'Do They Mean Us?' BME Community Engagement in Birmingham* (Birmingham: Birmingham Race Action Partnership, 2004).

Birmingham Stephen Lawrence Commission, *Challenges for the Future: Race Equality in Birmingham* (Birmingham: Birmingham City Council, 2001).

Black Public Sphere Collective, *The Black Public Sphere* (Chicago: University of Chicago Press, 1995).

Blair, T. *The Third Way* (London: Fabian Society, 1998).

Bore, A. *Speech to First Birmingham Race Summit* (Birmingham: Birmingham Race Action Partnership, www.brap.org.uk/files/uploaded_files/race-summit-2003/albert-bore-speech.doc, 2003).

Bourdieu, P. *Outline of a Theory of Practice* (Cambridge: Cambridge University Press, 1977).

Bourdieu, P. *Distinction* (London: Routledge, 1984).

Bourdieu, P. 'The Forms of Capital', in Westport, J. (ed.), *Handbook of Theory and Research for the Sociology of Education* (New York: Greenwood, 1986).

Brah, A. *Cartographies of Diaspora: Contesting Identities* (London: Routledge, 1996).
Brandolini, A. and Smeeding, T. 'Patterns of Economic Inequality in Western Democracies: Some Facts on Levels and Trends', *PS: Political Science and Politics*, 39, 1 (2006), 21–26.
Bristol, T. and Fenn, E. 'The Effects of Interaction on Consumers' Attitudes in Focus Groups', *Psychology and Marketing*, 20, 5 (2003), 433–454.
British Sociological Association, *Language and the BSA: Ethnicity & Race* (Equality and Diversity Resources: www.britsoc.co.uk/user_doc/Non-Racist%20Language%20.doc, 2005).
Brooks, L. 'Kid Power', *The Guardian*, 26th April (2003).
Bulpitt, J. *Territory and Power in the United Kingdom* (Manchester: Manchester University Press, 1983).
Butler, J. *Gender Trouble: Feminism and the Subversion of Identity* (New York: Routledge, 1999).
Bynner, J., Elias, P., McKnight, A., Pan, H. and Pierre, G. *Young People's Changing Routes to Independence* (York: Joseph Rowntree Foundation, 2002).
Cannadine, D. *Class in Britain* (New Haven: Yale University Press, 1996).
Cantle, T. *Community Cohesion: A Report of the Independent Review Team* (London: Home Office, 2001).
Carby, H.V. 'White Woman Listen! Black Feminism and the Boundaries of Sister-hood', in Centre for Contemporary Cultural Studies, *The Empire Strikes Back* (London: Hutchinson, 1982).
Carey, M. 'Comment: Concerns in the Analysis of Focus Group Data', *Qualitative Health Research*, 5, 4 (1995), 487–495.
Castles, S. 'Towards a Sociology of Forced Migration and Social Transformation', *Sociology*, 37, 1 (2003), 13–34.
Clark, J. 'Creating Citizen-Consumers: The Trajectory of an Identity', paper delivered to CASCA conference (Ontario: May 2004).
Clark, J. and Newman, J. 'What's in a Name? New Labour's Citizen-Consumers and the Remaking of Public Services', paper delivered to CRESC Conference (Manchester: July, 2005).
Coleman, S. *A Tale of Two Houses* (London: Hansard Society, 2003).
Coles, R. *Youth and Social Policy: Youth Citizenship and Youth Careers* (London: UCL Press, 1995).
Connell, R.W. *Masculinities* (Cambridge: Polity Press, 1995).
Cornwall, A. 'Locating Citizenship Participation', *IDS Bulletin*, 33, 2 (2002), 49–58.
Crick, B. *Education for Citizenship and the Teaching of Democracy in Schools: Final Report of the Advisory Group on Citizenship* (London: Qualifications and Curriculum Authority, 1998).
Crompton, R. *Class and Stratification* (Cambridge: Polity Press, 2nd Edition, 1998).
Crompton, R. and Scott, J. 'Introduction: the State of Class Analysis', in Crompton, R. *et al.* (eds), *Reviewing Class Analysis* (Oxford: Blackwell, 2002).
Crompton, R., Devine, F., Savage, M. and Scott, J. *Reviewing Class Analysis* (Oxford: Blackwell, 2002).
Cruickshank, J. (ed.) *Critical Realism: The Difference it Makes* (London: Routledge, 2002).
Cunningham, S. and Lavalette, M. ' "Active Citizens" or "Irresponsible Truants"? School Student Strikes Against the War', *Critical Social Policy*, 24, 2 (2004), 255–269.
Curtice, J. and I.C.M. *The June 2004 Elections – The Public's Perspective* (London: The Electoral Commission, September, 2004).

Dalton, R. *Democratic Challenges – Democratic Choices. The Erosion of Political Support in Advanced Industrial Democracies* (Oxford: Oxford University Press, 2004).

Deacon, A. *Perspective on Welfare* (Buckingham: Open University Press, 2002).

Dean, H. *Welfare Rights and Social Policy* (Harlow: Prentice Hall, 2002).

DeLuca, T. *The Two Faces of Political Apathy* (Philadelphia: Temple University Press, 1995).

Dennison, C., Crosier, A., Goodrich, J., McVey, D. and Forrest, S. *Involving Young People in Peer Education: A Guide to Establishing Sex and Relationships Peer Education Groups* (London: Department of Health, 2002).

Desai, A. *We are the Poor: Community Struggles in Post-Apartheid South Africa* (New York: Monthly Review Press, 2002).

Devine, F. and Savage, M. 'Conclusion: Renewing Class Analysis', in R. Crompton *et al.* (eds), *Reviewing Class Analysis* (Oxford: Blackwell, 2002).

Dikeç, M. 'Voices into Noises: Ideological Determination of Unarticulated Justice Movements', *Space and Polity*, 8, 2 (2004), 191–208.

Dryzek, J. *Deliberative Democracy and Beyond: Liberals, Critics, Contestations* (Oxford: Oxford University Press, 2000).

Dryzek, J. and Berejikian, J. 'Reconstructive Democratic Theory', *American Political Science Review*, 87, 1 (1993), 48–60.

Du-Bois-Reymond, M. '"I Don't Want to Commit Myself Yet": Young People's Life Concepts', *Journal of Youth Studies*, 1, 1 (1998), 63–79.

Dudrah, R. K. 'Birmingham (UK): Constructing City Spaces Through Black Popular Cultures and the Black Public Sphere', *City*, 6, 3 (2002), 335–350.

Durish, P. (2002), "hhtp://www.cortlnd.edu/wagadu'issue1/miraftab 'Citizenship and Difference: Feminist Debates' *Annotated Bibliographic series of Transformative Learning Center* (Ontario: Ontario Institute for Studies in Education, University of Toronto, 2002).

Dwyer, P. *Welfare Rights and* Responsibilities (Bristol: The Policy Press, 2000).

Eden, K. and Roker, D. *'You've Gotta Do Something . . .': A Longitudinal Study of Young People's Involvement in Social Action* (Keele: Youth Research 2000 Conference, University of Keele, 2000).

Elander, I. and Blanc, M. 'Partnerships and Democracy: A Happy Couple in Urban Governance?', in Andersen, H. and van Kempen, R. (eds), *Governing European Cities: Social Fragmentation and Governance* (Aldershot: Ashgate, 2001).

Electoral Commission, *Election 2001: The Official Results* (London: Portico's, 2001).

Electoral Commission, *Black and Minority Ethnic Survey* (London: The Electoral Commission, 2005a).

Electoral Commission, *Understanding Electoral Registration: The Extent and Nature of Non-Registration in Britain* (London: The Electoral Commission, 2005b, www.electoralcommission.org.uk/files/dms/Undreg-FINAL_18366-13545__E__ N__S__W__.pdf).

Equal Opportunities Commission, *Sex and Power: Who Runs Britain?* (London: Equal Opportunities Commission, 2006, www.eoc.org.uk/pdf/sexandpower_ GB_2006.pdf).

Fahmy, E. *Ethnicity, Citizenship and Political Participation in Britain: Findings from the 2001 Home Office Citizenship Survey* (London: ESRC/ODPM, 2004, www.bris.ac.uk/sps/ESRC-ODPM/welcome.htm).

Faulks, K. *Citizenship* (London: Routledge, 2000).

Finch, J. 'It's Great to Have Someone to Talk to', in Bell, C. and Roberts, H. (eds), *Social Researching: Problems, Politics and Practice* (London: RKP, 1985).

232   *Bibliography*

Finch, L. *The Classing Gaze: Sexuality and Surveillance* (NSW, Australia: Allen & Unwin, 1993).
France, A. *Youth Researching Youth: The Triumph and Success Peer Research Project* (Leicester: Youth Work Press, 2000).
Franklin, M. *Voter Turnout and the Dynamics of Electoral Competition* (Cambridge: Cambridge University Press, 2004).
Fraser, N. *Justice Interruptus: Critical Reflections on the 'Post-Socialist' Condition* (London: Routledge, 1997).
Furlong, A. and Cartmel, F. *Young People and Social Change: Individualisation and Risk in Late Modernity* (Buckingham: Open University Press, 1997).
Gamble, A. 'Why Social Democrats Need to Rethink the State', in Browne, M. and Diamond, P. (eds), *Rethinking Social Democracy* (London: Policy Network, 2003).
Gamble, A. 'The Constitutional Revolution in the United Kingdom', *Publius*, 36, 1 (2006), 19–35.
Gaskill, G. *Qualitative Researching with Text, Image and Sound* (London: Sage, 2000).
Geertz, C. *The Interpretation of Cultures: Selected Essays* (London: Fontana, 1993).
Giddens, A. *Beyond Left and Right* (Cambridge: Polity Press, 1994).
Giddens, A. *The Third Way* (Cambridge: Polity Press, 1998).
Gilroy, P. *There Ain't No Black in the Union Jack* (London: Hutchinson, 1987).
Gilroy, P. *Small Acts: Thoughts on the Politics of Black Cultures* (London: Serpent's Tail, 1993).
Giroux, H.A. 'Betraying the Intellectual Tradition: Public Intellectuals and the Crisis of Youth', *Language and Intercultural Communication*, 3, 3 (2003), 172–186.
Goldberg, D.T. 'Polluting the Body Politic', in Cross, M. and Keith, M. (eds), *Racism, the City and the State* (London: Routledge, 1993).
Goldberg, D.T. *The Racial State* (Oxford: Blackwell, 2002).
Gottschalk, P. and Smeeding, T. 'Cross-National Comparisons of Income and Earnings Inequality', *Journal of Economic Literature*, 35, 2 (1997), 633–687.
Gottschalk, P. and Smeeding, T. 'Empirical Evidence on Income Inequality in Industrial countries', in Atkinson, A. and Bourguignon, F. (eds), *Handbook of Income Distribution* (Amsterdam: New Holland, 2000).
Gould, P. 'Labour Party Strategy', in Bartle, J., Atkinson, S. and Mortimore, R. (eds), *Political Communication: the General Election Campaign of 2001* (London: Frank Cass, 2002).
Griffiths, V. *Adolescent Girls and Their Friends: A Feminist Ethnography* (Aldershot: Avebury, 1995).
Hall, S., Critcher, C., Jefferson, T., Clarke, J. and Roberts, B. *Policing the Crisis: Mugging, the State and Law and Order* (London: Macmillan, 1978).
Harden, J., Scott, S., Backett-Milburn, K. and Jackson, S. 'Can't Talk Won't Talk? Methodological Issues in Researching Children', *Sociological Research Online*, 5, 2 (2000), http://www.socresonline.org.uk/5/2/harden.html.
Hay, C. *Political Analysis* (Basingstoke: Palgrave, 2002).
Haywood, C. and Mac an Ghaill, M. *Men and Masculinities: Theory, Research and Social Practice* (Buckingham: Open University Press, 2003).
Hebdige, D. *Cut 'n' Mix: Culture, Identity and Caribbean Music* (London: Comedia, 1987).
Henn, M., Weinstein, M. and Wring, D. *Young People and Citizenship: A Study of Opinion in Nottinghamshire* (Nottingham: Nottinghamshire County Council, 1999).

Henn, M., Weinstein, M. and Wring, D. 'A Generation Apart? Youth and Political Participation in Britain', *British Journal of Politics and International Relations*, 4, 2 (2002), 167–192.

Held, D., McGrew, A., Goldblatt, D. and Perraton, J. *Global Transformations: Politics, Economics and Culture* (Cambridge: Polity Press, 1999).

Henry, N., McEwan, C. and Pollard, J.S. 'Globalisation from Below: Birmingham – Postcolonial Workshop of the World?', *Area*, 34, 2 (2002), 117–127.

Hewitt, M. 'New Labour and Social Security', in Powell, M. (ed.), *New Labour, New Welfare State* (Bristol: The Policy Press, 1999).

Hiscock, D. 'The Apathy Generation', *The Guardian*, 9th May (2001).

Home Office *Guidance on Community Cohesion* (London: Community Cohesion Unit, 2002).

Hussain, Y. and Bagguley, P. 'Citizenship, Ethnicity and Identity: British Pakistanis after the 2001 "Riots"', *Sociology*, 39, 3 (2005), 407–425.

Hutnyk, J. 'Hybridity', *Ethnic and Racial Studies*, 28, 1 (2005), 79–102.

IDEA, *Youth Voter Participation: Involving Today's Young in Tomorrow's Democracy* (Stockholm: Institute for Democracy and Electoral Assistance, 1999).

Inglehart, R. *Culture Shift in Advanced Industrial Society* (Princeton: Princeton University Press, 1990).

Inglehart, R. *Modernization and Postmodernization: Cultural, Economic and Political Change* (Princeton, NJ: Princeton University Press, 1997).

Inglehart, R. and Welzel, C. *Modernization, Cultural Change and Democracy* (New York and Cambridge: Cambridge University Press, 2005)

Islin, E.F. and Turner, B.S. (eds) 'Citizenship Studies: An Introduction', *Handbook of Citizenship Studies* (London: Sage, 2002).

Istituto di Ricerca, *Study on the State of Young People and Youth Policy in Europe* (Milan: Istituto di Ricerca, 2001).

Janoski, T. and Gran, B. 'Political Citizenship: Foundation of Rights', in Isin, E.F. and Turner, B.S. (eds), *Handbook of Citizenship Studies* (London: Sage, 2002).

Johansson, H. and Vinden, B. 'Welfare Governance and the Remaking of Citizenship', in Newman, J. (ed.), *Remaking Governance: People Politics and the Public Sphere* (Bristol: Polity Press, 2005).

Jones, G. and Wallace, C. *Youth, Family and Citizenship* (Buckingham: Open University Press, 1992).

Jowell, R. and Park, A. *Young People, Politics and Citizenship: A Disengaged Generation?* (London: Citizenship Foundation, 1998).

Keith, M. *After the Cosmopolitan? Multicultural Cities and the Future of Racism*, (London: Routledge, 2005).

King, D. and Wickham-Jones, M. 'Bridging the Atlantic: The Democratic Party Origins of Welfare to Work', in M. Powell (ed.), *New Labour, New Welfare State?* (Bristol: Policy Press, 1999), 257–280.

King, G., Keohane, R. and Verba, S. *Designing Social Inquiry: Scientific Interference in Qualitative Research* (Princeton: Princeton University Press, 1994).

Kitzinger, J. and Barbour, R.S. *Developing Focus Group Research: Politics, Theory and Practice* (London: Sage, 1999).

Knowles, C. and Mercer, S. 'Feminism and Antiracism: An Exploration of the Political Possibilities', in Donald, J. and Rattansi, A (eds), *'Race', Culture and Difference* (London: Sage, 1992).

Kooiman, J. ' "Societal Governance" Levels, Models and Orders of Socio-Political Interactions', in Pierre, J. (ed.), *Debating Governance: Authority, Steering and Democracy* (London: Sage, 2000).

Krueger, R. and Casey, M. *Focus Groups: A Practical Guide for Applied Research* (London: Sage, 3rd Edition, 2000).

Kymlicka, W. *Contemporary Political Philosophy: An Introduction* (Oxford: Oxford University Press, 1990).

Laclau, E. *New Reflections on the Revolution of Our Time* (London: Verso, 1990).

Laclau, E. and Mouffe, C. *Hegemony and Socialist Strategy* (London: Verso, 1985).

Lamb, M. *Young Conservatives, Young Socialists and the Great Youth Abstension: Youth Participation and Non-Participation in Political Parties* (Unpublished PhD thesis, Department of Politics and International Studies, University of Birmingham, 2002).

Langford, B., Schoenfeld, G. and Izzo, G. 'Nominal Grouping Sessions Vs Focus Groups', *Qualitative Market Research*, 5, 1 (2002), 58–71.

Le Lohé, M. 'Ethnic Minority Participation and Representation in the British Electoral System', in Shamit Saggar (ed.), *Race and British Electoral Politics* (London: UCL Press, 1998).

Leach, S. and Wingfield, M. 'Public Participation and the Democratic Renewal Agenda', *Local Government Studies*, 25, 4 (1999), 46–59.

Lees-Marshment, J. *The Political Marketing Revolution* (Manchester: Manchester University Press, 2004).

Leftwich, A. *What is Politics: The Activity and Its Study* (Cambridge: Polity Press, 2004).

Li, Y. and Marsh, D. 'Bang to Rights: Searching for Expert Citizens and Everyday Makers' (Mimeo: Department of Sociology, University of Birmingham, 2006).

Lister, M. (2005) *The Social Foundations of Democratic Participation*, 'PhD. Department of Political Science and International Studies, University of Birmingham'.

Lister, R. *Citizenship: Feminist Perspectives* (Basingstoke: Palgrave, 2003).

Mahony, P. and Zmroczek, C. (eds) *Class Matters: Working-Class Women's Perspectives on Social Class* (London: Taylor and Francis, 1997).

Mair, P. and van Biezen, I. 'Party Membership in Twenty European Democracies, 1980–2000', *Party Politics*, 7, 1 (2001), 5–21.

Marquand, D. 'Marxism', in Marsh, D. (ed.), *The Decline of the Public* (Cambridge: Polity Press, 2004).

Marsh, D. 'Ideas and Institutions: The British Political Tradition and Constitutional Reform under New Labour' (Mimeo: Department of Political Science and International Studies, University of Birmingham, 2005).

Marsh, D. and Furlong, P. 'A Skin Not a Sweater: Ontology and Epistemology in Political Science', in Marsh, D. and Stoker, G. (eds), *Theory and Methods in Political Science* (Basingstoke: Palgrave, 2002).

Marsh, D. and Hall, M. 'Political Tradition(s): Beyond Bevir and Rhodes', paper delivered at Australian National University, Canberra (Mimeo: University of Birmingham, March, 2006).

Marsh, D. and Read, M. 'Quantitative Versus Qualitative Methods?', in Marsh, D. and Stoker, G. (eds), *Theory and Methods in Political Science* (Basingstoke: Macmillan, 2002).

Marshall, T.H. *Citizenship and Social Class and Other Essays* (Cambridge: Cambridge University Press, 1950).

Matthews, H. and Limb M. 'Another White Elephant? Youth Councils as Democratic Structures', *Space and Polity*, 7, 2 (2003), 173–192.

McAdam, D., McCarthy, J.D. and Zald, M.N. (eds) *Comparative Perspectives on Social Movements* (New York: Cambridge University Press, 1996).

McDonald, W.J. 'Focus Group Research Dynamics and Reporting: An Examination of Research Objective and Moderator Influences', *Journal of the Academy of Marketing Science*, 21, 2 (1994), 161–164.

McKinnon, C. and Hampsher-Monk, I. 'Introduction', in McKinnon, C. and Hampsher-Monk, I. (eds), *The Demands of Citizenship* (London: Continuum, 2000).

McRobbie, A. 'Sweet Smell of Success? New Ways of Being Young Women', in McRobbie, A. (ed.), *Feminism and Youth Culture: From Jackie to Just Seventeen* (London: MacMillan, 2nd Edition, 2000).

Merton, R., Fiske, M., and Kendall, P. *The Focused Interview* (Glencoe: Free Press, 1956).

Micheletti, M., Follesdal, A. and Stolle, D. (eds) *Politics, Products, and Markets: Exploring Political Consumerism Past and Present* (New Brunswick: Transaction Publishers, 2004).

Miraftab, F. 'Invented and Invited Spaces of Participation: Neoliberal Citizenship and Feminists' Expanded Notion of Politics', *Wagadu: Journal of Transnational Women's and Gender Studies*, 1, 1 (Spring, 2004), http://web.cortland.edu/wagadu/vol1-1toc.html (accessed July 2006).

MORI, *British Public Opinion: General Election June 2001* (London: MORI, 2001).

MORI, *Final Aggregate Analysis* (London: MORI, www.mori.com/polls/2005/election-aggregate.shtml, 16th May, 2005a).

MORI, *Black and Minority Ethnic Survey* (London: The Electoral Commission, May–July, 2005b).

Morrow, V. *Understanding Families: Children's Perspectives* (London: National Children's Bureau, 1998).

Mortimore, R. and Gill, M. *Don't Count On My Vote!* (London: MORI, www.mori.co.uk/pubinfo/rmm/dont-count-on-my-vote.shtml, 16th February, 2005).

Mouffe, C. *The Return of the Political* (London: Verso, 1993).

Mulvey, S. *The EU's Democratic Challenge* (London: news.bbc.co.uk, Friday, 21 November, 2003).

Munday, J. 'Identity in Focus: The Use of Focus Groups to Study the Construction of Collective Identity', *Sociology*, 40, 1 (2006), 89–105.

Murji, K. and Solomos, J. (eds) *Racialization: Studies in Theory and Practice* (Oxford: Oxford University Press, 2005).

Nayak, A. 'Performing Whiteness: Skinhead Culture and The Defence of White Masculinities', in Brah, A., Hickman, M.J. and Mac an Ghaill, M. (eds) *Thinking Identities: Ethnicity, Racism and Culture* (Basingstoke: Macmillan, 1999).

Newman, J. *Modernising Governance: New Labour Policy* (London: Sage, 2001).

Newman, J. (ed.). *Remaking Governance: Peoples, Politics and the Public Sphere* (Bristol: Polity Press, 2005a).

Newman, J. (ed.) 'Introduction', *Remaking Governance: People Politics and the Public Sphere* (Bristol: Polity Press, 2005b).

Newman, J. (ed.) 'Participative Governance and the Remaking of the Public Sphere', *Remaking Governance: Peoples, Politics and the Public Sphere* (Bristol: Polity Press, 2005c).

Newman, J. (ed.) 'Conclusion' *Remaking Governance: Peoples, Politics and the Public Sphere* (Bristol: Polity Press, 2005d).

Newman, T. 'Rights, Rites and Responsibilities: The Age of Transition to the Adult World' in Roberts, H. and Sachdev, D. (eds), *Having Their Say – The Views of 12–19 Year Olds* (Ilford: Barnardos, 1996).

news.bbc.co.uk 'Young "not turned off" by politics' (news.bbc.co.uk/1/hi/uk_politics/2541327.stm, 4 December, 2002).

Norris, P. *Critical Citizens* (New York: Oxford University Press, 1999).

Norris, P. *Democratic Phoenix: Reinventing Political Activism* (New York: Cambridge University Press, 2002).

Norris, P. 'Young People and Political Activism: From the Politics of Loyalties to the Politics of Choice?' (Mimeo: Harvard University, Report for the Council of Europe Symposium, 27–28 November, 2003).

Norris, P., Walgrave, S. and Von Aelst, P. 'Who Demonstrates? Antistate Rebels, Conventional Participants, or Everyone?', *Comparative Politics*, 37, 2 (2005), 89–205.

Okin, S. M. 'Humanist Liberalism', in Rosenblum, N. (ed.), *Liberalism and the Moral Life* (Cambridge, MA: Harvard University Press, 1991).

Operation Black Vote, *Into the Millennium* (London: Operation Black Vote, www.obv.org.uk/info/millmain.html, 1997).

Operation Black Vote, *Ethnic Minorities and the British Electoral System Research Report* (London: Operation Black Vote, www.democratic.org.uk/obv/docs/anwar.html, 1998).

Operation Black Vote, *Hopes and Fears of Ethnic Minorities in Britain* (London: Operation Black Vote, www.obv.org.uk/europe/euelection1999/hothouse.html, 1999).

Orton, M. 'Irresponsible Citizens? New Labour, Citizenship and the Case of Non-Payment of Local Taxation', *Critical Social Policy*, 24, 4 (2004a), 504–525.

Orton, M. 'New Labour, Citizenship and Responsibility: Family, Community and the Obscuring of Social Relations', in Dean, H. (ed.), *The Ethics of Social Welfare: Human Rights* (Bristol: The Policy Press, 2004b).

O'Toole, T. 'Engaging with Young People's Conceptions of the Political', *Children's Geographies*, 1, 1 (2003), 71–90.

O'Toole, T. and Gale, R. *Participative Governance and the Democratic Inclusion of Young Black and Minority Ethnic 'Active Citizens'* (Nicosia: European Consortium for Political Research Joint Sessions of Workshops, Intercollege, Cyprus, 2006).

O'Toole, T., Marsh, D. and Jones, S. 'Political Literacy Cuts Both Ways', *Political Quarterly*, 74, 3 (2003), 349–360.

O'Toole, T., Lister, M., Jones, S., Marsh, D. and McDonagh, A. 'Tuning Out or Left Out? Political Participation and Non-Participation among Young People', *Contemporary Politics*, 9, 1 (2003), 45–61.

Ouseley, H., *Community Pride Not Prejudice* (Bradford: Bradford Race Review, www.bradford2020.com/pride/report.pdf, 2001).

Pakulski, J. and Waters, M. *The Death of Class* (London: Sage, 1996).

Park, A. *Young People's Social Attitudes 1998: Full Report of Research Activities and Results* (Keele: ESRC, 1998).

Park, A., Curtice, J., Thomson, K., Jarvis, L. and Bromley, C. *British Social Attitudes, the 19th Report* (London: Sage, 2002).

Parker, D. *Through Different Eyes: The Cultural Identities of Young Chinese People in Britain* (Aldershot: Avebury, 1995).

Parry, G., Moyser, G. and Day, N. *Political Participation and Democracy in Britain* (Cambridge: Cambridge University Press, 1992).

Pattie, C., Seyd, P. and Whiteley, P. *Citizenship, Democracy and Participation in Contemporary Britain* (Cambridge: Cambridge University Press, 2004).

Peterson, R. and Kern, R. 'Changing Highbrow Taste: From Snob to Omnivore', *American Sociological Review*, 61 (1996), 900–907.

Phelps, E. 'Young Citizens and Changing Electoral Turnout, 1964–2001', *Political Quarterly*, 75, 3 (2004), 238–248.

Phelps, E. 'Young Voters at the 2005 British General Election', *Political Quarterly*, 76, 4 (2005), 482–487.

Philo, C. and Smith, F.M. 'Political Geographies of Children and Young People', *Space and Polity*, 7, 2 (2003), 99–115.

Pierre, J. (ed.) 'Introduction: Understanding Governance', *Debating Governance* (Oxford: Oxford University Press, 2000).

Pilkington, H. and Johnson, R. 'Peripheral Youth: Relations of Identity and Power in Global/Local Context', *European Journal of Cultural Studies*, 6, 3 (2003), 259–285.

Pirie, M. and Worcester, R.M. *The Millennial Generation* (London: MORI/ Adam Smith Institute, 1998).

Pirie, M. and Worcester, R.M. *The Big Turn-off: Attitudes of Young People to Government, Citizenship and Community* (London: Adam Smith Institute, 2000).

Power Inquiry, *Power to the People*, Report of Power: An Independent Inquiry into Britain's Democracy (London: Power Inquiry, March, 2006).

Punch, K. *Introduction to Social Research: Quantitative and Qualitative Approaches* (London: Sage, 1998).

Purdam, K., Fieldhouse, E., Kalra, V. and Russell, A. *Voter Engagement among Black and Minority Ethnic Communities* (London: The Electoral Commission, July 2002).

Putnam, R. 'Bowling Alone: America's Declining Social Capital', *Journal of Democracy*, 6, 1 (1995), 65–78.

Ram, M., Jones, T., Abbas, T. and Sanghera, B. 'Ethnic Minority Enterprise in its Urban Context: South Asian Restaurants in Birmingham', *International Journal of Urban and Regional Research*, 26, 1 (2002), 24–40.

Rasmussen, C. and Brown, M. 'Radical Democratic Citizenship: Amidst Political Theory and Geography', in Isin, E.F. and Turner, B.S. (eds), *Handbook of Citizenship Studies* (London: Sage, 2000).

Rhodes, R.A.W. *Understanding Governance* (Buckingham: Open University Press, 1997).

Richards, L. *Handling Qualitative Data: A Practical Guide* (London: Sage, 2005).

Richards, L. and Marshall, B. *Political Engagement among Black and Minority Ethnic Communities: What We Know, What We Need to Know* (London: The Electoral Commission, 2003, *http://www.electoralcommission.org.uk/files/dms/* BMEresearchseminarpaper11354-8831_E_N_S_W_.pdf).

Richardson, J., Seyd, P. and Whiteley, P. *True Blues: The Politics of Conservative Party Membership* (Oxford: Oxford University Press, 1995).

Rojek, C. *Celebrity* (London: Reaktion Books, 2001).

Rose, N. *Powers of Freedom: Reframing Political Thought* (Cambridge: Cambridge University Press, 1999).

Rubin, H.J. and Rubin, I.S. *Qualitative Interviewing: The Art of Hearing Data* (London: Sage, 1995).

Saggar, S. (ed.) *Race and British Electoral Politics* (London: UCL Press, 1998).

Sanders, D. 'Behaviouralism', in Marsh, D. and Stoker, G. (eds), *Theory and Methods in Political Science* (Basingstoke: Palgrave, 2002).

Savage, M. *Class Analysis and Social Transformation* (Buckingham: Open University Press, 2000).

Savigny, H. 'Political Marketing: A Rational Choice', *Journal of Political Marketing*, 3, 1 (2004), 21–38.

Saward, M. 'Governance and the Transformation of Political Representation' in Newman, J. (ed.), *Remaking Governance: Peoples Politics and the Public Sphere* (Bristol: Polity Press, 2005).

Seyd, P. and Whiteley, P. *Labour's Grassroots: The Politics of Party Membership* (Oxford: Clarendon Press, 1992).

Shapiro, V. 'Economic Activity as Political Activity', paper delivered to Annual Meeting of the American Political Science Association (Washington DC: APSA, 2000).

Shklar, J. 'The Liberalism of Fear', in N. Rosenblum (ed.), *Liberalism and the Moral Life* (Cambridge, Mass.: Harvard University Press, 1991).

Skeggs, B. 'Rethinking Class: Class Cultures and Explanatory Power', in Haralambos, M. (ed.), *Developments in Sociology* (Ormskirk: Causeway Press, vol. 16, 2000).

Smith, M. A. 'Ethics in Focus Groups: A Few Concerns', *Qualitative Health Research*, 5, 4 (1995), 478–487.

Smithson. J. 'Using and Analysing Focus Groups: Limitations and Possibilities', *Social Research Methodology*, 3, 2 (2000), 103–119.

Solomos, J. *Black Youth, Racism and the State* (Cambridge: Cambridge University Press, 1988).

Solomos, J. *Race and Racism in Britain* (Basingstoke: Palgrave, 2003).

Solomos, J. and Back, L. *Race, Politics and Social Change* (London: Routledge, 1995).

Somerville, P. 'Community Governance and Democracy', *Policy and Politics*, 33, 1 (2005), 117–144.

Spence, J. 'Women, Wives and the Campaign Against Pit Closures in County Durham', *Feminist Review*, 60 (1998), 33–60.

Spivak, G. 'Can the Subaltern Speak?' in Williams, P. and Chisman, L. (eds), *Colonial Discourse and Post-Colonial Theory: A Reader* (Brighton: Harvester Wheatsheaf, 1994).

Squires, J. *Gender in Political Theory* (Oxford: Polity Press, 2000).

Standing, G. *Beyond the New Paternalism* (London: Verso, 2002).

Sterling, R. 'Promoting Democratic Governance Through Partnerships', in Newman, J. (ed.), *Remaking Governance: Peoples, Politics and the Public Sphere* (Bristol: Polity Press, 2005).

Strother, R. 'Tell Your Customers That You Have Listened, Learned and Responded', *Media Asia*, 11/28/2003.

Tarrow, S. *Power in Movement: Social Movements and Contentious Politics* (Cambridge: Cambridge University Press, 1998).

The Daily Telegraph, 'Rioters Dishonour War Heroes' (May 2nd, 2000).

Thomas-Slater, B. 'A Brief History of Participatory Methodologies', in Slocum, R., Wichart, L., Rocheleau, D. and Thomas-Slater, B. (eds), *Power, Process and Participation-Tools for Change* (London: Intermediate Technology Publications, 1995).

Thomson, R., Bell, R. Holland, J., Henderson, S., McGrellis, S. and Sharpe, S. ' "At this point everyone turned against me": Critical moments in young people's narratives of transition', paper presented to *Making and Breaking Borders* conference (Helsinki: 2000).

Tisdall, E.K. and Davis, J. 'Making a Difference? Bringing Children's and Young People's Views into Policy-Making', *Children and Society*, 18 (2004), 131–142.

Tolman, D. 'Doing Desire: Adolescent Girls' struggle for/with Sexuality', *Gender & Society*, 8, 3 (1994), 324–342.

Toynbee, P. 'Mrs. Thatcher's Airhead Revenge', *The Independent* (28th April, 1997).

Turner, B.S. 'Contemporary Problems in the Theory of Citizenship', in Turner, B.S. (ed.), *Citizenship and Social Theory* (London: Sage, 1993).

Turner, L. 'From the Classroom to the Ballot Box', *The Guardian* (13th January, 2004).

Urban75, www.urban75.net/ubb/forum1/HTML/001443.html, accessed:28.03.01. (2001).

Van Aelst, P. and Walgrave, S. 'Who Is That (Wo)man in the Street: From the Normalisation of Protest to the Normalisation of the Protestor', *European Journal of Political Research*, 39 (2001), 461–486.

Van Drenth, A. 'Citizenship, Participation and the Social Policy on Girls in the Netherlands', in Bussemaker, J. and Voet, R. (eds), *Gender, Participation and Citizenship in the Netherlands* (Aldershot: Ashgate, 1998).

Voet, R. *Feminism and Citizenship* (London: Sage, 1998).

Walby, S. *Gender Transformations* (London: Routledge, 1997).

Walker, D. 'The Party's Over', *The Guardian* (16th January, 2001).

Walsh, V. 'Auto/biographical Imaginations and Social Change', in Mahony, P. and Zmroczek, C. (eds), *Class Matters 'Working-Class Women's Perspectives on Social Class* (London: Taylor and Francis, 1997).

Walters, W. 'Some Critical Notes on Governance', *Studies in Political Economy*, 73, Spring/Summer (2004), 27–46.

Werbner, P. 'Black and Ethnic Leadership in Britain: A Theoretical Overview', in Werbner, P. and Anwar, M. (eds), *Black and Ethnic Leaderships: The Cultural Dimensions of Political Action* (London: Routledge, 2001).

White, C., Bruce, S. and Ritchie, R. *Young People's Politics: Political Interest and Engagement Amongst 14–24 Year Olds* (New York: Joseph Rowntree Foundation, 2000).

Wilkinson, H. and Mulgan, G. 'Freedom's Children and the Rise of Generational Politics', in Wilkinson, H. and Mulgan, G. (eds), *Life After Politics: New Thinking for the Twenty-First Century* (London: Fontana, 1997).

Wilkinson, S. 'Focus Group Methodology: A Review', *International Journal of Social Science Methodology*, 1 (1987), 181–203.

Wilks, T. 'The Use of Vignettes in Qualitative Research into Social Work Values', *Qualitative Social Work*, 3, 1 (2004), 78–87.

Wilson, D. 'Exploring the Limits of Public Participation in Local Government', *Parliamentary Affairs*, 52, 2 (1999), 246–259.

Wring, D. 'Images of Labour: The Progression and Politics of Party Campaigning in Britain', *Journal of Political Marketing*, 1, 1 (2002), 22–37.

Wyn, J. and White, R. *Rethinking Youth* (St. Leonards, NSW: Allen & Unwin, 1997).

Wyness, M., Harrison, L. and Buchanan, I. 'Childhood, Politics and Ambiguity: Towards an Agenda for Children's Political Inclusion', *Sociology*, 38, 1 (2004), 81–99.

Young, I.M. *Justice and the Politics of Difference* (Princeton: Princeton University Press, 1990).

Index